CLASSIFIED SECRETS

Writing Real Estate Ads that Work

CLASSIFIED SECRETS

Writing Real Estate Ads that Work

William H. Pivar
Bradley A. Pivar

Real Estate
Education Company
a division of Dearborn Financial Publishing, Inc.

While a great deal of care has been taken to provide accurate and current information, the ideas, suggestions, general principles and conclusions presented in this text are subject to local, state and federal laws and regulations, court cases and any revisions of same. The reader thus is urged to consult legal counsel regarding any points of law—this publication should not be used as a substitute for competent legal advice.

Executive Editor: Kathleen A. Welton
Acquisition Editor: Wendy Lochner
Project Editor: Roseann P. Costello
Copy Editor: Maija Balagot
Interior Design: Karen Yops
Cover Design: Karen Yops

Published by Real Estate Education Company,
a division of Dearborn Financial Publishing, Inc.

Printed in the United States.

10 9 8 7 6 5 4

LIBRARY OF CONGRESS
Library of Congress Cataloging-in-Publication Data

Pivar, William H.
Classified secrets: writing real estate ads that work/William H. Pivar, Bradley A. Pivar.
p. cm.
Includes index.
ISBN 0-88462-112-X
1. Advertising—Real Estate business. 2. Advertising, Newspaper.
3. Advertising, Classified. I. Pivar, Bradley A. II. Title.
HF6161.R3P58 1988 88-10105
659.13'2—dc19 CIP

Contents

Preface

Classified Secrets: Writing Real Estate Ads That Work is a desktop tool to place beside your telephone, calculator and listing book. Used first as a workbook and then as a reference, it will help you consistently write classified real estate advertisements that draw inquiries from the right buyers at the lowest possible cost—ads that work.

The secrets of writing effective classified ads are not exotic or very complex, but they are highly valuable—U.S. real estate firms waste millions of dollars on useless ads and missed opportunities. You can avoid others' mistakes—and sharpen your competitive edge—by learning and applying the techniques spelled out in this book.

Classified Secrets takes you through the entire process of writing classified ads. You will gain an understanding of the reasoning behind effective ads by learning to analyze the parts of an ad and the functions of each. The book also presents a highly detailed examination of the features, benefits and potential targets for hundreds of residential property types and situations. Similar methods can be applied to nonresidential properties as well. An extensive chapter on investment properties shows you how to apply your knowledge of classified ad writing to get the attention of investors.

Throughout the book, examples are highlighted along with brief comments explaining the sample ads or headlines. This provides an understanding of the *concept* behind a particular ad. A quick reference guide to synonyms and descriptive terms is included at the end of the book. This handy word list quickly reviews the wording and methods you learned earlier—and enables you to use your knowledge in practical ways. Special practice exercises challenge you with property descriptions and ask you to define your audience and write ads for the properties. The authors follow up with ads they wrote and an explanation of their choices.

As you use this book and absorb its techniques, you'll find your own ideas keep coming—some of them variations on material in the book and some completely original. With the basic skills developed through your use of *Classified Secrets,* you'll realize the only limitations to writing successful classified ads are the boundaries of your own imagination.

An Invitation To Show Your Stuff Soon you'll be writing classified ads that make you proud. We'd like to include your outstanding creations in future editions of this book, giving you appropriate credit, of course. If you think your ads are terrific, send the cream of the crop to:

William H. Pivar
75-496 Desert Park Drive
Indian Wells, California 92210

The authors would like to express special thanks to Ian L. Price for openly sharing his research and ideas. Mr. Price is an Australian real estate educator (Gold Coast College of Technical and Further Education in Queensland, Australia) and has written extensively on preparing real estate classified advertisements.

The photographs in the book are by Corinne E. Pivar, API.

1 Understanding Classified Advertising

Consumers are assaulted daily by hundreds or thousands of advertisements on television and radio, in newspapers and magazines and through signs attached to almost any vertical object that will hold a nail. What makes classified ads stand out from all the rest is that they are not thrust upon a hostile or indifferent consumer. Classified ads are, in fact, eagerly sought out and willingly read. As a result, the reader comes to them in an entirely different state of mind. Buyers know the classifieds are *the* market for real estate.

Highly motivated real estate buyers read the classified ads every day, while those whose need to buy is less urgent may check them intermittently. Still others have no interest in buying but read the ads out of curiosity; these curious readers often tell others about interesting ads or even become buyers themselves when an ad excites them.

Never forget, though, that classified advertising does not sell real estate—people do. The ad is a teaser that should convey just enough information to make the reader want more. An effective ad triggers an emotional response that results in a phone call. This, in turn, gives the salesperson a chance to identify the prospect, determine his or her needs and try to turn the prospect into a buyer of either the advertised property or another.

Most brokers recognize the value of that opportunity and so invest heavily in classifieds. Unfortunately, many of those dollars are wasted because few brokers understand what makes an ad work or how to evaluate its effectiveness. Ads that work have one thing in common: They strike a special emotional chord in the reader for whom they are written. When an ad works, its author has almost certainly defined his or her target audience, then presented the property's features and benefits in a way that evokes the desired response.

The process sounds almost ridiculously simple, yet failure to attain this straightforward goal results in a glut of ineffective or marginal ads. The inescapable fact is that writing ads that work requires energy, time and thought. A common shortcut has been to copy from others, tailor old ads to new listings or delegate ad writing to the listing salesperson. Such efforts are generally inefficient in that they result in less than the maximum possible return on advertising dollars.

This book aims to take you step-by-step through the tried-and-true secrets of writing ads that work. It isn't a collection of good ads to fit every occasion and property, but a working tool that will enable you to properly analyze the needs of likely buyers and then quickly and efficiently write effective classified ads that address those needs.

This chapter guides you through the practical realities of classified advertising and provides you with guidance toward writing and placing effective ads—ads that produce the maximum return for your advertising dollar. The later chapters teach you the art of targeting your advertising and the skill of writing ads that produce the responses you want from the audience you have targeted.

Where To Advertise

When people think of classified advertising, most of them think of the large metropolitan newspapers. Since these papers have huge circulations and classified sections, they are sought out and read by prospective buyers. This makes them an extremely effective advertising medium but not inexpensive: A ten-line ad appearing one Sunday in the *Los Angeles Times* costs $160. While the price per reader is a bargain, these papers cover tremendous geographic areas, including those where readers are unlikely to become buyers.

Putting all your advertising in the one dominant metropolitan paper may mean you are missing readers who don't see the major papers on a regular basis. While cost per reader is higher with a paper of lesser circulation, ads there can contribute to a better overall profit.

When two papers reach the newsstands at the same time, cross-readership will be low, making it more important to advertise in both papers. Separate morning and afternoon papers tend to have more cross-readership. By knowing which placements gave you which calls, you can evaluate the value of ads in alternative newspapers.

Special Editions

Newspapers periodically push special editions for special events, often with special advertising rates because of increased circulation. Even though such an issue may attain phenomenal circulation, it may not deliver meaningful readership if most of the increase is from copies sold for shipment outside of your advertising area.

Some papers also publish special real estate supplements several times each year. Because these supplements are likely to be studied by prospective real estate purchasers, they can be a wise ad choice.

Along with the widely distributed metropolitan papers in your area, consider other media:

Neighborhood Papers

Many communities within major metropolitan areas have their own newspapers, usually weeklies. Their readership, while much smaller than that of the major papers, is concentrated in a particular geographical area. Even though ad rates per reader are higher than with the larger newspapers, cost per response is likely to be significantly lower because of the precise distribution in a target area.

Local papers often have the further advantage of being read more thoroughly than larger newspapers because they are smaller and less frequent. Readers tend to read the want ads in local weeklies even when they are not particularly interested in buying.

Foreign-Language Papers

Foreign-language papers should not be ignored. They can carry effective advertising for the broker who takes the time to become acquainted with the general needs of the papers' readers. The advertiser may find, for example, that the readers of publications catering to the longer-established immigrants—Polish- and German-language papers, for example—seem to prefer solid homes of stone or brick, and quality duplexes, as well as income and investment property.

The readers of papers catering to more recent residents may have different wants. Arabic newspapers—and there are many of them—have proven to be excellent media for advertising businesses, luxury homes and income and investment properties. Vietnamese papers are excellent media for advertising low-cost homes, small-income property and family-type businesses. Spanish-language papers can be effective for advertising single-family housing and small farms.

If you have someone in your office who speaks the paper's language, point that out in your advertisement. This will have a strong impact on readers who are not yet comfortable speaking English.

Black Papers

Major metropolitan areas have black newspapers. Some sellers make the mistake of stereotyping blacks as low-income buyers, forgetting there are blacks at all economic levels. In fact, advertising luxury property in black newspapers can be very effective, since it indicates to the readers that not only are you willing to work to meet their needs, but that you are willing to do so in a "color-blind" manner.

Advertising only properties that are located in predominantly black areas in black publications would be steering, a violation of the Civil Rights Act of 1968. If you wish to advertise in black-oriented publications, you should make certain you include properties in predominantly white areas.

Gay Publications

A number of papers serve our gay communities. These papers can be productive advertising media for condominiums, luxury smaller homes, resort properties and businesses. Advertising in these papers will indicate to the readers that you are willing to actively meet their real estate needs.

Throwaways

As the advertising rates of the large newspapers have risen, there has been remarkable growth in the weekly throwaway shoppers either delivered to the home, mailed or available free at markets and newsstands. These papers usually reach specific geographical areas and seldom segregate their classified ads by category but spread them throughout the paper. Readers looking for a particular item are often forced to read hundreds of classified ads.

Your ads in the throwaways will reach a great number of readers who would not have seen them in other media. For these throwaways, consider ads that grab the attention of readers who otherwise had not considered themselves possible home buyers.

OWN FOR LESS THAN YOUR RENT

LOW DOWN PAYMENT—PAYMENTS LIKE RENT

TRY $1,000 DOWN

Throwaways can be fantastically effective ad media and advertisers are beginning to recognize this. The editor of a daily newspaper in a community of about 20,000 people told us his publication just reduced its classified rates to compete with throwaways. He estimated that at least a third of the area's real estate advertising dollars now go to throwaways. He also pointed out that many people don't buy newspapers at all. The way to reach this group is through the throwaways.

Specialized Publications Specialized throwaways such as mobile home news circulate in some communities. These make excellent media for mobile home lots, land zoned for mobile homes, larger mobile homes for buyers moving up and homes where the sellers are willing to take a mobile home in trade.

Other Papers If you check your local yellow pages, you might be surprised at all the special papers listed in the *Newspaper* category.

Special Magazines

Many magazines carry classified ads. These can be extremely effective if you are aiming at specific interest groups. A print shop advertised in a magazine for the printing trade will be read by thousands of printers, just as ads for kennels in a magazine devoted to dogs will reach dog fanciers.

There are magazines and trade publications for just about every group imaginable. *Gales's Encyclopedia of Associations,* available at most public libraries, tells you about associations that have publications. The price per reader in such specialty publications is high, but the effective cost is low because you are paying only for the readers you want to reach.

Ad Books

Sometimes it's impossible to refuse a plea to buy space in an ad book or program. Such a donation can be turned into a source of prospects if you do more than just give the ad taker your card to be reproduced. Instead, consider a classified ad for one or more properties. The ad will stand out among the display ads and is likely to be read. Relate the ad as closely as possible to the group that will see it. For a concert, a tax shelter or a luxury property might be appropriate. A horse show program might be just the place to describe properties where horses can be kept. Properly aimed, your "charity" ad can produce real benefits.

Television and Radio

When we think of classified ads we think of printed matter. Many brokers, though, have found that radio can be a verbal classified ad and television can be effectively used to provide a picture that enriches the commentary. Many stations have programs, usually on Sunday mornings, in which they feature individual properties.

The fact that an ad is being heard or watched instead of read does nothing to change the importance of your choice of words. The skills of targeting your audience and stimulating a response are essentially the same in any medium.

Customizing Ads to the Medium

Writing effective ads is a demanding task, so it is always tempting to use the same ad everywhere you buy space. However, by using different ads with different appeals in different papers for the same property, you increase your odds of zeroing in on your buyer. In cases of cross-readership you will appear to be offering several attractive properties and, thus, will increase the chance that one of the appeals will strike a chord in the right reader.

When placing an ad, keep in mind the likely age, special interests and economics of the readers of each advertising medium. Then write for that audience. An ad in a laborers' union paper, for example, might feature sale terms; for a paper aimed at singles, you might appeal to life-style; second homes could be advertised in publications appealing to the affluent, as well as in out-of-town papers circulated where the second-home buyers are likely to live.

The Mechanics of Classified Advertising

Classified ads typically have no color or photographs. Most are single column, though advertisers may purchase blocks of space several columns wide for a display ad.

Some newspapers have a number of standard cuts. They'll give you copies of what's available. Some examples:

Cuts can be repeated for a border.

More than one cut can be combined for a border.

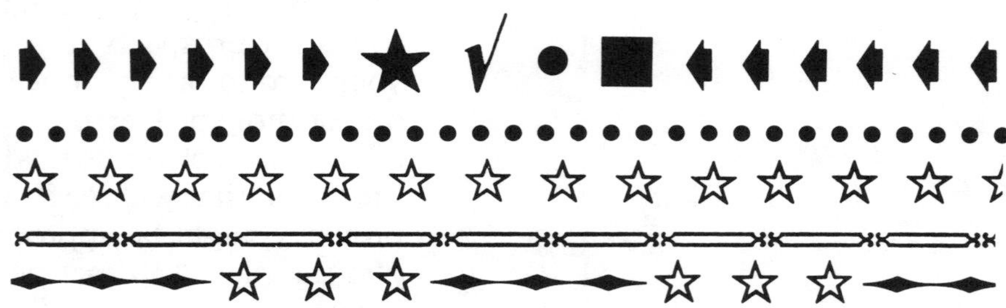

Some newspapers allow advertisers to use special cuts and logos:

Reverse cuts are allowed in some papers, usually for the logo only. The white print stands out from the black background:

Some papers also allow dark borders around ads to give them emphasis.

Type styles and sizes are generally limited. Your local newspaper will provide you with samples of their available choices. Note that larger-size type means more lines to pay for. The following type samples are reprinted courtesy of the *Chicago Sun-Times:*

CLASSIFIED TYPE SIZES

Each letter, punctuation mark and each space between words must be counted as one character.	Average letters and spaces per line	This type size counts as
AGATE LOWER CASE—5½ PT the chicago sun-times	30	1 line
AGATE CAPITALS—5½ PT PEOPLE-REACHER WANT ADS	21	1 line
TYPE No 2 LOWER CASE—8 PT get better results than ever	25	2 lines
TYPE No 2 CAPITALS—8 PT OVER 3½ MILLION READERS	19	2 lines
TYPE No 3 LOWER CASE—12 PT lowest combination cost	20	3 lines
TYPE No 3 CAPITALS—12 PT READERSHIP—RESULTS	16	3 lines
TYPE No 4 LOWER CASE—18 PT classified want ads	15	4 lines
TYPE No 4 CAPITALS—18 PT GIVE YOU MORE	11	4 lines
TYPE No 5 LOWER CASE—24 PT sell it faster	12	5 lines
TYPE No 5 CAPITALS—24 PT LOWER COST	9	5 lines
TYPE No 6 LOWER CASE—30 PT with want ads	11	6 lines
TYPE No 6 CAPITALS—30 PT YOU'LL FIND	9	6 lines
TYPE No 7 LOWER CASE—36 PT many of	9	
TYPE No 7 CAPITALS—36 PT CHICAGO'S	8	
TYPE No 8 LOWER CASE—42 PT big buyers	9	
TYPE No 8 CAPITALS—42 PT WITH ADS	7	

Numbers 7 & 8 are billed on a measured line basis

Type No. 9 (48 point). Type No. 10 (60 point) and Type No. 11 (72 point) of the same type face are available for use in multiple column classified advertisements that are at least 194 lines deep.

MINIMUM SIZE OF ADVERTISEMENTS
The minimum size of an advertisement is 2 lines

When No. 2 type is used	4 lines
When No. 3 type is used	6 lines
When No. 4 type is used	8 lines
When No. 5 type is used	10 lines
When No. 6 type is used	12 lines
When No. 7 type is used	14 lines
When No. 8 type is used	16 lines

Because of varying type and column sizes, a five-line ad in one paper might require only four lines in another. Caps are usually available and should generally be used for the ad heading or first line. Don't use caps for the entire ad, though, or they will lose their impact. Caps can also be used for a key feature or word to provide greater emphasis.

The most legible type faces are generally serif styles. (Serifs are the little feet on the bottom of the letters.) Many experts claim that serif type is more readable, providing greater comprehension in a single reading. However, benefits of serif type are disputed by other reading experts. The ads in this book are sans serif (without feet) because the trend in large newspapers seems to be away from serif type for classified ads.

Typically, newspapers categorize classified ads under headings such as *Business Opportunities, Investment Property, Lots and Acreage, Farms, Single-Family Homes,* etc. In larger papers single-family homes are further categorized by areas. Decide where your ad belongs. Ask yourself, "If a prospective buyer were looking for such a property or features, what category would that buyer look under?" A home with a rentable guest house could be advertised under both residential and income property. If most ads for a type of property are under one classification, follow the crowd. If most of the motels in a particular newspaper are advertised under *Business Opportunities,* don't place your listing under *Investment Opportunities,* where prospective buyers would be unlikely to look. Again, it pays to study the medium and the market.

Deadlines and Accuracy

It doesn't take great genius to write a good ad but it does take time. If you don't prepare your ads when you first take a listing, you must allow yourself sufficient time well before the advertising deadlines.

Rushed ad writers tend to repeat old ads or to run hastily prepared, ineffective copy. Worse yet, brokers often use ads prepared for other properties with slight or no modifications. Ads should be written to fit property, not property fitted to the ads. In 1784 Samuel Johnson wrote, "Words written without effort are read without pleasure." It takes time to write truly effective ads, although this book will make the task less burdensome.

You should know the due times for advertising and get your ads to the paper early. If the paper's office is located close to yours, dropping off ads in person, rather than using the phone, reduces the chance of error. In many papers, late ads are published in a special, mixed-category late-ad section. Ads run there are money-wasted, as house hunters are unlikely to notice them.

The person who writes the ads should review them for correctness and correct any mistakes for future insertions. Most papers will adjust rates if they make a mistake and are notified promptly.

Some newspapers provide advance proof sheets upon request. By checking these, you can correct mistakes before they happen. This is especially important for weekend ads, special issues or ad supplements and open house ads.

The Economics of Classified Advertising

In terms of results, classified ads can be a bargain. They are the one sure way to reach people who want to buy real estate. Not every person buying is buying because of a classified ad, but nearly every buyer has at least checked them.

Rates vary widely from small weekly papers where a six-line ad might run three dollars, to the *Los Angeles Times* where a Sunday insertion of six lines costs almost $100.

The Long-Run "Bargain"

Most papers offer advertising contracts which provide reduced rates if you agree to take a specific number of lines over a period of time. The more lines, the lower the rate. Some contracts also require ads be kept in for a minimum number of insertions.

Noncontract advertisers can also obtain significant discounts by keeping the same ad in unchanged for a protracted period of time. The daily rate for a 30-day insertion is usually about 1/2 the normal daily rate. Local papers will provide you with rate cards and contract information.

Savings obtained by running the same ad over and over usually turn out to be false economy. Ads lose their appeal when they are repeated day after day. The longer the ad is repeated the weaker the response becomes. The benefits of repetition are far outweighed by the "What's wrong with it?" or "There's nothing new" attitude generated by the ad. After a while, the ad will reach only those just entering the home search process.

Besides being generally ineffective, long insertions can be costly. Suppose you have contracted for a 30-day, special rate, six-line ad in the *Los Angeles Times.* Your cost would be:

Weekdays:	26 days	×	$6.30	×	6 lines	=	$982.80
Sundays:	4 days	×	8.25	×	6 lines	=	198.00
							$1,180.80

As you can see, the bargain 30-day rate has the potential to eat up your entire advertising budget. A bargain rate is not a bargain if it fails to generate an adequate response. Furthermore, being tied to a few long insertion ads could mean the loss of your advertising flexibility.

Our recommendation: Don't repeat ads more than three days in succession in a daily paper. After that, take them out and leave them out for at least three weeks. You can advertise the same property in the interim, if you want to, with a different ad. If you write several ads on each property when it is first listed, you will be less likely to take the easy way out by simply repeating and repeating the same old thing. As the rest of this book will explain in detail, ads can be written to stress various benefits. A new ad emphasizing different appeals has the freshness and excitement of a new listing. Potential buyers who passed over the earlier ads may be drawn to the benefits named in the new version. Thus, by changing the ad's approach, you can attract several types of potential buyers to the same property.

It is important that the owners understand your advertising approach. They should realize that it is not necessary to advertise their home every day. Advertising similar property in the same price range will suffice. Prospective buyers are qualified and other properties meeting their needs are also shown. Therefore, just a few ads in a range of types and prices can cover numerous other properties.

Budgeting

Your advertising budget should be based upon a percentage of your anticipated gross commissions. Many brokers budget between 20 and 25 percent of the office commission, but since ad costs vary, there are no rigid guidelines. Base your percentage on what you think is needed to reach your sales volume goals.

Set your budget for each advertising medium and review it at the end of each month. Then you can adjust your planned expenditures based on the previous month's volume as well as the anticipated volume for the coming month.

New brokerage offices generally have to advertise more heavily when they start out in order to build up a clientele of owners and prospective buyers.

Adjusting to the Market

Market conditions change rapidly and you have to be ready to change strategies when they do. In real estate you must make hay while the sun shines. Periods of great activity are the time to expand advertising. When there is a general real estate decline, consider a retrenchment. Some firms do successfully expand sales and profit during hard times, but far more who have tried it have failed.

Your newspaper advertising manager might tell you that the time to increase your advertising is when business gets slow and that you can advertise yourself out of a recession. But the advertising manager doesn't pay your bills, and going to the poorhouse is not the way out of a recession. While increased advertising will produce increased sales even in the worst of times, the gains are likely to be more than offset by higher costs.

When business is slow, brokers worry about their advertising and devote the time and effort necessary to come up with better ads. As business improves, however, they tend to get sloppy. When sales are being made, mediocre ads start to look okay even though good ads would make business even better. Staying aware of this natural tendency will help you avoid the lethargy of success.

Avoid Rigid Limits

Don't set advertising limits on a property-by-property basis. A property that hasn't sold may be bringing in prospects who end up buying your other listings. We'll look at ways to analyze ad responses later in this chapter.

Keep in mind that when you took the listing you agreed to use diligence in obtaining a buyer, not diligence up to a particular dollar amount. If you intend to cease further advertising on a property, you should in good conscience return the listing to the owner.

Keep the Real Goal in Mind

Don't advertise to please your salespeople. Most salespeople are primarily interested in today, not tomorrow. They want bigger ads, and more of them, to get more leads. Advertising leads come in without any effort on their part but use up your dollars. Salespeople should not rely on advertising alone for their leads but use it as just one of many sources. Increasing an advertising budget to keep salespeople happy or to match the ad coverage of a competitor during slow periods is a formula for failure. The goal of a good advertising program is sales, not pleasing others or feeding your ego.

Too Many Leads?

If your advertising is producing more business than your staff can adequately handle, it might be tempting to reduce your ad budget. A better solution might be to increase your sales staff so salespeople spend fewer hours getting telephone leads and more hours out selling.

New brokers with inexperienced sales staffs waste a great percentage of the responses received because they lack the knowledge to turn inquiries into showings and showings into sales. The advertising budget is meaningless unless your sales staff can take advantage of it.

The Best Size

You can analyze your ad results by ad size. Will a 12-line ad bring double the response of a six-line ad? If not, two separate six-line ads might be preferable. We are not advocating bare-bones ads. Bare-bones ads are short ads with minimum facts and no adjectives. Such ads lack punch; in a competitive environment ten four-line bare-bones usually get less response than five eight-line ads that include adjectives packing an emotional appeal.

Ads should be written for effective messages, not to fit into preset spaces. Cutting adjectives or feature descriptions to keep within a line limit might cut an ad's effectiveness 50 percent or more and just save one line of type.

Block Ads Many brokers place large block ads, some taking up a whole page, advertising a great number of their properties. These ads are really institutional ads saying, "Hey! Look at us—we are big and have a great number of properties available!" as well as being classified to sell specific properties. Unless all of the properties in a large block ad relate to the category under which the block ad is placed, people looking under different categories may ignore the big block ad.

The block ads used by some brokers don't resemble classified ads in appearance and are often missed, despite their huge size, by prospective buyers checking the classified ads. We have received better results from many smaller ads than from one larger ad. While the smaller ads are probably more effective in sales, the large block ads are impressive to owners with property to list.

Who Should Write the Ads

Whoever writes the ads should actually visit the property. Writing an ad from secondhand knowledge misses opportunities to consider all of the property's features and to formulate ads appealing to different groups of potential buyers. After a listing is taken, several ads should be immediately prepared on the property stressing different features and/or appealing to different categories of prospective buyers. You may want to supply copies to the owners to show them how you are preparing to show their property.

One person should be responsible for writing all the office ads. Many offices allow the listing salespeople to write their own ads, but this eliminates your control over quality. While you will get some excellent ads, you will also get many average ads and some really poor ones. You can also expect some ads written more to please an owner than to sell the property.

Logically, the person who pays for the ad—usually the broker—should write it. This is a duty easily delegated, but such an extremely important function requires that the broker have absolute faith in the ability, energy and willingness of the ad writer to come up with the best ads within his or her ability. Some brokers successfully delegate ads to a talented sales manager; most feel the job is up to them.

Most newspapers have employees who will be very happy to help you write your ads. Make use of their knowledge, but keep in mind that the newspaper's goals are not necessarily the same as yours: They want to sell you as much advertising space as they can—you want to sell property. Used as a substitute for your own hard work and good judgment, the "free" assistance could end up literally costing you a fortune.

Which Properties To Advertise

Don't advertise property you don't control. The only properties you control are properties on which you have signed exclusive right-to-sell listings or properties you own. Advertising open listings, exclusive agency listings and verbal vest-pocket listings has been enough to turn independent brokers into salespeople working for wiser brokers.

Don't advertise a property until it is ready for showing, with all planned cleanup or renovation done. A premature showing could lead a good prospect to dismiss the property from further consideration. The only exception to this is when you advertise a fixer-upper prior to the work being completed. (See Chapter Nine.)

After a listing has expired, don't continue your advertising in hopes of getting an extension. Your ad book should be coded with expiration dates so you don't accidentally advertise too long.

As soon as an offer has been accepted, your office should go through a checklist of actions, including stopping the ads. Simple though this is, thousands of real estate offices pay millions of dollars for advertising they could have cancelled.

Many offices choose the properties they will advertise by price; they might advertise one very low-cost, low-down-payment property, one property in a desirable middle-price area and one luxury property. In this way just a few ads will bring responses applicable to the majority of their inventory.

Even though prospective buyers are often switched from the property they call on to other properties that better meet their needs, your advertising decisions should be based upon salability. If you advertise your probabilities rather than possibilities, your chance for success will be enhanced.

Don't advertise property you don't reasonably expect to sell. In fact, don't even list it. If the price and terms are not competitive, advertising will simply waste your money, bring few responses and reflect negatively on your firm.

Make sellers understand that during periods of low activity there are many sellers and few buyers; if their properties are to have a chance, they must do more than just compete with others that are not selling. A property must have very definite advantages, such as price, terms, features or the property's condition.

Never promise exceptional ad coverage to owners in order to obtain listings that are not exceptional. You will end up with a big advertising bill and owners of similar properties expecting the same treatment.

When To Advertise

In daily newspapers, weekend ads are more effective than weekday ads. Weekend editions have greater circulation and many house hunters have only weekends to shop. Because of the larger classified sections in the Sunday papers, many home hunters save them and refer to them through the entire week.

For evening newspapers, a Friday night paper can be very effective as it will be used by Saturday house hunters.

Saturday evening papers are not very effective for classified ads because the large Sunday edition usually comes out very early the next morning and will be used by the Sunday house hunters.

People do read the classified ads and buy during the week. This is especially true of people relocating into the area. In the summer months with daylight savings, weekday ads are much more effective than in winter. The longer days are conducive to after-work house hunting.

Many daily papers run food store ads on a particular day. This day usually has much higher circulation because of newsstand sales. Daily advertising rates are usually the same, so an insertion on the higher circulation day could be more productive even though much of the increased readership is just interested in food specials and coupons.

Many brokers have preferences for morning or afternoon papers. Despite deep-seated feelings, there does not appear to be any worthwhile statistical data justifying either belief. Evening papers have the advantage that they are more likely to be read at home by more than one member of the family. Morning papers are often read on the way to or at work and discarded. However, people spending the entire day looking for houses will usually start with the morning papers.

The time of year will also affect advertising response on some properties. Advertising is best kept up year-round, but seasonal considerations should influence your ad budget.

Some brokers stop advertising before Christmas because sales are usually slow. Actually, the reduced number of ads will help your ads reach the "must-buy" prospects. You can reduce your number of ads but don't eliminate them during slow periods.

Vacation homes should receive the greatest advertising emphasis in the months just before and during the normal vacation period.

Family housing ads generally do best starting about a month before the end of the school year and continuing through the vacation period. Buyers often wish to relocate without disturbing their childrens' education.

Tax-sheltered-investment advertising becomes more effective as you approach April 15, when people realize their needs for tax shelters. Toward the end of the year is also a good time to advertise tax shelters.

Winter is a good time to increase farm ads, as many farmers are interested in buying prior to spring planting.

In northern areas, lot advertising is very effective when started prior to the building season.

Analyzing Advertising Results

Just about every broker believes that he or she writes good ads. This belief is encouraged by the fact that even the worst possible classified ads bring at least some responses. Poor ads succeed because classified ads reach interested readers.

In smaller communities with few available properties, potential buyers often check everything that is advertised. The quality of the ad becomes more important as the market becomes more competitive. The more properties advertised in a medium, the more important it becomes that your ads have a competitive advantage. You can't change the properties you control, but you can advertise them in a way that evokes the maximum positive response.

Every salesperson should indicate on a simple daily check sheet (similar to the one included here) the source of calls received and the results.

You can't learn by results unless you know results. Advertising is too expensive to be based upon gut feelings; you must have data. Regular use of the check sheet will provide data on the effectiveness of the ad, the advertising medium and sales techniques of your staff.

The demographics of areas differ as to age, family size, income and special needs, so success of an ad in one area or medium does not ensure success in another. By evaluating responses to your ads, you can determine the features or appeals that work in particular areas and media.

When an ad brings an exceptional response, ask yourself why. Check with your salespeople on what the callers were most interested in. Exceptional appeals should be noted for further use with other, similar properties.

An ad that provides many calls and few showings probably gives a false impression of the property. Ads that seem too good to be true, and are not true, bring calls but turn off buyers to you and your firm when the truth comes out.

An ad that results in many showings but no sale, on the

other hand, may be appealing to the wrong group of buyers—or the property might be overpriced. In either case, corrective action is needed.

DAILY CHECK SHEET

Salesperson ______________________ Date __________

Time	Property Called On	Source of Call	Name and Phone Number of Caller Obtained	Appointment Made to Show Advertised Property	Appointment Made to Show Other Property

Abbreviations

Abbreviations detract from comprehension. The more you use abbreviations, the more difficult it will be for readers to follow your message. In competitive ad situations, abbreviations can be false economy.

Some abbreviations are well understood and do not greatly harm an ad, but consider the following, in which only the broker's name and phone number have been changed. This is not an example of a good ad. It is included only to illustrate problems of abbreviation.

> LG. VW. hm with pvc 4 bdrm, 3 ba, 3 C Gar. Lg. Ms. Suite, Gr. Hs. Lg. pool, Guest qtrs. Newly decor, 17 citrus, 10 lg. palm etc. Rm for tns crt. Blo mkt. $189,000.
>
> **Clyde Realty 476-8200**

We believe the ad is supposed to read:

> Large view home with privacy, 4 bedrooms, 3 baths, 3-car garage, large master suite, greenhouse, large pool, guest quarters. Newly decorated, 17 citrus, 10 large palm etc. Room for tennis court. Below market $189,000.
>
> **Clyde Realty 476-8200**

As you can readily see, excessive abbreviations reduce readability and effectiveness. I suggest that you put yourself in the shoes of a reader who has had no previous involvement in a real estate purchase and who is reading the classified ads for the first time. If that person doesn't instantly understand your abbreviations, don't use them. Don't expect the reader to make the effort to decipher your ad when there are many more on the page that make sense at first glance.

Instead of trying to save a line with abbreviations, you would more likely be money ahead by adding words that heighten the image of the property and increase its desirability.

Bare-bones ads are not going to produce significant traffic in a competitive market.

Abbreviations can be used—and are used in this book—but not to excess, and never when the reader cannot immediately comprehend the meaning.

Numerals are not really abbreviations—in fact numerals are clearer than words and save space as well. You would not say "*Two* baths" when "*2* baths" takes less space and provides instant understanding.

Keep Alternative Properties on Hand

While many people buy the homes they see advertised, more buy alternative properties, often at a higher price. When people see what they really want, emotions tend to take over and strict price limitations loosen up. You can prepare to deal with this pattern by writing the best ad you can for the house being advertised, but being ready with alternative properties to show prospective buyers the ad attracts. Generally these properties should not be more than 20 percent higher in price. You should provide all salespeople with a copy of the ad as well as recommended alternative properties to show prospective buyers.

Targeting Your Ads

When you go through a newly listed home, try to build up a mental picture of its most likely buyer. Ask yourself, "What features of the house appeal to that buyer?" You will probably find that particular features appeal to more than one group. An oversized fenced backyard with six fruit trees, for example, could strongly appeal to:

Gardeners
Would-be gardeners
Families with small children
Families with dogs
Retirees

Once you have a firm picture of the kinds of people you want to attract, write your ad(s) on that basis.

At this stage it is important to avoid letting your own personal tastes and preferences influence your ads. You might regard a small older home in a transition area as substandard housing or even a slum dwelling, but there is someone out there who will find it the answer to a housing dream or a prime investment opportunity.

Don't worry about being overly enthusiastic in your choice of descriptive adjectives: The eventual buyer will find your adjectives just right.

Some Other Hints

Because most ads are written by economy-conscious brokers or owners, the classified pages of many papers are a mass of fine type. If this is the case with the papers you use, consider one or more slugs. A slug is a line of blank type that can set your ad apart from other ads. A slug can fall between the ad heading and the ad body and between the ad and the signature line.

Some brokers simply run all their properties together in a one-column ad. The ad on the left is taken from an actual example (with the broker's name removed). The one on the right is the same except for the addition of a slug between each property. You can see how just a few extra lines add to the visual impact of an ad to make it stand out in a competitive environment.

NOTE: This ad is not meant as a model of a good ad, but as a way to show how extra space can increase visual impact. As you progress through this book, you might want to rewrite these ads using what you've learned to make them more effective.

To make a strong feature stand out you can capitalize one word. If you capitalize too much it loses effectiveness.

Many brokers count letters so they don't waste half a line. Some use their word processors to compose their ads. They can

RESIDENCES

A MUST SEE
Don't pass on this 3 bdrm. 2 ba. home w/cov. patio, fenced yd. A great starter home. Probate—Owner may finance. $34,500.
GREAT STARTER HOME
Charming 3 bdrm., family room home—all elec. stainless steel kit—original owner—will sell V.A. or F.H.A. $49,500.
SUPER FINE
A mint condition 3 bdrm., 2 ba. home under 2 yrs. old. Carefree yard. Nicest home in area. Owner wants to sell—Priced at only $65,000.
NEW LISTING
Choice 3 bdrm., den, 2 ba. home w/many built-in features. Newer roof & Ext. Stucco—Full sprinklers—A Great Buy at only $67,500.
V.A. OR F.H.A. TERMS
Choice 2 bdrm., Spanish style home on cor. lot. 20 × 15 family room—too many extras to mention. Owner anxious—submit offers $69,500.

RESIDENCES

A MUST SEE
Don't pass on this 3 bdrm., 2 ba. home w/cov. patio, fenced yd. A great starter home. Probate—Owner may finance. $34,500.

GREAT STARTER HOME
Charming 3 bdrm., family room home—all elec. stainless steel kit—original owner—will sell V.A. or F.H.A. $49,500.

SUPER FINE
A mint condition 3 bdrm., 2 ba. home under 2 yrs. old. Carefree yard. Nicest home in area. Owner wants to sell—Priced at only $65,000.

NEW LISTING
Choice 3 bdrm., den, 2 ba. home w/many built-in features. Newer roof & Ext. Stucco—Full sprinklers—A Great Buy at only $67,500.

V.A. OR F.H.A. TERMS
Choice 2 bdrm., Spanish style home on cor. lot. 20 × 15 family room—too many extras to mention. Owner anxious—submit offers $69,500.

then consider addition of an adjective that will not only fill up the space, but strengthen the ad as well.

The more ads your local papers carry, the more care you must take in preparing your ads—to make them stand out from all the similar ads for similar properties

The Rules of Good Ads

You don't have to be a genius to write good ads as long as you follow the seven general rules:

1. **Say it clearly.** After you have written the ad, ask yourself, "Can I say it more clearly?" Don't use technical terms that your prospective buyer might not understand. *Wraparound mortgage* would probably confuse most prospective buyers. If a prospective buyer is confused, he or she is unlikely to respond to the ad with a phone call.
2. **Emphasize features likely to appeal to the eventual buyer.**
3. **Use adjectives that enhance the ad.**
4. **Don't repeat the newspaper's classification in your ad.**
5. **Don't copy ads of others.** Even good ads lose effectiveness when overworked.
6. **Don't use words that fail to benefit the ad.**
7. **Be absolutely honest in your ads.**

Anatomy of a Classified Ad

Generally, a classified ad consists of a heading to grab the attention of the reader, an ad body that tells about the property and a close that moves the reader to act.

Getting Attention: The Heading

The heading is there to get the reader's attention and get him or her to read the rest of your ad. It accomplishes this when it strongly promotes the qualities most likely to appeal to the ultimate buyer. These could be price or terms.

LOW DOWN PAYMENT

ONLY $47,500

$1,000 DOWN

LOWEST INTEREST

The headings could be special features.

4 BEDROOMS

HOUSE + GUEST HOUSE

Or a combination of features.

4BR—SOUTHERN COLONIAL

4BR—$98,500

You can expect your good headings to be copied by others. When a number of ads use the same heading, the effectiveness of all of them is reduced. This is a good reason for changing ads often.

Even when you advertise a number of properties in a larger block ad, each property should have its own heading or larger type. While headings should be in larger type to stand out, they don't have to be capitalized. In fact, lowercase letters are more legible than capitalized letters. For clarity in this book, however, headings are shown in all caps.

In a desirable area, the property's location is usually the main feature. There are exceptions, however:

1. Where the newspaper has categorized the areas so that prospective buyers immediately know that the home is in a desirable area;
2. Smaller newspapers where all of the ads are likely to be read because there are so few; or
3. A home located in an obscure or less-desirable-sounding area—an inquiry and visit might well reveal that the home and area meet the needs of a prospective buyer who would not have inquired at all had the area been emphasized.

When these exceptions do not apply and the location is a positive feature, the location *should be* in the heading. You can use a subheading to cover other features, or they can be combined.

BEVERLY HILLS $385,000

WESTWOOD COLONIAL

WESTWOOD 4BR COLONIAL

When a home has a special desirable feature, such as four bedrooms, commercial zoning, zoned for horses, swimming pool or even an unusually attractive price or terms, your heading should generally reflect that strong feature. The remainder of this book will give examples of effective headings for every imaginable feature.

However, there are many homes that, while desirable, just don't have the kind of features for creating instant appeal on paper.

If you've tried hard to find special features but they don't lend themselves to a heading, you can resort to an attention-getting line that reveals little about the house but intrigues the reader to read on and get the total story. Cutesy headings such as *Sugar & Spice* don't really say a thing or grab the reader's attention. They are best avoided.

The ideal way to present the property without outstanding features is to find words that either set a mood or perk the interest of the reader to examine particular strengths of the house. Chapter Five includes numerous examples of general headings.

Describing the Benefits: The Body

The ad body should flow naturally from the heading. The body of the ad gives facts and sets a mood. Keep in mind the ad is simply a teaser to induce the reader to call for further information. Positive features and words that trigger emotional responses accomplish this.

Miles of sand beach for barefoot walking

Child-safe cul-de-sac

Mouth-watering family orchard

Rocking-chair front porch

Sun-drenched kitchen

Lazy fish-filled river

Snuggle-up fireplace

Sassy French Provincial

Room for bikes and trikes

On a winding country lane

Embodies the charm and romance of a bygone era

Restored to capture the aura of yesteryear

Nestled beneath towering pines

In writing your ad you must be the eternal optimist. Mentioning an undesired feature or negative aspect reduces the likelihood of a call and does a disservice to the prospective buyer as well. Any analysis of home-buying patterns shows that many, if not most, buyers end up with features they didn't want and without features that were "must-haves"—and they are happy with their homes. When these buyers saw the house they purchased, they had an opportunity to realize that there were positive benefits they had underestimated and "must-haves" that didn't really matter. However, if they had heard about the negatives in advance, they might never have even looked at the property that ultimately became their home. A notable exception to this rule is negative ads, covered in Chapter Nine.

Prospective buyers often are nervous—a real estate purchase is, after all, likely to be the largest decision of their lives. Giving them a negative feature provides them with an escape, an opportunity to avoid a decision.

Your ads should avoid trivial detail. The fact that there are new gutters and the air conditioner has a new compressor will not sell a house. The more details your ads contain, the greater the likelihood that you will include information that appears negative or undesirable to a prospective buyer.

Mentioning that a new home includes a bath is not necessary—people expect it to have one. It could even be a negative feature if a prospect wants two baths.

Mentioning that a basement is unfinished is not necessary. A finished basement, however, might be a plus.

Ads should always be honest and highly positive, extolling the virtue of a property. There are exceptions, however, such as the fixer-upper, where a home is often pictured as worse than it actually is. (See Chapter Nine.)

The purpose of the ad body is to sell benefits. You must show homeseekers that the property fulfills their needs. The ad should contain information that interests them enough to call for more. The most effective ways of describing particular benefits are illustrated throughout the rest of this book.

Where specific features don't work, you can get results with more general language. Chapter Five includes examples of generalized language to be used in the ad body.

Addresses? Except for open house ads, your ad generally *should not* include the address. Buying a home is a big decision and can be very scary, so many people unconsciously look for reasons not to buy. If they have a chance to drive by for a "look-see," any negative factor can turn into a reason to avoid further inquiry. You have then lost the opportunity to overcome a real or imaginary fault and to show the benefits the property offers.

When an address is given, the prospective buyer may actually go to the door and try to talk to the owner. Unsupervised buyer/seller contact is likely to mean no sale, even though the property is perfect for the buyer's needs.

When you don't provide the address, prospective buyers must contact you for details. You then have the opportunity to find out their specific needs and to sell the advertised property or show another property that better meets their needs.

Price? The price of the property generally *should be* included in ads. Some brokers believe that leaving out a price brings in responses from a wider spectrum of potential buyers. This provides them the opportunity to switch callers to properties more appropriate to their needs. Other brokers feel that mentioning price downgrades quality properties.

However, tests by newspapers have consistently shown that unpriced ads result in fewer responses than priced ads, even for luxury property. Many serious buyers are turned off when they don't see a price. Some—often quite accurately—regard unpriced ads as a sure sign of an overpriced property. And most people hesitate to put themselves in the position of being told their perfect house is way beyond their financial capacity.

If price is a prime feature it can be included in the ad heading.

SHOREWOOD—$165,000

Otherwise, price generally should come after the closing statement ending the ad.

With expensive homes, many brokers like to indicate the price range without mentioning an exact figure. They feel that this enhances prestige.

Over $200,000

In the 90's

Mid-90's

Motivating Action: The Closing

An effective closing either sums up the features, helps set the mood, gives a reassurance of value or asks for action. Closings that accomplish these goals appear throughout this book. Chapter Five includes many closings, categorized by purpose.

The Signature Use your firm name in all your ads. Blind ads by brokers without a firm name are unethical—and, in some states, illegal.

Some brokers simply put "agent" or "broker" in their ads along with a phone number. Don't do it. Many prospective buyers will believe that the property belongs to the advertising broker, and so offers little likelihood of a good deal.

There is institutional value in having your name in ads. The name recognition helps in dealing with prospective buyers as well as owners.

Some ads have the broker's name and phone number immediately after the last word of the ad. This reduces the number of lines in the ad but produces a cramped look that detracts from its general effectiveness. The preferred form is a signature line that makes your name stand out. You may want to put your firm name in capital letters for greater contrast with the ad body.

Many newspapers accept cuts of the broker's logo. A number of your logos on one page show the reader that you can offer several properties. Logos do serve as institutional advertising and provide greater name recognition, but their advantages must be weighed against their higher costs.

You can include a specialty in your signature block, such as:

Investment property specialists

The motel specialists

Shorewood exclusively

The specialty line will tell prospective buyers you have other properties.

Some firms include image-building information that doesn't help sell.

Since 1922

A half century of service

Serving Shorewood for 40 years

We make house calls

While the above information on office signs can be beneficial, it really doesn't do much to increase ad response.

The "Realtor®" term and symbol takes little space and should be included with your name if you are a member of the National Association of Realtors®. It shows you are bound to a course of moral conduct far beyond the bare legal requirements.

Putting It All Together

The remainder of this book will show you how to write ads aimed at specific buyers and how to stress particular features of a wide spectrum of real estate.

2 Location, Privacy and View

You have undoubtedly heard that the three most important factors in determining value are location, location and location. This statement isn't just rhetoric. Buyers generally regard location as their top priority above architectural style, floor plan or amenities.

A desirable location deserves to be noticed by ad readers. If your property is in a particularly attractive part of an area that your newspaper uses as a heading, then that subdivision or subarea should be part of your own heading.

NOTE: The boxed comments in the left margin correspond to the sample ad headings listed on the right (and also boxed).

Neighborhood

Keep in mind that desirability of location is a relative factor. Desirability directly relates to price range. A highly desirable area for a $50,000 home would not necessarily be a desirable area for a home selling for $500,000. If the location is a plus factor for a particular property, then the location should be included in the ad if it is not in the paper's heading category.

When an area is a negative factor or just marginally desirable, don't emphasize the area in your ads. Prospective buyers who actually see a home are often sold by the emotional appeal of one or more of the features. Had they known the (what they consider marginal or negative) location in advance, they probably would not have even inquired.

Headings Ad headings that emphasize the desirability of an area include:

A MALIBU ADDRESS

If the price seems reasonable for a very desirable area, it should be included in the heading.

MALIBU—*$198,000*

This approach can make a little-known area more desirable.

BE FIRST TO DISCOVER VISTA

LA JOLLA TRENDSETTER

HEART OF BEVERLY HILLS

BEL AIRE ADDRESS

PRESTIGIOUS SAN MARCOS

FABULOUS INDIAN WELLS

THE BEAUTY OF WESTWOOD

THE LUXURY OF PALM SPRINGS

FALLBROOK'S FINEST

MOVE UP TO WESTWOOD

COUNTRY CLUB AREA

PREFERRED LAKE DRIVE ADDRESS

This ad gives special class to an old area.

OLD SAN DIEGO

MIDDLETON'S FINEST

Body Copy A desirable area can be covered in the ad body with:

In highly prized Westlake Village

In sought-after Westview

In the small exclusive community of Fallbrook

Nearby suburb

The weekends start earlier in. . .

In the coveted community of Westlake Village

The most prestigious street in Bel Aire

For the price of an ordinary home you can live in. . .

The only available home in much-sought-after Westwood Village

On a private lane in. . .

Set in the estate area of Mount Vernon

In the friendly community of Westwood where neighbors still know each other by name

In the master-planned community of. . .

Better

In the masterfully-planned community of. . .

On the best block of the most-sought after street in. . .

The name of a desirable or desirable-sounding subdivision also makes an excellent heading.

THE WOODLANDS

VILLAGE WOODS

STONEHAVEN

DELAWARE PINES

STRAWBERRY HILL—$98,500

BEACON POINT

MARINER'S WALK

COACHLIGHT VILLAGE

A desirable street can be emphasized.

MISSION ROAD—$89,500

ALBERTA COVE ROAD

Often particular streets are boundaries of economic subareas. You could emphasize particular desirability with:

NORTH OF CAPITAL DRIVE

WEST OF TRUESDALE BLVD.

It is possible to emphasize the desirability of an area without specifying the area. You would do so in the ad heading or body when the location has no special known identification which distinguishes it from less desirable areas.

PRESTIGIOUS ADDRESS

THE RIGHT ADDRESS

AN ELEGANT ADDRESS

A SUCCESS ADDRESS
You will be proud of the address.

ELITE LOCATION

AN ESTATE-LIKE AREA

FAIRY-TALE SETTING

COVETED LOCATION

VERY "IN" LOCATION

This phrase is appropriate for a close-in location.

LIVE WHERE IT'S AT

ELITE AREA

GOLD COAST ADDRESS

THE BEL AIRE OF TOLEDO

THE BEVERLY HILLS OF AKRON

AAA LOCATION

EXCITING LOCATION

PREMIER LOCATION

MILLIONAIRES' ROW

LOCATION—LOCATION

DISCOVER YOUR OWN SHANGRI-LA

PREFERRED LOCATION

A most rare setting

In an architecturally controlled community

A very special neighborhood

This makes an older area seem attractive.

ESTABLISHED NEIGHBORHOOD

An established community of fine homes

Established neighborhood of prestige homes

In an exclusive community of fine residences

Family-oriented neighborhood

SOUGHT-AFTER LOCATION
set amidst horse farms and fine estates

Closeness of places to other areas can be emphasized in your ad heading or in the ad body.

BEL AIRE (ALMOST)

These emphasize closeness to a desirable area.

ON THE EDGE OF BEVERLY HILLS

BORDERING BEVERLY HILLS

ALMOST IN BEVERLY HILLS

ACROSS FROM MISSION HILLS

You can make the fact that property is close to a major employer a positive feature.

WALK TO LOCKHEED

WALK TO WORK

This location is not as close as a walk to work.

BIKE TO WORK

Just a couple minutes from Pinewood Plaza

Convenient to everything

Less than 30 minutes from everything

Walking-close to schools and shopping

Super schools are walking-close to this . . .

Late for school? Not from this . . .

Close to beach, ski lift, recreational area, baseball stadium, etc.

8 MINUTES TO HEAVEN

CUT YOUR COMMUTE

A desirable school district can be a strong plus for family housing.

KILDARE SCHOOL DISTRICT

WALK TO MALL

The plaza is not there yet.

WALK TO PLANNED PLAZA

E-Z DRIVE TO PLAZA

Convenience to medical facilities is a major concern to many buyers.

ACROSS FROM MEDICAL CENTER

This could be a strong plus feature.

Adjacent to jogging trail

Leave your car in the garage. Walk to the station from this. . .

Walk to train

Almost in the park

Around the corner from the park

Walk to worship

Short walk to St. Mary's

Walking-close to synagogue

Backs to woods

10 minutes to shops

Walk to courts

Bike to beach

Closer than a walk to beach

Just steps to beach

Adjacent to riding trails

Borders national park

Just minutes from the quaint village of. . .

Short drive to famed *Lake La Belle*

30-minute drive to blue waters and white sand beaches

Closeness to a well-known home can be emphasized.

Across the street from the *Kincaid Estate*

Just down the road from the *Kincaid Estate*

You will be neighbors with bank presidents and physicians in this. . .

Adjoins the former *Bing Crosby* ranch

ENJOY WALKING
This. . .is close to everything.

Location Special Features

A location's special features can be stressed in the ad heading or in the ad body with:

ON THE GREENBELT

GREENBELT LOCATION

CORNER LOCATION

SOUTHERN EXPOSURE

ON A SUNNY CORNER LOT

NESTLED IN THE HILLS

IN THE HILLS

ON TOP OF THE HILL

PERCHED ATOP A HIGH KNOLL

KNOLLTOP SETTING

Sited high on a ½-acre knoll on the prettiest street and the friendliest neighborhood in town

Majestically perched on a knoll

SITTING PRETTY
on an oversized lot, this...

Majestically perched on a 1½-acre site overlooking...

HILLTOPPER

YOUR OWN EAGLE'S NEST

ABOVE ALL

TOP OF THE MOUNTAIN

TOP OF THE WORLD

BE KING OF THE HILL

HILLTOP SHOWPLACE

ABOVE THE SMOG

Nestled in secluded elegance on an estate-size lot in *Rolling Hills*

A natural undisturbed setting

On a quiet dead-end street

Stroll the peaceful village streets from this...

A little bit of Cape Cod

Waterscaped setting

Your oasis in the city

Where the trees grow tall and the sun meets the sea

Nestled in a peaceful wooded setting

Nestled in the *pines*

On a no-traffic street

The gently rolling hills create a haven for this...

Cantilevered over a magnificent 2-acre estate

Set in a sun-streaked wooded glen

HOME IN THE WOODS

In the planned residential community of *Westwood*

Set in the pastoral seclusion of *Westville*

Offers the excitement of city living in a quiet country-like setting

COUNTRY SETTING
for a city sophisticate

PASTORAL TRANQUILITY

Country ambiance with all of the conveniences of the city

You will be proud to give this address.

Proudly situated on over *4* rolling acres

On *2* prestigious acres

Pastoral setting

Tucked away on *3* enchanted wooded acres

On a wooded cul-de-sac

On a peaceful cul-de-sac

ON A QUIET CUL-DE-SAC

NO FLOODS—NO SLIDES—NO SMOG

OVERLOOKS 17th FAIRWAY

ON THE BLUFF

On a quiet residential block

On a quiet country lane

In a family-oriented community

Major highway frontage

In a neighborhood of fine homes

In a select community of fine homes

Located in an exclusive conclave of fine homes

Set in a serene residential enclave

In one of the most desirable areas of . . .

Established neighborhood of prestige homes

In a cloistered community of fine homes

In an area of handsome executive homes

In a small community of quality homes

Located in an area of large estates

In a Williamsburg-like setting

Scenic and secluded setting

Generalities governing location include:

Indeed a superb location

The setting for your future happiness

A beautiful setting for a superb estate

A very special home in a special neighborhood

An address to be envied

In a pleasantly secluded neighborhood of winding boulevards and intimate culs-de-sac

Postcard setting

Storybook setting

Sited for excellence

Where location is used as a heading, a subheading can be used for another desirable feature.

HEART OF BEVERLY HILLS

FIXER-UPPER ESTATE—$820,000

Golf-Related Locations

Proximity to a golf course will overwhelm all other considerations for a certain segment of the population. Appropriate ad headings:

FORE

TRY FOR PAR

TEE OFF FOR FREE

Include this if home owners' fee includes golf.

THUNDERBIRD GOLF COURSE

Other body copy:

Just off the 7th tee

Just off the Emerald Green Fairways

Just a chip shot from the course

Golf-cart-distance from the course

Not on the course

On the 13th fairway

The golf course is right in your front yard.

Executive course

Smaller course

World-class golf course

Championship golf course

27-hole course

Designed by *Jack Nicklaus*

In a country-club setting

Not on golf course

Located in an exclusive golf community

In the golf-course community of. . .

Completed Ads Stressing Location

If greater details about the location would have conveyed a positive image, then the details should have been included.

SO NEAR YET SO FAR

Convenient to shopping, churches and busline, yet this friendly 2-bedroom Cape Cod is far from the city's bustle and noise. An oversized two-car garage and a delightful garden are just two of the many features that make this home desirable at $79,500.

Clyde Realty 476-8200

The desirable location is the strongest attraction, so must be emphasized.

BEVERLY HILLS

This stately Mediterranean is situated in a cloistered enclave of prestige homes. Offering 4 bedrooms, 4½ baths, living and family rooms for entertainment on a grand scale, a separate guest suite, 4-car garage, pool, hot spa, tennis court and more amenities than you could possibly imagine. It comes complete with an address to be envied.
$1,200,000

Clyde Realty 476-8200

This ad, with its attention-getter heading, sells the benefits of an older home in an urban location.

THERE IS MORE TO LIFE

than commuting. This picture-perfect Victorian town house boasts everything the suburbs can offer except the driving. On a quiet tree-canopied street in a sought-after area, it offers 2 bedrooms, huge studio (or 3rd bedroom), 2 massive baths and several fire-places. The sun-drenched kitchen opens onto a dining patio in the private walled garden. City living at its finest for an affordable $96,000.

Clyde Realty 476-8200

The heading is an attention-getter indicating the property is golf-related.

DUFFER'S WIDOW

Keep that golfer close to home with this condo overlooking the 17th fairway. Dual master suites, den, wet bar and a delightful patio with hot spa are just a few of the amenities which will make this your home for the good life. $187,500.

Clyde Realty 476-8200

Privacy

To many prospective buyers, privacy is a prime concern. There are those who wish to escape the boxed-in feeling of the cities. They don't want to have to talk in whispers for fear of being overheard. They want to know they can turn up their stereos if they want to. They want to know the feeling of actually being alone. People who have lived with in-laws or in a large apartment complex know the true value of privacy.

Headings Privacy can be promoted effectively in ad headings.

This also makes a good closing.

ULTIMATE IN SECLUSION

ENCHANTING HIDEAWAY

ESCAPE
to this enchanting hideaway.

SERENE HIDEAWAY

SERENITY

WANT TO BE ALONE?

BE A HERMIT

HERMIT'S CHOICE

END OF THE ROAD

END-OF-THE-ROAD SECLUSION

END-OF-THE-ROAD PRIVACY

SECLUDED SLEEPER

CLOSE-IN SECLUSION

GET LOST

A PRIVATE WORLD

More than one feature can be combined in your heading.

SUPER VIEW—PRIVACY TOO

LOVE YOUR PRIVACY

THE IDEAL SANCTUARY

A PRIVATE WORLD

YOUR PRIVATE OASIS

YOUR OASIS OF PRIVACY

NUDIST'S DELIGHT

THE SOUND OF SILENCE

If the price is likely to attract interest, it can be included in the heading.

SANCTUARY $49,500

PRIVACY PREVAILS

ELEGANCE & PRIVACY

PICTURESQUE AND PRIVATE

SECLUDED VILLA

A WORLD OF PRIVACY

ON A SECLUDED ROAD

ON PRIVATE ROAD

WALLED ESTATE

ABSOLUTE PRIVACY

DISAPPEAR

DESERT ISLAND
It just seems that way at this...

This is aimed at a particular segment of privacy-seekers and could be very effective for a low-priced starter home.

ESCAPE YOUR IN-LAWS

ESCAPE TO TOTAL SECLUSION

Body Copy The ad body can emphasize privacy by including phrases such as:

Master suite exits to private pool and spa.

The name of the development can be an important selling point.

In the private world of *Cedarbrook*

Located on a very private corner of *Westwood*

On an acre of privacy

The privacy of a single-family home for the price of a condominium

Very private pool

Very private Jacuzzi off master bedroom

Tucked away amidst the pines

Where neighbors maintain their property and your privacy

On *3.8* very private acres

Set in a very private glade

Privacy garden

Ancient oaks create a screen of privacy and gently filter the morning light.

A secluded place where there is time to ponder

Privacy so complete one could swim in nature's garments

A very private world of your own

Set in a private wooded enclave

In a private wooded preserve

Expansive privacy in a luxury setting

Through the *stone gates* to your own world of private elegance

Cloistered behind high stone walls

Scenic and secluded setting

Privacy shutters
Providing pampered privacy

Where the air is cleaner, water bluer and privacy still exists

End-of-the-road privacy

One-way vision

One-way walls of glass

Leave the city for this very private hideaway.

A most rare private setting for this...

The ideal retreat from hectic city life

Private master suite

Master suite with his-and-her baths

Privacy of a walled patio

Very private patio

Children's wing

Guest wing

You will revel in the privacy of this...

Electric gates open to this private villa.

You will be captivated by the quiet beauty of this very private villa.

Even the revenuers couldn't find this one...a really remote...

Secluded yet only 20 minutes from the Civic Center

Set on a hillside to give you that little extra privacy

Situated for utmost privacy

This...home is hidden from view by its large wooded lot.

A very private sunporch

A very private end unit

This is an excellent description for a starter home.

Anyone who has ever lived with in-laws will appreciate the privacy and tranquility of this...

Closings For ad closings emphasizing privacy, consider:

Tranquility and privacy await you $________.

Your private escape kit $________.

A very private place $________.

Serenity can be yours $________.

This can be your sanctuary $________.

Completed Ads Stressing Privacy

A PRIVATE WORLD

The tree-canopied drive will lead you to a world of beauty and absolute privacy. The 2-story brick authentic English Tudor home features 3 bedrooms, den, formal dining room, 2½ baths plus a 3-car attached garage. The home, which reflects the finest in craftsmanship and care, is completely shielded from the street by its park-like setting. Tranquility and privacy await you for $225,000.

Clyde Realty **476-8200**

This attention-getting heading says privacy.

WANT TO BE ALONE?

A world of privacy can be yours. This 3BR, 4-year-old Cape Cod is tucked away on a wooded, full-acre lot on a secluded tree-lined street. Amenities include an oversized attached double garage, 1½ baths, full basement, country kitchen, wood-burning fireplace and a huge screened and glassed back porch that looks out over your own forest. The perfect family sanctuary at $89,800.

Clyde Realty **476-8200**

If the reader is living with in-laws, this ad hits home, selling the benefits of an affordable house.

ESCAPE THE IN-LAWS

Tired of whispering? Yearn for the personal freedom of your own home but think you can't afford it? Privacy can be yours in this 2BR expandable in Westover Heights that offers an oversized garage, full basement and a huge second floor bonus room. Your chance to stop whispering at only $43,800 with low-down FHA or no-down VA financing.

Clyde Realty **476-8200**

This ad has an attention-getting heading. The price was included in the heading because it is an attractive feature. Privacy can be emphasized in urban as well as suburban and rural property.

NUDIST'S DELIGHT—$89,500

A high-walled garden resplendent in a myriad of colors can be your private oasis in the city. The impressive 3-bedroom, 2½-bath residence offers the traditional charm and detailing of a time when leisurely living was a way of life. Don't let this opportunity for sanctuary escape you. Call today for a private showing.

Clyde Realty **476-8200**

View

Homes and lots with a view attract buyers. Advertising featuring a view provides an aura of quality, even with buyers who don't especially care about the vista. To most buyers, however, the view is very important. Many homes are sold looking out from the windows rather than looking in. A good view can overcome many deficiencies in a property.

Headings These headings emphasize the view:

These headings give the visual picture of looking down on a blanket of beautiful lights.

ABOVE THE LIGHTS

SEA OF LIGHTS

CITY LIGHTS

THE CITY AT YOUR FEET

PALACE IN THE SKY

CABIN IN THE SKY

ABOVE ALL

WHITE-WATER VIEW

OCEAN VIEW

CITY VIEW

RIVER VIEW

These headings indicate a view without really saying the property has one.

HIGH ON A HILL

ATOP THE HILL

THE TOP OF THE HILL

A VIEW OF THE WORLD

EXHILARATING VIEW

INCOMPARABLE VIEW

MILLION-DOLLAR VIEW

This would be good for English architecture.

SMASHING VIEW

OVERLOOKING THE WORLD

UNREAL VIEW

AWESOME VIEW

MAGICAL VIEWS

DAZZLING VIEWS

These headings indicate an uninterrupted wide view.

CINEMASCOPE VIEW

PANORAMIC VIEW

360° VIEW

SWEEPING VIEW

MILE-WIDE VIEW

These indicate that nothing can be built to obstruct the view.

PERMANENT VIEW

GUARANTEED VIEW

VIEW PRESERVED BY DEED COVENANTS

YOU CAN SEE FOREVER

SEDUCTIVE VIEW

VIEW-TIFUL

VIEWS—VIEWS—VIEWS

VIEW LOVERS

These headings can be modified. (Example: Unsurpassed ocean *view).*

UNSURPASSED VIEW

INCREDIBLE VIEW

WATCH THE SHIPS
from this ocean view. . .

UNPARALLELED VISTAS
await you with this. . .

FOREVER VIEWS

BIRD'S-EYE VIEW

EAGLE'S-EYE VIEW

These headings indicate another feature besides the view.

NEW—VIEW

COOL POOL AND VIEW

SERENE VISTAS

PASTORAL VISTAS

SERENE PASTORAL VISTAS

SEVENTH HEAVEN VIEWS

FAIRY-TALE VIEWS

PICTURE BOOK VIEWS

GLORIOUS VIEW

Body Copy The view can also be featured in the ad body. For water-related ads, see Chapter Eight.

Up high on a picturesque knoll, this...

Overlooking the ruggedly beautiful...

Your opportunity to live among the most beautiful scenery in the world...

This...offers magnificent sightseeing right out your windows.

What a view from this...

View the city lights from your private patio.

Set high on a hill with a view of the valley below

A view from every window and the world at your feet from this..., situated...

Spectacular views from every window of this...

A commanding view of...

Kitchen windows overlook...

Sunrise view

Unspoiled view

A breathtaking hilltop panorama of...

High atop..., everything else is downhill.

You can almost see...from the redwood deck of this...

Unobstructed...view

Breathtaking view of...

Watch the ships from the...

Watch the sailboats, from the deck of this...

Commanding over *10* acres of *pastoral splendor*

Let the rest of the world live in your shadow.

Overlooks a variegated fairyland of lights

Carefully sited to offer superb views of...

Tranquil view of...

Framed by spectacular *mountain* views

Garden views from the picture window of this...

Your first glimpse of the magnificent *ocean* view will convince you that truly this is an unparalled place to live.

Watch the morning sunrise from your very private deck.

Watch the evening sunset from your very private deck.

An almost fairy-tale diorama

Surrounded by stunning vistas

Views don't necessarily have to be natural.

The dining area overlooks the sparkling pool.

The sliding window wall of the great room opens to the lush landscaping of a tropical garden.

The window wall makes the lush garden a natural extension of the living room.

Birds and animals are a definite plus in selling property.

The breakfast area overlooks the well-frequented hummingbird feeders.

You will be able to look out the windows and see quail and doves at the well-frequented bird feeders.

The backyard features a magnificent oak tree that is home for at least one family of squirrels.

(Deer/Wild Turkeys/Eagles) have been seen on the property.

Closings Closings related specifically to views include:

Million-dollar view included in the price of only $________.

The house is included with the million-dollar view for only $________.

You can be above it all for $________.

Your own eagle's nest at $________.

The city at your feet for only $________.

Celestial view with a down-to-earth price of $________.

The view will last forever but your opportunity is now.
Call ______________________________

Completed Ads Stressing View

This ad sets a mood while telling very little about the house. Its purpose is to evoke an inquiry.

NATURE WILL BE YOUR DECORATOR

Magnificent window walls appear to bring the great outdoors into this exciting natural stone and cedar 3-bedroom home. You will look out over a wooded ravine inhabited by squirrels, raccoons and even deer. A rare offering that is truly at peace with nature, $149,800.

Clyde Realty **476-8200**

The heading is an attention-getter leading directly into the ad body.

COUNT EVERY STAR

and every flickering light of the valley. You are bound to feel on top of the world living in this sprawling 3BR, 2½-bath hillside ranch. It has everything on your want list plus a view that is forever. Unexcelled at $97,400.

Clyde Realty 476-8200

Colorado *gives an image of stone, glass and mountains.*

This ad is directly aimed at readers with an interest in photography.

A PHOTO VIEW

The hundreds of sq. ft. of glass in this 3BR, 2½-bath Colorado contemporary comes completely decorated with mountain vistas that would be worthy of Ansel Adams. Situated on an estate-size lot dotted with towering pines, this 3-year-old home is enhanced by central air, all the built-ins imaginable, a 3-car garage and a darkroom with stainless steel sinks in the full basement. Picture yourself as owner at $175,000.

Clyde Realty 476-8200

HIGH ON A WINDY HILL

Your private road leads to this glass and stone estate that gently blends into the rugged mountainside. You will look down upon the city from every room of this 4BR, 11-room residence enhanced with every imaginable convenience. Your own eagle's nest offered at $269,000.

Clyde Realty 476-8200

3 Architecture, Security and Grounds

The first impression prospective buyers get of a house is when you take them up the front walk. Your classified ads set the mood for a positive response to this introduction. Even more important, they can help you generate inquiries from people to whom the outside features of a property are especially important. This chapter shows you how to make effective use of these features in your ads, and the following chapters do the same for all the other aspects of a residential property.

Architecture

The fact that a home was designed by an architect, rather than taken from a plan book at the local lumber yard, can become a significant plus in ads. One way to achieve this is to use a heading or ad body that points out that a property was specially designed by an architect.

ARCHITECTURALLY PERFECT

ARCHITECTURALLY FRESH

ONE OF A KIND

ARCHITECTURAL MASTERPIECE

ARCHITECTURALLY DESIGNED

DISTINCTIVELY DESIGNED

An ad which mentions the name of the architect is even stronger.

FRANK LLOYD WRIGHT-DESIGNED

The name of a well-known architect should always be given, but even a little-known name can add desirability and prestige.

Designed by *Thomas Kemper,* this home captures the spirit of the Southwest.

Designed by *Thomas Kemper* in *1923*

An outstanding home designed by *Thomas Kemper*

Artistic masterpiece designed by the reknowned *Thomas Kemper*

You can also allude to well-known architects when the house is designed in a style similar to that of the architect.

FRANK LLOYD WRIGHT-INSPIRED

If a home has ever been featured in a newspaper or magazine or other promotions, make mention of it.

Featured in *Architectural Digest*

Featured in *House & Garden*

Featured in 1982 Parade of Homes

On 1981 home tour

For homes whose designs have won awards you could state:

ARCHITECTURAL AWARD WINNER

DESIGN AWARD WINNER

AWARD-WINNING DESIGN

Architectural Styles

An advertisement naming an architectural style has a distinctive touch that creates a mental picture in the mind of the reader. The architectural statements are shown below as ad headings but can also be used in the ad body if you feel another feature will make a stronger heading.

Colonial

This creates the mental image of soaring columns.

RHETT BUTLER COLONIAL

GONE WITH THE WIND

COME HOME SCARLETT AND RHETT

TARA

SOUTHERN MANOR

SOUTHERN BELLE

PILLARED COLONIAL

SOUTHERN COLONIAL

SOUTHERN TRADITIONAL

NEW ORLEANS COLONIAL

DOUBLE-STAIR COLONIAL

COLONIAL WITH A CONTEMPORARY FLAIR

COLUMNED COLONIAL

7-COLUMNED COLONIAL

SUBSTANTIAL COLONIAL

COLONIAL CLASSIC

CLASSIC COLONIAL

NOSTALGIC COLONIAL

NEW ENGLAND CHARMER

CLAPBOARD COLONIAL

OLD NEW ENGLAND

FEDERAL COLONIAL

COLONIAL SPLENDOR

DISTINCTIVE COLONIAL

IMPECCABLE COLONIAL

PICTURE-BOOK COLONIAL

This creates a very pleasant image.

A TOUCH OF WILLIAMSBURG

ATTENTION: WILLIAMSBURG BUFFS

WILLIAMSBURG-INSPIRED

MT. VERNON COLONIAL

CONNECTICUT YANKEE

CENTER-HALL COLONIAL

EXECUTIVE COLONIAL

STATELY COLONIAL

TIMELESS COLONIAL

MONUMENTAL COLONIAL

NANTUCKET COLONIAL

NANTUCKET REVISITED

SALTBOX COLONIAL

QUAKER VILLAGE COLONIAL

ROTUNDA COLONIAL

CLAPBOARD AND SHUTTERS

HEAD-TURNING COLONIAL

GEORGIAN COLONIAL

VIRGINIA COLONIAL

STATELY GEORGIAN

CLASSIC GEORGIAN

QUAKER CHARMER

PENNSYLVANIA DUTCH

DUTCH COLONIAL

PAMPERED DUTCH COLONIAL

NEW ENGLAND IN OHIO

NEW ENGLAND SALTBOX DESIGN

MISSISSIPPI GAMBLER
This southern colonial features. . ., . . ., . . .,

CURRIER & IVES
would have loved this picture-book colonial.

A heading for the literate reader

NATHANIEL HAWTHORNE
would have loved this multigabled 9-room colonial.

This could be used for other architectural styles.

CHAMPAGNE COLONIAL
Absolute elegance in this. . .

This is an excellent approach for a newer home.

COLONIAL PURIST
You will think this center-hall New England colonial was built in the 1700s.

COLONIAL FLAVOR
at a pre–Civil War price

EUROPEAN COLONIAL

Cape Cod

FRIENDLY CAPE COD

CAPTIVATING CAPE

NEW ENGLAND CAPE COD

Contemporary *Contemporary* is just another name for a very modern design. The following can be used as headings for contemporary homes or as descriptions within the body of the ad:

RERESHING CONTEMPORARY

SKYLIT CONTEMPORARY

TREETOP CONTEMPORARY

DRAMATIC CONTEMPORARY

OUTSTANDING CONTEMPORARY

STUNNING CONTEMPORARY

SOPHISTICATED CONTEMPORARY

CUSTOM CONTEMPORARY

UPBEAT CONTEMPORARY

THE AMERICAN DREAM — *This really fits any house.*

EASTERN STYLE — *This adds prestige to a house in the West.*

WESTERN STYLE — *This adds prestige to a house in the East.*

COLORADO CONTEMPORARY

CALIFORNIA CONTEMPORARY

CALIFORNIA-INSPIRED CONTEMPORARY

ARIZONA CONTEMPORARY

NEW MEXICO CONTEMPORARY

The Southwest has a positive design image.

TOMORROW'S HOUSE

A TOUCH OF GLASS

TONS OF GLASS

CONCRETE AND STEEL

IMAGINATIVE DESIGN

GLASS AND REDWOOD

STONE AND CEDAR

HILLSIDE A-FRAME

PICTURESQUE A-FRAME

TRI-LEVEL

SPLIT-LEVEL

SPLIT-LEVEL SPLENDOR

EARTH SHELTER

RUSTIC CONTEMPORARY

SOLAR HOME

The old art deco modern rounded buildings of the pre–World War II era have become very much in demand today.

ART DECO

BEAUX-ART

Stunningly conceived

Innovative without being trendy

Clean sleek uncluttered design

Stunning contemporary architecture features a unique combination of fine family living and entertainment on the grand scale.

Free-flowing contemporary design sculptured of stone and glass

The stone and glass exterior blends harmoniously into the wooded countryside.

Or Spanish, Italian, French Renaissance, etc.

Contemporary with a hint of Oriental

Excitingly different

Contemporary elegance casually designed in the flavor of the Southwest

Imaginative floor plan

Sleek and sophisticated, yet warm and cheerful

Rustic board-and-batten exterior blends with the golden hills surrounding this. . .

Spanish Red tile roofs and arches are the two key features of Spanish architecture. The following headings should be considered:

JUST A TOUCH OF SPAIN

A TOUCH OF SPAIN

OLD WORLD SPANISH

"OLÉ"

OLD MONTEREY

SPANISH HACIENDA

ADOBE HACIENDA

SPANISH EYES

PRESIDIO SPANISH

THE CHARM OF MEXICO

SPANISH INDULGENCE

MASSIVE ARCHES

TONS OF TILE

MISSION TILE

English For brick and/or stone homes with a Norman, Tudor, Cotswold or Elizabethan flavor, the following can be used as headings:

ENGLISH CHATEAU

ENGLISH COUNTRY

UPSTAIRS DOWNSTAIRS
an English estate set in. . .

TO THE MANOR BORN

COTSWOLD MANOR

STONE MANOR HOUSE

ENGLISH COTTAGE

ENGLISH MANOR

ENGLISH MANOR HOUSE

ELIZABETHAN TOWN HOUSE

SMASHING

ANGLOPHILE'S DELIGHT

This conservative approach creates a solid feeling.

PROPER ENGLISH

A TOUCH OF OLD ENGLISH

PROPER ENGLISH BRICK

ENGLISH BRICK

YORKSHIRE TUDOR

TIFFANY TUDOR

HANDSOME TUDOR

FLAWLESS TUDOR

SMASHING TUDOR

OLD ENGLISH

COUNTRY ENGLISH

ENGLISH COLONIAL

QUEEN ANNE

ARCHITECTURALLY SMASHING

Your ad body might say:

Distinctively designed with a touch of Tudor

Old-world charm prevails with its leaded glass, slate roof and architectural detailing.

Authentic English manor

Reminiscent of an English country estate

Smashingly impressive *English Tudor*

Patterned after the noble houses of England where entertaining and hospitality were inseparable from a gracious tradition

French A French architectural description creates a very positive mental image in the minds of most readers.

CHATEAU

FRENCH CHATEAU

SASSY FRENCH PROVINCIAL

FRENCH COLONIAL

TURRETED CASTLE

FLEMISH COTTAGE

FRENCH COUNTRY HOME

The words sumptuous *and* tantalizing *have a sexual connotation.*

SUMPTUOUS FRENCH COUNTRY HOME

TANTALIZING FRENCH COUNTRY HOME

FRENCH REGENCY

TWO-STORY FRENCH REGENCY

FRENCH NORMANDY

TURRETED FRENCH NORMAN

FRENCH MANOR

FRENCH CONTEMPORARY

Used as a closing it would be Fantastique at $________.

FANTASTIQUE

Used as a closing it would be Magnifique at $________.

MAGNIFIQUE

Italian Italian architectural descriptions tend to create an image of a very formal home.

VENETIAN GOTHIC

STATELY MEDITERRANEAN

MEDITERRANEAN COLONIAL

OLD-WORLD MEDITERRANEAN

THE GLORY OF ROME

LAVISH VILLA

ITALIANATE ARCHITECTURE

BRICK ITALIANATE

Traditional Many American homes can't really be placed in any particular architectural style. You can cover these styles in a positive manner in the body or heading with words such as:

TRADITIONAL ESTATE

NEW TRADITIONAL

AMERICAN TRADITIONAL

This provides a positive image for older homes.

AMERICAN BUNGALOW

IMPRESSIVE TWO-STORY

OLD-WORLD CHARM

ELEGANT BRICK TRADITIONAL

DIGNIFIED 4BR TRADITIONAL

American Ranch Single-story long homes with a low roof pitch can be described with headings such as:

LONG, LOW AND LUSCIOUS

CALIFORNIA RANCH

RAISED RANCH

This means the basement is exposed.

EXCITING RAMBLER

BRICK RANCHER

Victorian This turn-of-the-century style with its gingerbread and turrets is very much in demand because of the nostalgia craze. Productive headings:

VICTORIAN

COUNTRY VICTORIAN

CHARMING VICTORIAN

GRAND VICTORIAN

This attention-getting heading really fits.

A DIGNIFIED LADY

TURRETED VICTORIAN

VICTORIAN SHOWCASE

STATELY VICTORIAN

BOW-FRONT VICTORIAN

GRANDIOSE VICTORIAN

VINTAGE VICTORIAN

QUEEN ANNE VICTORIAN

STORYBOOK VICTORIAN

COMMANDING VICTORIAN

GINGERBREAD VICTORIAN

A GINGERBREAD HOUSE

Other Styles

A good closing would be European splendor at $______.

EUROPEAN SPLENDOR

BROWNSTONE CLASSIC

FRONT-STOOP BROWNSTONE

EUROPEAN INSPIRED

EUROPEAN TOWN HOUSE

A BIT OF BAVARIA

SWISS CHALET

ORIENTAL CHARM

GREEK REVIVAL ESTATE

ELEGANT GOTHIC

Special Features Headings may mention just one architectural feature.

GOTHIC COLUMNS

SOARING COLUMNS

BLUE SHUTTERS

SHUTTERS & BRICK

STONE & REDWOOD

VINTAGE CARVED DOORS

ANCIENT ARCHES

COLUMNED PORTICO

Body Copy The body of ads emphasizing architectural style can include language like this:

Exquisite architectural details

Handsome detailing

Authentic decor

Classic exterior

Features *colonial* grace with modern comfort

This is a way to emphasize it isn't a big old house.

A charming not-too-big *colonial*

The most authentic *French Regency* we have seen

Traditional with a contemporary touch

An exciting blend of contemporary and traditional

Remarkably distinguished design

A much-sought-after but seldom available *federal colonial*

This meticulous *colonial* exemplifies the elegance of *Southern* charm.

Narrow

San Francisco–style town house

Distinctively designed

12-foot ceilings

Victorian parlor

Front parlor

Daringly designed

A masterful example of *Elizabethan* architecture

A feeling of old-world charm is evident as you enter this . . .

This meticulous *colonial* exemplifies the elegance of Southern charm.

Dramatically different yet brimming with charm

Colonial with a contemporary flair

The aesthetic allure of classic design

Blending the traditional with the timeless

Detailing and finishing that will appeal to the most discriminating purchaser

Built with delightful *European* flair and style

More than just crown molding, this . . .

Innovative floor plan

Ageless dignity of proud *English Tudor*

A home that is as one with its surroundings

Creative use of form and space

Patterned after the noble houses of *Virginia*

Magnificent in concept, unique in design

Cut stone and *cedar*

Flexible floor plan

This describes a home in which the master bedroom is separated from other bedrooms.

Split plan

Fieldstone accents

Slate and shake

An attractive way to describe glacial or fieldstone

Crab orchard stone

A home that makes a statement as individual as you are

Provocative floor plan

Packed with architectural excitement

Over *3,000* square feet of living space that flows for entertaining yet maximizes privacy

You will love the old-world character of this delightful property.

Fluted *Corinthian* columns

Beveled glass

Fluted pilasters

Roman columns

Greek columns

Corinthian columns

Capturing nature's essence

Multilevel

Designed for flexibility and functionality

Architecturally unique

Be prepared for something tastefully different.

Aesthetically pleasing

This could describe a new home.

Designed to become legendary

A home that breaks the monotony of the ordinary

Merging aesthetic form with efficiency of function

Classical embellishments

The embodiment of simple elegance

A home of unparalleled design in a setting of unsurpassed beauty

Set in harmony with nature

Hill and home merge in natural harmony

You will be as excited as the judges when you see this award-winning home.

The stone turrets recall European grandeur.

Sophisticated 3-bedroom *French Regency*

The graciousness of yesterday is reflected in this grand new *Victorian* beauty.

With a distinctive *Oriental* flair

The distinctive design creates the ambiance of a quiet European villa.

Colonial architecture that will excite the heart of a purist

There is a fantastic feeling of openness and elegance in this . . .

Wide open and bright throughout

Open-living design

Open rustic design

Open-concept planning

Open floor plan

Free-flowing floor plan

. . . planned for easy living

The most livable floor plan you have seen

Versatile floor plan

Airy and spacious floor plan

Designed to bring the beautiful outdoors right into the living areas

Awe-inspiring design

Designed to delight

Masterful design

Exuberant design

Distinctively designed

Worthy of *House & Garden*

Exciting and spacious

Closings

A house of tomorrow today $________.

Your chance to escape from the commonplace $________.

Your escape from the commonplace $________.

A home as individual as yourself $________.

This one-of-a-kind masterpiece can be yours at only $________.

This bold statement requires your action today $________.

An American dream at $________.

Your touch of New England at $________.

Be the first to inspect this rare find $________.

Designed for easy living and priced for today at $________.

A space-age design at the down-to-earth price of $________.

An elegant design for living at $________.

Exciting individuality at $________.

A very unique offering at $________.

Designed to please at $________.

This unique lifestyle can be yours $________.

Completed Ads Stressing Architectural Style

WILLIAMSBURG-INSPIRED

Massive end fireplaces, pegged hardwood floors, towering ceilings and all of the desired detailing are tastefully combined with the conveniences of today in this newer 3BR, den, 2½-bath residence. Set on a wooded ½-acre site, the home is enhanced by a brick and copper country kitchen with all of the built-ins including microwave, central air and a 2½-car carriage house. Designed to excite the heart of a colonial purist, this is truly an American dream. Offered at $142,500.

Clyde Realty 476-8200

VICTORIAN OUTSIDE

But with a contemporary flair for easy living. The leaded glass, gingerbread woodwork and its wraparound rocking-chair-covered porch gives this almost new Victorian the gracious elegance of homes of long ago. The interior of this 3BR, 3½-bath home is a light and airy blend of the classic with contemporary convenience. There is a matching coachhouse with a studio and bath above. A one-of-a-kind architectural masterpiece proudly offered at $220,000.

Clyde Realty 476-8200

This ad carries the proper English theme throughout without being cutesy. It's likely to appeal to conservative people of means—the group it is aimed at.

A PROPER RESIDENCE

This conservatively elegant brick and stone English traditional is very likely a step above anything you have seen. There are 4 baronial-size bedrooms, 3½ luxurious baths, library, drawing room, huge living room, an authentic English pub room, a 4-car garage for your motor cars and a very correct location. An extremely civilized way to live at $290,000. See your estate agent or contact:

Clyde Realty 476-8200

OLÉ!

Capturing the old with its tile, arches and courtyard fountain, this 3BR, 2-bath Spanish contemporary offers a bright and open concept for easy living. Enhanced by flowing tile floors, ranch-size kitchen, formal dining area, step-down living area with its adobe fireplace and all the extras you would expect in a fine Larado Hills residence. Its exciting individuality can be yours at $97,600.

Clyde Realty 476-8200

This attention-getting heading fits a contemporary.

TOMORROW IS TODAY

with this stunning Peter Holmes–design contemporary in exclusive Highland Estates. Set on a spectacular view site, its free-flowing form of native stone and glass blends into the rocky hillside. Open-concept planning and soaring ceilings make this 3,000-sq.-ft. residence seem even larger. 4BR, 3½ baths, study, fitness room, formal dining area, skylighted atrium and huge living areas highlight this architectural masterpiece. At last there is a home as individual as yourself, offered at $260,000.

Clyde Realty 476-8200

Security

The use of scare tactics to sell real estate can never be condoned. Ads that focus on the dangers of a neighborhood encourage exodus rather than the solution of its problems. As people leave, further decline usually occurs.

Advertising of security benefits should be avoided in rental advertising since it could possibly be construed as a promise. If security is promised, the owner could be held liable should a loss occur because of failure in the security system. Your sale ads must also not promise security or indicate that the buyers will be safe: There is simply no way safety can be guaranteed.

While security should never be used to evoke fear, security can be used in a positive manner to sell benefits. You can stress security in ad headings with phrases such as:

These ads sell a pleasant and secure mood.

BEHIND THE GATES

BEHIND THE WALLS

HIGHRISE SECURITY

BEHIND GUARDED WALLS

BEHIND A GATE-GUARDED ENTRY

If a property has security protection, your ad body could make reference to security with statements such as:

Situated in a gate-guarded enclave of prestige homes

24-hour security patrol

24-hour guard gate

24-hour doorman

Security gate

This doesn't mean a guard; it could be a card or key gate.

A controlled-access community

Behind electronically controlled gates

Security shutters

Monitored security

Video security

State-of-the-art security

Intercom security

Behind massive stone walls

Security gates open to reveal. . .

Honeywell alarm system

Worry-free security

Police-connected alarm system

Secure residential area

Highrise security

Behind guarded walls

24-hour parking attendants

Underground security parking

Key-operated elevators

Latest in electronic security

Smoke detectors

Intercom security system

'Round-the-clock electronic surveillance

Sonic alarm system

Security cameras

Ultrasonic security system for your peace of mind

Alarm system on all windows and doors

Central security system

Armed response alarm system

Foyer security

Full security system

Sophisticated security system

Electronic alarm system

Intercom

Security windows

Lower-level security bars

Security gates with intercom

Behind a decorative wrought iron security gate

Completed Ads Stressing Security

This ad is for a condominium.

BEHIND THE GATES

living is easy with the worry-free happy life of this all-adult enclave. Just steps from the community recreation center, it has 2BR, 2 baths and it's decorator-fresh. The answer to carefree living $79,500.

Clyde Realty **476-8200**

This ad is for a condo or planned unit development.

MARINER'S VILLAGE

There is a place where you can take a peaceful evening stroll and greet your neighbors. Let your tensions disappear in this 3BR, 2-bath brick rambler in the quiet and private gate-guarded community of Westbrook. The attractive home features landscaping to be envied, a natural stone fireplace and a sun-drenched country kitchen that opens onto a brick paved patio that is the perfect spot for outdoor dining, entertaining or just plain relaxation. Offering enjoyment and peace of mind at $89,500.

Clyde Realty 476-8200

Grounds

Lot Size While *.37 acres* or *16,117 square feet* might be accurate size descriptions, they will be lost on the average reader who only knows that an acre or a half acre is large. You can better indicate that a lot is large by:

Estate-size lot

Country-size lot

Tribe-size lot

Family-size lot

Orchard-size lot

Garden-size lot

Double-size lot

Huge lot

An average-size or smaller lot should not usually be mentioned. However, you might want to mention other special features.

Corner lot

200′ deep

Gardens Gardens sell many homes. There are buyers who would not consider a home without a garden or a place for one. Even people who have never planted anything often have a yearning to till the soil. Therefore, mentioning a garden in your ads can put many readers in a receptive frame of mind.

Headings You can feature the garden in your heading with one of the following:

GARDENER'S SHOWCASE

PROMISE HER (*OR HIM*) A ROSE GARDEN
Fulfill your promise with this...

IF YOU ENJOY FLOWERS

TOMATOES AND ROSES

BUY HER (*OR HIM*) A ROSE GARDEN

SMELL THE FLOWERS
and enjoy this...

GARDEN LOVERS

GREENHOUSE LOVERS

GARDEN-LOVER'S PARADISE

GARDENER'S PARADISE

GARDEN-LOVER'S DELIGHT

PLANT YOUR GREEN THUMB HERE

ATTENTION GREEN-THUMBERS

HARVEST
in your own backyard, the huge garden includes...

GOOD PICKINS

Body Copy Your ad stressing a garden could include these phrases:

Family-size garden

Tribe-size garden

A super-size vegetable garden comes with this...

A garden that's just waiting for you

The productive garden will take care of all your vegetable needs.

The garden is ready for your harvest.

The *family room* opens onto a private garden.

English garden

This is an ideal reference for a small or more formal garden.

Private-walled garden

Organic garden

There is a great interest in organic foods among health-oriented people.

A garden that will be the envy of your friends

A lush tropical garden

A lush tropical setting
Formal rose garden
South garden
Exotic plantings
Hawaiian garden
Oriental garden
Bonsai garden
A garden of surprises
Grape arbor
A botanical garden setting
Lattice-canopied garden aisle
Perennial gardens provide a starburst of color.
Flower-bedecked *courtyard*
Formal garden
Award-winning azaleas
Rockscaped garden
A garden setting for this...
Lots of sunshine and flowers
Skylighted atrium provides you with a year-round garden spot
2 acres of trees and flowers

This would make a good closing.

The perfect plant-and-putter place
Old-fashioned grape arbor
Terraced garden
Courtyard garden
Solar greenhouse
Your own greenhouse

Even if there is no garden, the fact that there is room for one is a positive feature.

Excellent garden spot
Great spot for a vegetable garden
Sunny garden spot
A quiet garden spot
Perfect spot for your garden
Garden-size yard

This turns a very small yard into an asset.

Space for an herb garden

Lawns Almost everyone likes a beautiful lawn. You can create a mental picture of an attractive lawn.

Expansive lawn
Expansive emerald lawn

Sweeping emerald lawn

Park-like setting

Finely manicured lawn

Luxuriously manicured lawn

Green velvet lawn

Croquet-size lawn

A forest of flowering trees and shrubs embroider the green velvet lawn.

Sweeping lawns and towering trees

Terraced estate

The manicured lawn defies all dandelions.

Luxuriously manicured lawn

A green velvet setting for this. . .

Lush green lawns laced with a profusion of color

Set among specimen plantings

Breathtaking grounds

Even when a lawn is very small or nonexistent, your ad can show the positive side.

Low-maintenance landscaping

Sprinkler systems can also be covered in your ad.

Underground sprinkler system

Automatic sprinkler system

Fully sprinkled by automatic system

Trees Trees can be effectively used in your ad heading or body to create a positive mental image of the property.

This makes an excellent closing.

YOUR HOME IN THE WOODS

BENEATH TOWERING PINES

NESTLED BENEATH THE TOWERING TREES

NESTLED IN THE FOREST

NESTLED IN THE TREES OF BEAUTIFUL WESTWOOD

PEACH, PEAR AND APPLE TREES
are included with this. . .

FRUITFUL

FRUITFUL RETIREMENT

TALL TIMBERS

BIG TREES
shade this. . .

You could use these to describe a country home or acreage.

LEAVE THE CITY FOR THE LEAVES

HARDWOODS HAVEN

WOODED WONDERLAND

WOODS & WATER WONDERLAND

WOOD ACRES

YOUR OWN FOREST

IN THE OAKS
of Sleepy Hollow, this...

TWO HUGE PINES
act as guardian sentinels for this...

This is a catchy way to mention apple trees.

JOHNNY APPLESEED

YOUR OWN PRIVATE WOODS
go with this...

BLUEBERRIES & TIMBER

AN ANCIENT OAK
is in the backyard of this...

THINK TREES

Additional effective words and phrases:

Towering *oak*

Soaring *pines*

Giant shade trees

Native timber

Huge trees on this lot

Captivating setting adorned by huge shade trees...

Tree-canopied drive

Tree-lined drive

Tucked away in the trees

Nestled on a large lot beneath *mature shade trees*

Flanked by towering *magnolias* and graceful *cedars*

Towering trees form a canopy over this...

Towering trees and flowering shrubs

Sheltered by towering *pines*

Shaded by a grove of *mature hardwoods*

100-year-old *oaks* and *pines* shade this...

There's a great place for a hammock between the elms in the pleasantly shaded backyard.

This provides a positive image for a family.

Trees for climbing

Lawn graced with shade and flowering trees

You will love the backyard, which has one of the largest (oldest) white pines in the region.

Mix of mature *pine, birch* and *hardwoods*

Century-old *oaks*

A tranquil wooded setting envelops this. . .

Tucked away on *3* enchanted wooded acres

A good action closing.

Bring your bird book and your checkbook.

Set among huge and capitivating hardwood trees

Framed by flowering *dogwoods*

Watch the leaves change from this. . .

Hardwood forest to provide for your fireplace (or home heating) needs

Lost in *3* wooded acres

Cherry blossoms and *maple* surround this. . .

Age-old trees and manicured lawns

Flanked by ancient *maples*

Specimen trees

Specimen trees and shrubs

Cloistered behind towering *hemlocks*

Set in a sun-streaked wooded glen

Nestled in a peaceful wooded setting

Nestled in the *pines*

A tapestry of flowering shrubs and magnificent trees

Tucked away amid century-old *oaks*

An oasis of palms and citrus

A lush oasis of towering trees and flowering shrubs

Hammock-ready trees

Two stately *walnut* trees provide the perfect spot for your hammock.

Stately *walnuts*

A Paul Bunyan–size forest

Rustic wooded

Sprinkling of *hickory* and *oak* trees in the sunlit meadow

Sprinkled with *oak* trees

This is an excellent image.

You will be able to cut your own Christmas tree in your family woods.

Woodlot is loaded with game

10 tree-studded acres

6 *oak*-covered acres

Virgin timber

This indicates the trees have never been harvested.

Mature hardwoods

Marketable timber

Timber cruised at estimated *$450* per acre

This is a forester's estimate of value.

No timber has been cut in over *40* years.

Meandering drive (or path) through your scenic woodlot

Your woodlot will keep you warm for many winters.

Ample woodlot for home heating

Mature orchard

Young orchard

Producing orchard

Mouth-watering family orchard

This provides an excellent image.

Organic orchard

No insecticides or artificial fertilizers

Young orchard just coming into the most productive years...

Young orchard ready to bear by 1990

Tax-shelter grove (or orchard)

Fruit trees can be depreciated.

You'll have bushels of fruit from your *apple, pear, peach* and *plum* trees.

The word "your" helps the reader imagine ownership.

The backyard is enhanced with *apple, pear* and *peach* trees.

The backyard is a tropical oasis of *palms* and *citrus.*

Many fruit and nut trees embellish this rolling parcel.

Level lot embellished with *pecan, fig* and *pear* trees

Maple trees for augering

You will enjoy your own maple syrup from the sugar maples in your backyard.

Completed Ads Stressing Trees and Plants

This is an ad for an unimproved wooded parcel. It appeals to privacy-seekers, nature-lovers and escapists.

A LOG HOME

could be built from the many tall and straight pine trees on these 6 wooded acres located less than an hour from the city. A forest clearing with a natural spring provides the perfect setting for your future home. A very private place you will appreciate at $23,900.

Clyde Realty **476-8200**

If the lot was large and had room for a vegetable garden, it should have been stated.

HORTICULTURISTS' DREAM

9 varieties of fruit and flowering trees plus many rare plantings accent this one-of-a-kind colonial home. 3 bedrooms, family room, den and root cellar are just a few of the features that you will love. Besides the oversized two-car garage there is a separate garden house for your outdoor tools. Pristine beauty can be yours at $86,500 with owner financing available.

Clyde Realty 476-8200

This simple yet effective heading sets a very positive mental picture in the reader's mind. If area is not shown by the newspaper ad category, it should be covered in the ad.

HOME AND ORCHARD

A picture-perfect 3BR Cape Cod enhanced by a fieldstone fireplace, gleaming hardwood floors and a separate two-car garage with a workroom, set on a full acre. The mouth-watering orchard boasts over 30 trees, 4 varieties of apple, 2 of plum, plus pear, peach and cherry. This can be your place for a bountiful harvest at $89,500.

Clyde Realty 476-8200

General Landscaping In addition to lawns and trees, general landscaping can be described positively with words such as:

Professionally landscaped

Estate-like setting

Park-like grounds

Unrivaled landscaping

Native landscaping

Natural landscaping

This means very little has been done.

Desert landscaping

This refers to no lawn—only plants.

Impeccably landscaped

Flawlessly maintained landscaping

Easy-care landscaping

EZ care landscaping

Extensively landscaped

Lush landscaping

Likely the most beautiful yard in town

The backyard was made for entertaining.

Breathtaking grounds

Rose hedge

Sculptured hedge

English hedge

Many of our common trees and plants are not native to this country.

You will picnic in the park right in your own backyard.

Grounds feature exotic plantings from all over the world.

The flowers are in bloom on the grounds of this...

Lush atrium

Towering plantings in the two-story atrium

Cathedral-domed atrium

Fencing Some effective words and phrases:

Cyclone fencing

White board fence

Hundreds of feet of white board fencing surround this...

Cedar rail fence

Split-rail fencing

White picket fence

The charming white picket fence leads to a rose-lined walk.

Privacy walls

Stockade fence encloses this...

Block walls

Completely fenced

Fully fenced

Fenced and cross-fenced

3-slat white wood fence

Old stone walls

High-walled garden

Open fields and stone walls

Stone gates guard the entry to this...

Hedged with stone walls

Embraced by stone walls

Estate rail fencing

Ranch rail fencing

Wrought iron fencing

Cedar shakes, maple trees and old stone walls enhance this...

Swimming Pools, Spas and Saunas The following ad headings can emphasize the fact that a property includes a pool:

SWIM AT HOME

BRING YOUR SWIMSUIT

BE COOL IN THE POOL

Don't underestimate this appeal.

ATTENTION SKINNY-DIPPERS
The sliding glass doors of the master suite open on the secluded pool and spa.

SPLISH—SPLASH

GET IN THE SWIM

The following headings are effective attention-getters but don't really indicate that the house has a pool:

THINK SUMMER
Swim in your own heated pool while your steaks are grilling on the BBQ.

SUMMER IN THE CITY
won't be too bad with your own swimming pool.

BACKYARD VACATION

WHY GO TO THE BEACH?

RESORT AT HOME

CALIFORNIA LIVING IN CHICAGO

TAKE THE PLUNGE

Additional words and phrases for swimming pools include:

Master bedroom opens to a very private pool and spa

Private skinny-dipping pool

Crystal-clear pool

Dazzling pool

Inviting pool

Cool blue pool

Shimmering pool

Sparkling pool

Heated pool

Heated and filtered pool

These are logical reasons to buy a wanted luxury.

A heated pool for exercise that is fun

Keep fit and enjoy your exercise in the heated pool.

People love the idea of getting something for free.

Solar-heated pool

Solar pool heater

Kidney pool

Oval pool

Olympic pool

This describes a large pool.

You will want to vacation in your own backyard owning this. . .

Free-form pool

Glass-domed swimming pool

Glassed-in pool

Caged pool

Lap pool

Fully fenced pool

This feature is important if there are small children in the family.

World-class pool

In-ground pool

Include this when many pools in the area are not in-ground.

Gunite pool

A Gunite pool is more expensive than a vinyl-lined pool.

New pool

Completed Ad Stressing Pool

This is a good attention-getter heading. In many areas of the country the presence of a pool has little effect on sales price.

> **FREE POOL**
>
> The $89,500 price compares favorably with other 3-bedroom, 2½-bath near-new homes in prestigious Westview Estates that don't have an in-ground heated pool. If you want to get in the swim, call now.
>
> **Clyde Realty** **476-8200**

Hot spas can be described by:

Jacuzzi

Very private Jacuzzi off master bedroom

Jacuzzi is a brand name.

Hot spa

Hydrotherapy spa

Pool and spa

Titillating hot spa

Tantalizing hot spa

Sumptuous hot spa

Hot bubbly spa

Relax in your own hot bubbly spa.

Therapeutic whirlpool spa for total relaxation

Hot tub

Hot tub holds 6–8

Redwood hot tub

California hot tub

A bathhouse would be described as a *Cabana.* Saunas could be described as:

Finnish sauna

Danish sauna

Swedish sauna

Automatic gas sauna

Redwood sauna

Cedar sauna

. . . sauna in master bath

Sauna for healthy relaxation

A luxury seems more of a necessity when tied to health.

Fountains Appropriate language for describing fountains include:

FOUNTAIN COURTYARD

BUBBLING FOUNTAIN

TILED FOUNTAIN

SPANISH FOUNTAIN

MEXICAN FOUNTAIN

FOUNTAIN POOL

SHIMMERING FOUNTAIN

GARDEN FOUNTAIN

COURTYARD FOUNTAIN

Tennis Here are some attention-getters for tennis facilities:

IS TENNIS YOUR GAME?

TENNIS ANYONE?

TENNIS-COURT ESTATE

TENNIS UTOPIA

LOVE—LOVE—LOVE

This could be too subtle for some readers.

CLOSE TO THE COURTS

Night-lighted tennis courts

Illuminated tennis court

Sunken tennis court

Sunken lighted tennis court

Championship tennis court

World-class court

Your own tennis court makes keeping fit fun.

This statement suggests a health reason for an extravagance.

Room for tennis court

There is no court yet, but the fact that there is room is a plus feature.

Patio These words and phrases describe patios:

Brick patio

Flagstone patio

Tiled patio

Family patio

Inviting patio

Enclosed patio

This is really a porch.

The lush patio becomes part of the living area through the extensive use of glass.

Picnic-perfect patio

Flagstone terrace

Covered terrace

This also refers to a porch.

Canopied terrace

Stone terrace

Sun terrace

Raised patio overlooks...

Covered patio

Awning-covered patio

Breakfast patio

Magnificent terrace enhanced with a secluded pool and spa

Courtyard

Sip a mint julep on the flagstone patio of this...

Enjoy the beauty of nature from the patio of this...

Brick BBQ on the...

Roads, driveways, walks and parking space are important to some buyers. Here are some words and phrases to describe them at their best:

Roads

All-weather road

This means the road is not necessarily paved.

The road is more than a pair of ruts.	Improved road

Paved road

Not necessarily paved	County-maintained road

Quiet tree-lined street

On a quiet no-thru street

On a children-safe cul-de-sac

Shaded cul-de-sac

On a very special street in...

On a private all-weather road

This makes an excellent heading.	Down a winding lane

Located on a private road

Coachlighted street

Well-lighted quiet street

Paved drive

Cobblestone driveway

Concrete drive

Circle drive

Circular drive

The circle drive will bring you right to your front door.

Sweeping circular driveway

Sweeping circular driveway frames this...

Tree-canopied drive

Tucked away on a quiet cul-de-sac

The most prestigious street in...

Perched at the end of a long secluded drive

A country lane weaves its way through this...

Walks

Flagstone walk

These are an asset as a security feature.	Lighted walkways

Shaded walk

Cobblestone walk

Quaint cobblestone paths

Ancient cobblestone walks

Covered walkways

Parking Covered parking could be described as:

Protected parking

Covered parking

Carport

Double carport

You would describe underground parking as:

Indoor parking for 2 cars

Underground parking

Secure underground parking

Unprotected parking is simply described as:

Off-street parking

Off-street parking for 2 cars

RV Parking Even people who don't have recreational vehicles are often interested in room for them because RVs are on their wish lists. RV parking can be included in an ad this way:

Room for your RV

RV parking area

Plenty of parking for your camper and boat

Garages

Heated garage

> *This is an important feature in cold climates.*

Double garage

Attached 2-car garage

> *This is a two-car garage. If it is a one-car garage, you would simply describe it as* attached garage *or* separate garage.

Full 2-car garage

2½-car garage

Oversized double garage

> *Makes it seem larger than two-car garage.*

2+ car garage

2-car garage plus RV parking

Oversized 3-car garage has plenty of room for mom and dad's toys

Plenty of room in the oversized garage for 2 cars, your boat and snowmobiles

Room for bikes and trikes in the...

Outbuildings

Coach house

2-car coach house

Carriage house

Old Dutch barn

Horse barn

Aviary

Delightful aviary

Gazebo

Gazebo with wet bar and BBQ for your summer entertaining

Screened gazebo

Garden gazebo

Could be converted to separate guest facilities

Could be converted to guest house

Would make an ideal workshop

Many people dream of having their own studios.

Ideal as an artist's studio

Possible artist's/writer's studio

Would make an ideal studio

The perfect "sneak-away" studio

The perfect place for the hobbyist

A perfect playhouse for the children

Plenty of room for the collector with this. . .

Storage shed for your boat and snowmobiles

12′ × 40′ hobby building

Potting shed

Garden shed

English garden shed

4 The Home: Exterior, Rooms and Special Features

Exterior

Roof

You would mention a roof in an ad only if it is of unusual quality or adds to the architectural description.

Red tile roof

Spanish tile roof

Mission clay tile roof

A real slate roof

Hand-split cedar shakes

For architectural styles in addition to Spanish tile, you could mention:

Gambrel roof

Dutch gambrel roof

Pennsylvania gambrel roof

Mansard roof

French mansard roof

Multigabled roof

Siding

While you should not advertise the fact that a more expensive home has Masonite or aluminum siding, these sidings are appealing for lower-cost homes, retirement homes and income property. Language that can be used includes:

Low-maintenance Masonite siding

No-maintenance aluminum siding and trim

Maintenance-free vinyl siding

Other language for exterior treatments:

Western is an especially effective term in the East.

Western cedar siding

Maintenance-free redwood (or cedar) siding

The quality cedar exterior blends in with the natural setting.

Natural cedar siding

Cedar shakes

Weathered cedar shakes

Natural textured wood siding

Handsome brick exterior

Brick and cedar exterior

Brick beauty

Cedar and stone exterior

Brick and stone exterior

LIKE A ROCK
All brick. . .

Native stone exterior

Solid stone construction

Maintenance-free exterior

Maintenance-free brick exterior

Mom and Dad will appreciate the low maintenance of this brick and cedar. . .

Low-maintenance brick and cedar means more time to enjoy. . .

This brick. . .offers maximum luxury with minimum upkeep.

Stone can be described as:

Cut stone

Solid granite

Lannon is a type of limestone.

Lannon stone

Orchard stone

An attractive way to describe glacial or fieldstone.

Crab orchard stone

River rock

Tennessee stone

Marble

Travertine marble

Carrera marble

Fieldstone

California driftwood

Native stone

Massive stone

Split-stone

Entryway

The entryway often has a dramatic feature that can be emphasized to elicit a desired emotional response.

Arched entry

Shaded entryway

Trellised entryway

Dramatic entryway

Courtyard entry

Tiled entry

Slate entryway

Rose-lined walkway leads to the...

For French Norman

Turreted entryway

Better

Dramatic turreted entryway

The stone archway enhances the charm of this...

Massive double doors open onto this dramatic...

The entry is but an introduction to extraordinary architectural inspiration.

Gallery entry

Gracious entry

Separate entry to servant's quarters

Leaded-glass entry doors

Stained-glass entry doors

Opulent marble steps lead to this...

A picturesque columned entry enhances this...

Sculptured double-door entry

Portico entry

Massive entryway

Gated entry

Cathedral entry

Stone courtyard

Flower-bedecked courtyard

Grand entry

Enter through a stone portal

Drive-through portico

The estate entrance frames this...

The handcrafted front doors provide a preview of the luxury and craftsmanship that await you.

Wrought iron gates lead to this...

The *wrought iron gates* lead to your own private corner of the world.

Entry Hall

You can describe the entry hall as:

Foyer

Tiled foyer

Slate foyer

Impressive slate foyer

Soaring foyer

2-story foyer

3-story soaring foyer

Split foyer

Vestibule

The lovely slate foyer beckons you into this magnificent residence.

Rooms

Living Room

The living room is the place where the owners present themselves to the world. Among the most effective appeals are those that imply social grace, status and comfort.

36′ living room

Show the size in feet only when it is much larger than normally expected.

Great room

Adds prestige to a large or older home

Dramatic great room

Adjectives add a great deal to desirability.

Step-down living room

Sunken living room

Good

Elegant sunken living room

Better

Grand-piano-size living room

Room for a grand piano in this entertaining-sized living room

Mirrored living room

The glass wall brings the outdoors in, making the bright and cheerful living room ideal for entertaining.

2-story living room

Vaulted living room

A living room designed for the casual life

The living room centers on a majestic stone fireplace.

Dramatically proportioned living room

A vaulted ceiling adds magnificent dimensions to the stately living room.

Sweeping living room

Living room open to dining room and/or kitchen

Open-concept living area

Living room with conversation corner

Romantic conversation pit

Intimate conversation area

Alcove

Alcoves, which are generally off the living room, can be described as:

Music alcove

Sleeping alcove

Reading alcove

Library alcove

Sewing room

Language used for dens can also be applied to alcoves.

Family Room

The family room is usually a living space for family activities, much less formal than a living room. While the living room might be for guests, the family room is for living. Terms and phrases emphasize the recreational and casual living aspects.

Give size only if it is larger than usually anticipated.

30′ family room

The family room centers around a massive stone fireplace.

Warm family room

Game room

Leisure room

Club room

Entertaining room

Usually a basement family room

Recreation room

Exposed or partially exposed basement

Daylight creation room

Billiard room

Usually an exposed basement room in a water-related property

Marine room

A pub room includes a bar.

Pub room

Bar has a sink

Pub room with wet bar

English pub room

Cozy pub room with stone fireplace

Playroom

Adult playroom

Family playroom

Main-floor room used for more formal entertainment

Drawing room

A room for entertaining

Salon

Magnificent salon

Grand salon

A lounge is actually more of a waiting room.

Lounge

Window-wrapped lounge

These are good designations for a basement recreation room without a bar.

Fitness room

Home gym

Private gym

Kitchen

The kitchen is probably the most emotionally volatile part of a house. It is the place where preparations are made for the ritual of sharing food, where guests end up before and after a meal and where memories of childhood most readily come to the surface. Most people have very definite ideas of what a good kitchen is. This section suggests ways to appeal to a variety of images.

Size Some people dream of a great hall of a kitchen, while others want to take as few steps as possible. Any size of kitchen can be presented in a way that attracts one school of thought or another.

These descriptions make the fact that a kitchen is small a positive feature.

Step-saver kitchen

Efficient step-saver kitchen

One-step kitchen

Cozy kitchen

Galley *makes a small narrow kitchen a positive feature.*

Galley kitchen

Efficient galley kitchen

Efficiency-engineered kitchen

These descriptions fit larger kitchens.

Table-space kitchen

Eat-in kitchen

Gigantic eat-in kitchen

Country kitchen

Breathtaking country kitchen

Cheerful country kitchen

Bright-light country kitchen

Farm-size kitchen

Ranch-size kitchen
Spacious kitchen
Down-home kitchen
Tribe-size kitchen
French country kitchen

At last, a kitchen where the whole family can eat together

Ambiance A dream kitchen evokes thoughts of great gourmet cooking in a pleasant environment. Your ad can help buyers recognize that dream.

Superb culinary center
Gourmet kitchen
Dreamy gourmet kitchen
The gourmet kitchen is a cook's delight.
European kitchen
European-inspired kitchen
Eurostyle kitchen
Spouse-saver kitchen
Work-saver kitchen
Chef's kitchen
A real cook's kitchen

A kitchen facing the yard

Garden kitchen

Sunlight

Greenhouse kitchen

Skylit kitchen
Designer kitchen
Dream kitchen
Dream kitchen features an island cooking center

Remodeled kitchen

Updated kitchen

Space-age kitchen
Super-new kitchen

Brand name

St. Charles kitchen

Glamorous kitchen
Friendly kitchen

Open space

Open kitchen

Kitchen/family room
Country-fresh kitchen

A sunny kitchen creates a very positive image.

Bright and airy kitchen
Sun-filled kitchen

Sun-drenched kitchen

Brick and copper kitchen

Energy-efficient kitchen features . . .

Special Features Don't forget the kitchen extras:

Breakfast bar

Convenient dining counter

Built-in dining nook

Walk-in pantry

Butler's pantry

A good nostalgic feature

Old-fashioned pantry

A real old-fashioned pantry

Mudroom off kitchen

Custom cabinetry

European *oak* cabinetry

Imported European cabinetry

Rich cherry cabinetry

The custom kitchen features *gleaming ceramic tile* and *hand-finished oak* cabinetry.

Oak cabinetry

Custom *birch* cabinets

Custom hardwood cabinets

An extraordinary amount of handsome wood cabinetry

Soft *pine* cabinets

Older home

The original *pine* cabinets

Old *pine* cabinets

Maytag appliances

The Maytag appliances reflect the quality appointments of this . . .

Like-new appliances

Built-in washer/dryer and dishwasher

All the built-ins

Built-in everything

Double ovens

Self-cleaning oven

Built-in microwave

Jenn-Air range

Double-door refrigerator with icemaker

Soft ceiling of light gently illuminates the charming kitchen.

Greenhouse window in kitchen

Floor-to-ceiling greenhouse windows in breakfast area

Tiled kitchen

Delft tile kitchen

Dining Rooms

Words and phrases that can be used to describe dining rooms include:

Separate dining room

Dining area — *An open area*

Formal dining room

Elegant formal dining room

Chandeliered dining room

Crystal chandelier adorns the formal dining room

Banquet-size dining room

Gallery dining room — *A rectangular room, usually with high ceilings*

Solarium-style dining room — *Many windows*

Breakfast room

Cheerful breakfast room

Greenhouse-windowed breakfast room

Sun-drenched breakfast room

Bedrooms

Like kitchens, bedrooms carry heavy emotional baggage. Comfort, luxury, restfulness, spaciousness and sensuality are among the qualities that fit various buyer perceptions.

Master suite with morning room

Master suite with sitting room

26′ master bedroom — *Give the size only if it is larger than normally expected.*

Master suite — *A master suite is usually a bedroom with a separate bath.*

Breathtaking master suite — *Better*

Sensuous master suite — *More appropriate for adult-oriented housing*

Sumptuous master suite

Lavish master suite

Generous master suite

These wordings can make a positive feature out of only two bedrooms.

Double master suites

Dual master suites

Master suite plus guest room

Master suite features a "snuggle-up" fireplace.

Shows that the master suite has privacy

Master suite plus 2 bedrooms in the children's wing

Master bedroom with separate dressing areas

His-and-hers dressing rooms

A small bedroom close to master bedroom can be designated a nursery.

Nursery adjacent to master suite

Maid's room

Maid or guest room

Appropriate for larger house

Separate suite for guests or live-ins

Emphasizes privacy

Separate guest suite

3 king-size bedrooms

Indicates three bedrooms have their own baths (makes a good heading)

3 masters

A boy and his dog will love bunking in this rugged paneled bedroom.

Dormitory-size bedroom

Not large enough for a king-size bed

3 queen-size bedrooms

For a two-story home, one bedroom on the first floor is a positive feature.

3 up and 1 down

Second floor

Delightful dormered guest room

A guest suite could be so designated in a family-oriented ad.

Teen suite

Room for additional bedrooms in . . .

Elegant en suite

Lower-level bedroom

Closets

Mirrored wardrobes

Mirrored doors on the sliding wardrobes

Double sliding wardrobe closets in . . .

His-and-her closets

Huge closets

Generous closets

More closets than you have ever seen

Extravagant closets

Walk-in closets

Master suite with his/hers walk-in closets

Solves all your closet problems

Outrageous closets

Closets you can get lost in

Baths

A full bath includes a tub, commode and wash basin. A half-bath is generally just a commode and basin, and a three-quarter-bath is a shower, commode and basin. However, these general descriptions do vary in different localities.

Words and phrases applicable to baths are:

Note	Phrase
	Master bath
Good	Sensuous master bath
Better	Deliciously sensuous master bath
	Sinfully sumptuous baths
	Skylight bath
	Oversized garden tub
Opens on planted area	Garden bath
Better	Enchanting garden bath
Large bath with room for exercise equipment	Bath/fitness center
Grecian *gives an image of tiled luxury*	Grecian bath
Roman *denotes a large bath.*	Roman bath
Usually large and tiled	Oversize Roman bath Roman tub
	Antique tub
Nostalgic feature	Antique claw-footed tub
	Phoenician bath
	Opulent Phoenician bath
	Oval tub
	Luxuriate in the oversized tub of this decorator-inspired bath.
	Step-down tub
	Sunken tub
	Sunken tub with Jacuzzi
	Luxurious sunken tub
	Bath with separate shower
	Double shower
	Double vanities
	His-and-hers vanities

Dual vanities

Dressing room

Dual dressing rooms

A powder room is usually a half-bath.

Powder room

Plumbing stubbed in for future bath

Roughed-in bath in basement

Other deluxe bath features to emphasize:

Hot spa

Soothing spa

Sensuous hot spa

Jacuzzi tub

Whirlpool tub

Whirlpool tub for two

Therapeutic whirlpool spa for total relaxation

Built-in sauna

Gold fixtures

Skylights in bath

Skylit bath

Mentioning the make of the bath fixtures or the fact that they are colored is no help in attracting buyers.

Tile and Marble

Ceramic tile

Better

Sleek ceramic tile baths

Italian tile

Venetian tile

Mexican tile

Portuguese tile

Travertine tile

Italian marble baths

Extensive use of marble

Carrera *is a fine white Italian marble.*

Carrera marble

The sculptor's choice—Carrera marble—enriches the sumptuous baths.

Real marble vanities

Refers to gold-plated fixtures

Marble and gold

Imitation marble

Cultured marble sinks

Marble accents

Travertine marble

Sheathed in *Travertine* marble

Grecian marble

Guest Quarters

The following descriptions highlight separate guest accommodations:

Very cold

FATHER- OR MOTHER-IN-LAW SPECIAL

A warm heading

ROOM FOR GRANDMA

WITH A GUEST HOUSE TOO

COMPANY COMING?

GUEST HOUSE
included with this

HOUSE + GUEST HOUSE
Separate bungalow for guests

Guest room

Guest suite

Indicates privacy

Separate guest suite

Self-contained guest house

The garage would make a possible guest house or studio.

This could make the house very attractive to some economy-minded buyers.

Separate guest unit could be rented.

Separate servant's quarters

If there is more than one house, the larger house would be referred to as the *main house* or *manor house* while the smaller house would be the *guest house.*

Den

Generally, a den is a small room directly off one of the main living areas. It can be more than that, though:

For a larger room

Lion-size den

Paneled den *has a masculine appeal.*

Walnut-paneled den

Gives image of rich paneling

Courtroom-paneled den

A study has more status appeal than a den.

Study

Paneled study

The designation library *will have a strong appeal to many readers.*

Library

English library

Excellent for a paneled room

English drawing room

For English architecture

Drawing room

A drawing room is a room for entertaining guests and is usually associated with drinking.

Office

Home office

Office/den

Estate office

For a large prestigious property

Music room

Since these rooms frequently contain stereos, music room *is a proper and prestigious designation. Even though a den is used as a TV room, do not call it that in your ads.* TV Room *lacks prestige.*

Convertible den

Convertible *indicates it can also be used as a bedroom.*

Intimate den

For a small room

OFFICE AT HOME

The den can be featured in the heading

Special den features can be pointed out with language such as:

The warm paneled den features a friendly *orchard stone* fireplace.

Floor-to-ceiling bookcases line one wall of the richly appointed study.

The separate entrance makes the den ideal for a home office.

Dens imply privacy. Ad copy can emphasize the quality.

Your perfect quiet spot

Your "sneak-away" place for quiet relaxation

Darkroom

A darkroom is a strong feature for photographers and others who consider themselves pretty good with a camera. Your ad can appeal to both by using the right language.

ATTENTION: PHOTOGRAPHERS

CAMERA BUFF'S DELIGHT

Darkroom

Darkroom with sink(s)

Darkroom with double stainless-steel sinks

Photographer's darkroom

If a house has an interior or basement room which is suitable for darkroom use, even if the present owner does not use it as such, you could state:

. . . ideal for a photographer's darkroom

. . . would make the perfect darkroom

Workshop

For the hobbyist or would-be hobbyist, the home handyperson and the lover of machinery and tools, a workshop sounds a very attractive note. You can get a good response very simply.

Separate workshop

Huge workshop

24′ workshop

Built-in workbench

Workshop or hobby room

. . . would make an ideal workroom

Workshop area in oversized double garage

Plenty of room in the dry basement for a hobby shop

Hobbyroom

Porch

For those who like them, porches can be one of the most attractive features a house offers, overcoming a whole series of potential negatives. Here are some ways to present porches at their most inviting, from the viewpoint of a variety of wants.

Old-fashioned front porch

Just the place for your rocking chair or porch swing

Swing on the porch and lull your troubles away.

Rocking-chair porch

Bring the rocking chair.

Rocking-chair-ready front porch

A screen porch just made for summer dreaming

Lemonade-sipping front porch

Welcome-home front porch

Pillared front porch

Enjoy summer evenings on the veranda of this . . .

The pillared front porch welcomes you to comfortable living.

Country porch

You will love the large front porch of this . . .

Porch with roof and columns

Columned portico

Old-fashioned gallery porch

Front porch with swing

Fully screened porch

A screened porch for those hot summer nights

Screened and glassed porch

Glassed-in porch

Sleeping porch

Enclosed porch

Wraparound porch

Veranda — *A veranda is usually a covered porch on the side of a building.*

Columned veranda — *Good*

White-columned veranda — *Better*

Lanai — *Open-sided porch*

Glassed-in Porch A screened and glassed porch could also be described as:

Sun porch

Sun-room

Sun-room perfect for plants and wicker — *This phrase sets a positive mood.*

Sun gallery

Summer room

Jalousied porch

California room

Florida room

Arizona room

Hawaiian room

Garden room

Conservatory — *Glassed-in room where plants are grown*

Glass-roofed conservatory

Solarium — *Sun porch*

Water View An upper porch with a water view would be known as a:

Widow's watch — *This might convey a negative image to some readers.*

Captain's deck — *Better*

Deck An open porch is usually referred to as a *deck*.

Wraparound deck

Warm sunny deck

Inviting sun deck

Secluded deck
A very private sun deck — *Privacy appeals to sunbathers.*

Privacy deck

Extensive deck area

Redwood deck

Cedar deck

Wrapped on 3 sides by a redwood deck

Redwood balcony

Sunset deck

Sunrise deck

Barbecue deck

Cantilevered deck

Garden deck

Completed Ad Stressing Porch

Porches can become the focal point of an ad.

This nostalgia-type ad makes an older home seem very appealing.

Very little is told about the home itself. If there were strong positive features, they could have been included in the ad.

There is probably only one bath, or it would have been mentioned.

FRONT-PORCH LOVERS

Bring along your rocking chair; the gallery porch on this 3BR, American traditional was made for long summer evenings. Set on a quiet east-side street, you will love the ancient oaks, the garage workroom and the flower garden that's the envy of the neighborhood. A home you will cherish at $58,500.

Clyde Realty **476-8200**

Expansion Room

Many houses contain extra space that might be an added attraction, though in most cases this would not work well as a main theme for an ad. Many older homes had large walk-up attics. Some Cape Cod and other two-story homes were originally sold with unfinished second floors. Many houses turn up in which these areas are still unfinished.

Bonus room

Bonus room would make an ideal studio or 3rd bedroom

Walk-up attic could be 4th bedroom

Storage attic could be converted to studio or guest room

Room for 2 additional bedrooms in the walk-up attic

Full storage attic

Basement

Basements can make an important difference to buyers who want lots of storage, workspace or expansion room.

Full basement

Poured basement

Block basement

8′ basement

Dry basement

Sump pump in basement

Under part of the house

Partial basement

Fruit cellar

Most of basement is above ground.

Exposed basement

Walk-out basement

Many windows

Daylight walk-out basement

Finished rooms

Finished basement

Room for an English apartment

English apartment

Terrace-level *is an attractive way to say basement apartment.*

Terrace-level apartment

Finished basement could be converted to separate apartment

Unfinished basement would make possible in-law suite

Income possibility will appeal to many readers.

Possible rental unit

Basement could be finished for rental unit

Room for 2 additional bedrooms in the exposed basement

Expansion room in basement

Future game room

Turn unfinished into an asset.

Basement ready to be finished

Ready for your finishing touches

Wine cellar

If there are racks

600-bottle wine cellar

Temperature-controlled wine cellar

Daylight basement

Partially finished basement

Laundry room in basement

Basement roughed-in for bath

Stubbed for *third* bath in basement

Dry basement perfect for rainy-day playroom

Plenty of storage room in the dry basement

Loft

A loft is usually an open area overlooking a main area in a two-story building. Appropriate language for describing a loft could be:

Studio loft

Sleeping loft

Swiss loft over great room

Balcony sleeping area

Balcony studio

Library loft

A separate definition of a loft is a large open room over a commercial building usually covering an entire floor. Because these are in demand by artistic people, the best description is simply:

Artist's loft

Artist's loft—3,000 square feet

Huge artist's loft

Utility Room

A utility room is customarily used for laundry and may also contain the water heater and/or furnace.

No-steps utility room

Separate laundry room

Separate laundry room off kitchen

No-steps laundry room

Laundry room/darkroom

A laundry room is often also suited for darkroom use.

Special Features

Special features help set a mood and establish an image for a house, but in many cases they are not strong enough to be the focal point of an ad. Don't ignore them, though: These are the little touches that give a house—and the ad that describes it—its own special character.

Fireplace

A fireplace adds a special romantic touch, and can have appeal for the practical-minded, as well.

Floor-to-ceiling fireplace

16′ fireplace

Soaring fireplace

Wood-burning fireplace

Fieldstone fireplace — *Uncut stones*

Orchard stone fireplace

Native stone fireplace

Split-stone fireplace

River rock fireplace

Massive stone fireplace

Majestic stone fireplace

California driftwood fireplace

Tennessee stone fireplace — *Mentioning the state of origin adds a special touch.*

Antique brick fireplace — *Has a richer sound than* used brick

A warm rose brick fireplace

Marble fireplace

Travertine fireplace

Cheerful fireplace

Corner fireplace

2-way stone fireplace

Corn-poppin' family fireplace

Heartwarming brick fireplace

Cheerful hearth

Toe-warming fireplace

See-through fireplace

Heatilator fireplace — *Brand name for a type of hot air circulating fireplace*

Fireplace with heat exchanger

. . . fireplace has gas log starter

Free-standing fireplace

Dramatic Danish fireplace

Stove insert for fireplace — *A stove insert allows wood heating and is becoming desirable in rural areas.*

Franklin stove

Marble hearth and mantle

Sold walnut mantle

Massive mantle from 200-year-old barn

Brick-hearth fireplace

Raised-hearth fireplace

Built-in woodbox

Pre-Christmas ads

Wait for Santa in front of your own native stone fireplace.

A place to hang your stockings

This. . .comes with a cheerful fireplace.

The fieldstone fireplace will offer warmth and comfort on those snowy evenings.

Toast your toes by the huge log fireplace.

Sellers are usually willing to leave their firewood. Firewood stacked and ready can be an additional plus factor.

Snuggle-up fireplace in master bedroom

You will enjoy the cozy fireplace in the master bedroom.

Comes complete with 6 cords of firewood for winter heating

Bar

Many homes have built-in bars. Here is some wording:

Wet bar *means water and a sink.*

Wet bar

If serving window for patio

Inside/outside bar

This means there is a bar refrigerator that stays.

Refrigerated wet bar

For a smaller recreation room centering on a bar

Friendly pub room

Inviting pub room

Doors

The following words and phrases can be used to describe doors:

Double doors

Pocket doors

double pocket doors

Massive hand-carved doors

Solid *oak* entry doors

Handcrafted doors

Sculptured double-door entry

Stained-glass entry door

Leaded-glass entry door

French doors

Sliding patio doors

Sliding French doors

Double glass doors

Classic French doors

Crystal doorknobs

Leaded-glass accents

9′ doors

Massive *9′* doors

The *sliding glass* doors in the *master suite* open onto . . .

Windows

In describing windows, use words that convey positive images or reflect quality.

Soaring window walls

A wall of glass

Knee-to-ceiling wall of glass

Majestic wall of glass

Window wall

30′ window wall overlooks . . .

Andersen® window wall — *Name of well-known manufacturer*

Old-fashioned bay window

Greenhouse window — *A multipaned bay window*

A touch of glass — *Good ad heading*

Picture windows look out over . . .

Picture window frames a picturesque and private backyard

Thermal windows

Thermopane® windows — *A brand name of insulated glass windows*

Double-glazed windows

Triple-glazed windows

Self-storing storms and screens

Solar bronze windows

Clerestory windows

The *clerestory* windows bathe the rooms in warm natural light.

One-way windows — *Privacy feature*

One-way wall of glass

Palladian windows

Window-wrapped *solarium*

Many small panes — Mullioned windows

Diamond-lite windows

Sky light — Sky dome

Sky studio

Skylights

Glass-domed *atrium*

Glassed-in pool

Double doors with small panes of glass — French doors

Sliding glass doors

The sliding glass doors open to...

Vintage Glass Glass in older or period construction may fit some of these descriptions:

Beveled glass

Beveled and jeweled glass

Etched glass

Intricately etched glass

Frosted glass

Stained glass

Leaded glass

Leaded-glass accents

Vintage leaded glass

Such as The oval glass door... — Oval glass

Shutters Window shutters can be described as:

Privacy shutters

Security shutters

Plantation shutters

Colonial shutters

Full shutters

Bermuda shutters

Shutters and window boxes

Stairs

Stairways can boost a quality image, if carefully described.

Center staircase

Wide center staircase

Angular staircase

Good	Curved staircase
Better	Graceful curved staircase

Spiral staircase

Cantilevered staircase

Intricately carved banisters

Walk up to the. . .

Walk down to the. . .

Sweeping staircase

Dramatic curved staircase

Good	Floating staircase
Better	Dramatic floating staircase

Opulent *marble* steps lead. . .

Circular staircase

The circular staircase spirals to. . .

Mirrored staircase

Grand staircase

Grand *walnut* stairway

Banistered staircase

Center staircase

Solid *cherry* balustrades

In areas where basements are expected, the lack of one can be expressed positively.

No stairs

No steps to climb

Single level

Everything on one level

Stairless ranch

Ceilings

Normally, you would only mention ceilings when they are unusual.

Lighted ceiling

Softly lighted ceiling

Illuminated ceiling

Skylighted ceiling

Clerestory-windowed ceiling

Good

Cathedral ceiling

Better

Soaring cathedral ceiling

Impressive cathedral ceiling

Beamed ceiling

Open-beamed ceiling

Exposed-beam ceiling

9′ ceiling

The 10′ ceiling in the living room adds to the feeling of spaciousness and light.

Two-story living room

Coved ceilings

Vaulted ceilings

The *14′ vaulted* ceiling enhances the ambiance of the *great room.*

Colossal ceilings

Double-height *living room*

Dramatic vaulted ceilings

Tin ceilings

Ceiling fans

Paddle fans

Bermuda fans

A ceiling can even be used as an attention-getting heading.

A real attention-getter

TOPLESS
Soaring ceilings in this. . .

Sunlight

Bright sunlit rooms are a positive selling feature.

Sun-drenched

Sun-filled

Filled with sunlight

Flooded with afternoon sunlight

Bright with the morning sun

Sun can even be used in headings.

HERE COMES THE SUN
right into your kitchen.

BASK IN THE SUN
on the open *porch* of this. . .

Colors

A written description of colors can create a very positive image—it's a matter of word selection.

Comment	Phrase
Browns and reds	Soft terra-cotta tones
Reds, oranges and browns are warm colors.	Rich terra-cotta tones
	Warm and rich color scheme
Creamy *gives life to beige.*	Creamy beige tiled floor
	Buttercup yellow
Soft creams and beige	Muted tones
Yellows, beiges, browns	Soft tones
	Bathed in soothing pastels
	Softly decorated
	Warm, soft colors and a California mood
Browns, beiges and golds	Basic earth-tone decor
	Golden earth tones
	Warm earth tones
	The muted earth tones reflect the natural surroundings.
Soft beiges, browns, yellows	Desert colors
	Desert decor
Whites, greens, blues	Cool and fresh
	Cool tones
	Fresh
Light colors	Bright and light
Peach and off-whites	Peaches-and-cream decor
For light colors	A happy decor of. . .
Usually whites and off-whites	Tasteful neutral decor
	Subdued tones of ivory and beige
These statements actually say very little but appear positive.	Coordinated wall coverings
	Decorator-perfect
	Decorator colors
	Decorator-fresh
	Decorator-sharp

Ads Stressing Color

While colors are seldom the focal point of an ad, they can help create a mood that entices the reader to call.

A WARM MEDLEY

The soft earth tones instill a rhapsody of utter contentment throughout this unique 2-bedroom and den home . . .

TERRA-COTTA TONES

Softly decorated in the earth tones of the American Southwest, this authentic hacienda will provide a warm welcome.

Clean

Most people are attracted to super-clean, well-maintained houses that look like model homes. Exceptional cleanliness and perfect condition are such strong motivators that they make for highly effective headings.

FOR MR. (OR MRS.) CLEAN

STAR BRIGHT
This 3-bedroom ranch-style home sparkles.

PERSNICKETY?
Then you will love this squeaky clean . . .

DID YOU EVER SEE A HOUSE SPARKLING? WELL, I DID!

FRESH ON MARKET
Spotless inside and out

SPOTLESS COLONIAL

BRING YOUR WHITE GLOVES
This super clean contemporary will pass your inspection.

NOT JUST CLEAN
Immaculate—this . . .

PRISTINE

Additional language can make the point about cleanliness in any part of the ad.

Better than new

Antiseptic clean

It sparkles
White-glove clean
In pristine condition
In blue-ribbon condition
Superbly maintained
Impeccably maintained
Better than a model
Shows like a model
Immaculate
Impeccable
Flawless
Spotless
Squeaky clean
Reflects caring owners
Reflects the owner's pride
Whistle-clean
Pin-neat
Absolutely nothing for you to do but move in
Handsomely kept 3BR home
Move-in ready
Decorator-sharp
Freshly decorated

Furnishings and Interior Decorations

Furnishings and decorations sometimes provide additional appeal.

Completely furnished
Fully furnished and accessorized
Magnificently furnished
Magnificent furnishings
Extravagant furnishings
Extravagant appointments
Exciting accessories
Exquisitely furnished
Complete and exquisitely furnished
Custom-furnished without regard to cost

Price was no object on these fabulous furnishings.

Decorator-furnished

A wealth of luxurious appointments

Toothbrush-ready at $________.

Unprecedented appointments

Lavishly appointed

Decorator appointments

Turnkey-furnished

Richly detailed interior appointments

Impeccably decorated and furnished

California decorator

Decorator-furnished in peaches and cream

Designer-furnished

Totally furnished with numerous one-of-a-kind items

Furnished with everything

Walk-in ready

Much better than partially furnished

Most of the custom furniture stays.

Comes with most furnishings

Furnishings available

Cheerfully and charmingly decorated and furnished

Custom-decorated and furnished

Lavish use of wall coverings

Lavishly decorated

Tastefully decorated

Professionally decorated

Name of interior designer

Decorated by. . .

Dramatically decorated

Levolor blinds

Decorator drapes

THE PROFESSIONAL TOUCH
Professionally decorated and landscaped, this. . .

Unusual attention-getting heading

FORKS AND SALT SHAKERS
are all you will need in this completely furnished. . .

This has been overused in many areas.

BRING YOUR TOOTHBRUSH
Everything else is included in this. . .

Paneling

In describing wood paneling in a positive manner, mentioning the type of wood adds to desirability.

Walnut wainscoting — *Could be veneer*

Solid *walnut* wainscoting — Wainscoting *is paneling on the bottom half of a wall.*

Solid *cherry* paneling

Tongue-and-groove *walnut* paneling

Extensive wainscoting

Gleaming *mahogany* paneling

Solid tongue-and-groove *walnut* paneling

Barnwood paneling — *Barnwood paneling is becoming highly desirable.*

If the type of wood is unknown, use:

Mellow wood paneling

Warm wood paneling

Courtroom paneling

Tongue-and-groove paneling

Imported hardwood paneling — *Much of it is*

Trim Veneers are not used for trim, so *solid* can be used.

Solid *oak* and *chestnut* trim

Solid *oak* trim

Solid *oak* woodwork

Unusual woodwork should be mentioned.

Mortised and pegged timbers

Massive oak beams

Hand-carved banisters

Circular staircase of *oak* and *cherry*

Wall Coverings

In describing the decor of a home, you might want to mention wallpaper. Use the term *wall coverings*—it has much more positive appeal.

Imported wall coverings — *This sounds much better than saying the wallpaper was made in Taiwan.*

Textured wall coverings

Decorator wall coverings

Designer wall coverings

Lavish use of wall coverings

Flooring

The following words and phrases can be used to describe various floor treatments:

Random-plank flooring

Hardwood floors

Boasting hardwood floors

Pegged hardwood floors

Gleaming hardwood floors

Dazzling *oak* floors

Bleached *oak* floors

Heart *oak* floors

Varnished *oak* floors

Pegged *pine* floors

Random-width *pine* floors

Parquet floors

Gleaming parquet floors

Maple floors

Soft-tone *maple* floors

Hand-pegged floors

Mellow *pine* floors

Pine plank flooring adds a warm glow...

Graced with hardwood and richly carpeted floors

Stain Master carpeting

Plush neutral carpeting

Plush wall-to-wall carpeting

Top-line carpeting

Plush carpeting

Dense Karastan® carpeting — *A well-known quality brand*

All-wool carpeting

Berber carpets

Sculptured wool carpeting

Terrazzo floors

Mexican tile floors — *Good*

Mexican pavers

Mexican quarry tile floors flow through this... — *Better*

Flowing tile floors

Quarry tile

Travertine tile

Portuguese tile

No-wax Congoleum

Easy-care vinyl

Sun-baked *Mexican* tile floors

Heating and Air-Conditioning

In most areas of the country, people expect central heating except in cabins. In some localities they also expect central air-conditioning. You don't have to use ad lines on these features if they are standard for the area and property type. Features beyond the ordinary, however, should be emphasized.

Energy efficient *gas* heat

Forced-air heat

Dual heat/air

Hot-water heat

Hydronic heat

Sounds much better than hot-water heat

Baseboard heat

Does not tell type

Hydronic baseboard heat

Zone heat control

4-zone hydronic heat

Heat pump

5-ton heat pump for economy and comfort

Heat pump for economical heat and air

Economical natural gas heat

The economy of natural gas

Desert water cooler

Used in low-humidity areas for cooling

Both air-conditioning and water cooler

This is a plus because a water cooler uses far less electricity than an air conditioner and can be used much of the time.

Climate-controlled environment

Electronically controlled environment

Easy to heat with its. . .

Energy efficient 2-zone gas heat

Climate zone control

Low utilities

Attention-getting heading	**LOW UTILITY BILLS** are yours with this...
Be certain of your facts before you make such a statement.	Last year's heating cost only $_______.
Attic fans reduce air-conditioning costs and are even used alone to keep a house cool.	Attic fan Automatic attic fan
	Central air
Not necessarily central air	Fully air-conditioned
	Central air-conditioning
These could be window units; if it is a central unit, say so.	Air-conditioning

In many northern states, people are converting to wood heat and using gas or oil for backup. A wood heat source is now a very desirable feature.

Wood/gas combination furnace

Wood-burning stove

Wood-burning furnace with auxiliary gas heat

Wood stove heats entire house.

Backup wood stove

Buy a chain saw and heat for free.

Economical wood heat

Energy-saving wood heat

Wood stove with catalytic converter

Wood heater fireplace insert

Franklin stove

Solar heat has a positive image because everyone likes something for free.

Passive solar home

Solar heat

Partial solar heat

Let nature heat your home

Southwest window wall for solar heating

With higher fuel costs, ads such as the following are becoming extremely effective:

An alternative heading would be BUY A CHAIN SAW.

HIGH FUEL BILLS?

The combination wood/gas boiler in this 3BR, 2-bath contemporary situated on a wooded site in convenient Golden Hills will solve your problems. Super insulation, triple-glazed windows and a see-through native stone fireplace in the living room and family room will mean a warm, economical winter. There is plenty of room in the oversized double garage for a winter's supply of firewood. A hot property at $79,600.

Clyde Realty **476-8200**

Because of allergies and dust, many homes have electronic air cleaners added to their central heating and cooling system. These cleaners electronically remove particles of dirt and pollen too small for normal filters. If a house has such a system, you could make it the focal point of your ad with:

This describes almost a majority of us.

ALLERGY SUFFERERS
Built-in electronic air cleaner provides a dust- and pollen-free environment for hay fever and asthma suffers.

In some areas humidity must be added to the air in winter. A positive feature would be:

Power humidifier

Automatic humidifier

Furnace with power humidifier

In other areas humidity must be taken from the air.

Automatic power dehumidifier

Insulation

Because of higher heating and cooling costs, buyers are more concerned with insulation.

Mention this if all the homes in the area are not.

R is a resistance factor used to measure insulation. By being technical you add a quality factor to the home. This is especially good for new homes.

Fully insulated

R 21 insulation

Super-insulated

Double-insulated

Extra insulation

6″ sidewalls

12″ of ceiling insulation

Take advantage of the enormous energy savings and minimal maintenance on this. . .

Features state-of-the-art energy efficient construction

Utilities

In areas where some homes do not have city utilities, their presence in the advertised property becomes a plus factor.

County water

City water and sewer

City water and gas

For vacant lots

Utilities to property

Utilities available

Natural gas

In areas where utilities are expected, a plus factor could be underground utilities.

You can make the fact that city water is not available a positive feature with:

Pure well water

You will relish the cold pure water from your own well.

Even a septic system can be a plus with:

Oversized septic system

It is not a good idea to mention in your ad the fact that a home has a new septic system or well: It suggests there was a problem. While you want to avoid negative aspects in your ads, full disclosure of possible problems or defects must be made to the purchasers during a showing.

Still More Features

The list of features that can become the core of your ad's drawing power is endless. Your power of observation and ability to put yourself in a buyer's place will continually suggest new approaches. To get you started, here are a few more features to stay aware of:

Automatic garage openers

Central vacuum system

Built-in vacuum system

Cable television

Satellite dish

Ceiling fan (paddle fan)

Dog kennel

Dog runs

Gas Bar-B-Q

Exterior gas lights can set a positive mood.

Gas lights

Yard lights

Intercom system

Protective covenants

Handicapped conveniences

Wheelchair access

Handicapped-equipped

Levolor blinds

Includes Home Protection Plan

Includes structural and equipment warranty

Includes Homebuyer Warranty Protection

Cathedral atrium

Glassed-in atrium

Fountain atrium

Taxes

In areas where property is not automatically reassessed upon sale, you might want to mention low taxes. The same holds true for particular communities with lower-than-normal taxes.

Low taxes

Low-low taxes

Taxes only *$872* in *1986*

Benefit by *Clearwater's* low tax rate

Lowest tax rate in county

5 General Homes, Family Homes and Open House Promotion

General Homes

When a home's special feature does not deserve a heading, use more general terms to grab the reader's interest and encourage them to read the entire ad and call the agent.

General Headings

Examples of general headings include:

DON'T TOUCH A THING
It's perfect the way it is.

E.T.—EXTRA TERRIFIC
You don't have to be from outer space to recognize the value in this...

AAAH!
Words don't describe this...

THIS AD WILL NOT BE REPEATED
as this...is bound to be sold to its first viewer.

REWARD
yourself with the home you deserve.

W.O.W.
Wide Open and Wonderful

NOT THE LEAST BIT ORDINARY

DON'T BOTHER
looking any further. This...

U.S. PRIME

IT'S INCREDIBLE

DON'T DREAM TOO LONG
as this...won't last.

YARD SALE
Stately trees, flowering shrubs and sweeping lawns come complete with this...

WHY SETTLE FOR VANILLA
when your tastes will be delighted by this...

This simply means it is a new listing, but it creates a feeling of urgency.

JUST RELEASED FOR SALE

ONE LOOK—WE GOTCHA

NEEDLE IN A HAYSTACK
You've found it in this...

THIS IS IT

RIP VAN WINKLE DREAM HOUSE

Price reduction (not necessarily a bargain)

CHOP—CHOP—CHOP
There goes the price on this...

TRY THIS FOR SIGHS

COME SEE—COME SIGH

VOTED BY OUR SALES STAFF
as the home least likely to be still for sale next week

EXPECT TO BE ENVIED

If good-size lot

BREATHING ROOM

THE CURE
for your new home fever is this...

Indicates there is no room for price reduction

BARE BONES $89,500

HAPPINESS IS:

BUY LOW—LIVE HIGH

Vacant

MOVE IN TOMORROW

UTOPIA
You will look no further after viewing this...

This can turn the absence of a basement into a virtue.

NO STAIRS

A HOME FOR ALL REASONS

VALHALLA

PAINSTAKINGLY PERFECT

NOT FOR EVERYONE

Two homes, one lot

2 FOR 1

STOP DREAMING

DREAM NO MORE

PSST—STILL LOOKING?
Then hurry to see this...

A PRETTY FACE
And it's pretty on the inside, too

MORE THAN A PRETTY FACE
This one has it all, including...

OWNER-LOVED
and so will you. This...

WARMTH—STYLE—CHARM

FIVE-STAR VALUE

GOING—GOING—GONE
Don't let this one get away.

WAITING MEANS LOSING

The name of the builder, even if not well known, can add prestige to a home.

KINGSLEY-BUILT

EXPECT TO BE IMPRESSED
when you enter this...

YOUR TOMORROW MAY NEVER COME
if you don't see this...today.

A LITTLE ESTATE

GO FOR IT

ENJOY—ENJOY

REMBRANDT COULDN'T PAINT
a prettier picture than this...

ALL THINGS BRIGHT AND BEAUTIFUL
in this...

THREE R'S
Reduced, Ready and Really Nice

WELCOME TO PARADISE

PARADISE FOUND

PARADISE FOR SALE

A PIECE OF PARADISE

MODERN AS TOMORROW
YESTERDAY'S PRICE

STAR QUALITY

THE LAP OF LUXURY

JUST A CLASS ABOVE

A good pre-Christmas heading

HOME FOR THE HOLIDAYS

LOOKS LIKE A MILLION

WE FOUND IT—BELIEVE IT

AWARD WINNER
You will give first prize to this. . .

JOG, DON'T WALK
This. . .won't last long.

For older city home

CHARM—CHARACTER—CONVENIENCE

Good for a colonial

AS AMERICAN AS APPLE PIE

THE AMERICAN DREAM

HAPPINESS IS
finding a. . .

INVEST IN HAPPINESS

WELCOME HOME

LOVELY TO LOOK AT
Delightful to live in

Price of home

THE $64,000 QUESTION
Are you the family for this. . .

IF YOU EVER DREAMED
of having a. . .

IT'S LOADED
with extras. This. . .

CAREFUL, IT'S LOADED
with charm. This. . .

READY FOR ADOPTION
The owner has left this. . .

UP FOR ADOPTION

YOU CAN'T TOP THIS

YOU WILL NEVER KNOW
what you are missing unless you call today to see this. . .

Three-line heading

THE RIGHT HOUSE
THE RIGHT PRICE
THE RIGHT FINANCING

Good action heading

STOP—CIRCLE—CALL

CIRCLE THIS AD

SAVE THIS AD

ALL THE "I-WANTS"

CURB APPEAL

BE THANKFUL YOU READ THIS AD

IT'S GOT EVERYTHING
except an owner. This orphan *ranch* has...

QUALITY—COMFORT—CONVENIENCE
are just the beginnings of the good things about this...

IMPRESSIVE
That's the only way to describe this...

THROW AWAY YOUR WISHBONE
Everything you ever wanted is here.

JUST A LITTLE PEEK
and you will be sold on this...

TODAY YOU FOUND YOUR PERFECT HOME

AVAILABLE AGAIN
We sold this home in *3* days, but the buyer could not complete the purchase.

Name of your state

THE NEBRASKA DREAM

Indicates immediate occupancy

EMPTY AND LONELY

LOOKED AT THE REST
Now you can buy the best.

THE LIFE OF RILEY
will be yours in this...

THE ART OF LIVING

FANTASTIC FIND

TOO GOOD TO LAST

TOO NICE TO LAST

LOVE AT FIRST SIGHT

VALUE—BEAUTY—SPACE

For a specially designed home

ONE OF A KIND

DREAM HOUSE

PERSONALITY PLUS

GOOD TASTE

ONLY FOR THE DISCRIMINATING

A HOME FOR ALL SEASONS

SURPRISE!

A RARE OPPORTUNITY

CAPTIVATINGLY BEAUTIFUL

ONCE IN A LIFETIME
can you find...

This is an effective negative attention-getting heading.

DON'T BELIEVE US
See for yourself. This...

The fact that a house has just been placed on the market is appealing to many buyers. They feel they have first chance at it. Some people feel that if a home has been on the market a long time, there must be something wrong with the property.

JUST LISTED

NEW LISTING

FIRST TIME OFFERED

FIRST TIME ADVERTISED

LABOR DAY—NO
Carefree living in this...

FOREVER
You won't want to leave this...

HOUSE BEAUTIFUL

BETTER HOME AND GARDEN

In some areas this heading has been overworked.

LAST CHANCE
This new listing will sell fast.

PREPPY
This young *brick, 4-bedroom ranch* is ready to go. It features every "in" convenience, including...

PICK OF THE WEEK

STORYBOOK PERFECT

HER PALACE
She will love this...

WE CHALLENGE YOU
to compare this...with any other home on the market.

INCREDIBLE BUT TRUE

SOMETHING FOR EVERYONE

LOOK—LOOK

IT'S TIME TO LIVE

IN A CLASS BY ITSELF

SEEING IS BELIEVING

LIKE NO OTHER HOME

General Body Copy

Generalized statements that have reader appeal can also be used in the ad body. Examples include:

You won't want to leave this...

Country-style living in the city

A city home with a country flair

Everything for the good life, including...

"Instantly appealing" describes this...

Offers a captivating blend of *indoor and outdoor* living at its finest

This eye-appealing home features...

Every convenience and amenity

Every imaginable convenience

Exciting and spacious

You will feel warm and welcome in this...

Worthy of *House & Garden*

Perfect for roommates

If there are two master suites, this would be a strong ad for a singles' paper.

This...is enriched with every contemporary comfort imaginable.

All the amenities you would ask for enhance the elegance of this...

This eye-pleasing home is blessed with...

A classic residence built for the ages

Sophisticated design

Unassuming charm

Offering a charm that complements the environment

Entertain your friends, even if they are royalty, in this...

A home that captures your vision of tomorrow

Attention to detail is apparent in every glance in this...

Romance and flair run rampant in this...

Captivatingly different

Stunningly conceived

A much-sought-after but rarely available...

Amenities to enhance your living pleasure

Featuring all of the amenities you have dreamed of

Refreshingly different

Versatile floor plan

Offering heart-stirring warmth that will win you over

Built in the European tradition of fine craftsmanship

This bewitching home features...

Endowed with...

You will notice the unusual attention to detail.

With all the extras you would expect in an executive home

Includes all the special touches you desire

2 years new

This is a plus for buyers who need a home now.

Vacant and lonely

Owner is ready to pack

General Closings

General closings include:

This is as pretty as they get $_________.

Enjoy the good life and a wise investment $_________.

Affordable luxury at $_________.

A home with character $_________.

Something very special $_________.

To see it is to love it $_________.

We are proud to offer this fine home at $_________.

An exceptional offering at $_________.

A truly exceptional offering at $_________.

The fact that immediate possession is possible is a strong feature for people being transferred into an area.

Move-in ready at $_________.

Available now at $_________.

Immediate possession at $_________.

Ready to move in at $_________.

Move right in at $_________.

Available yesterday $_________.

A very special place at $_________.

A very special home at $_________.

Welcome home $_________.

You will never say you're sorry at $_________.

A seldom-available opportunity at $_________.

A value with excellence at $_________.

Picky buyer's pick at $_________.

A spectacular choice at $_________.

For the best move of your life $_________.

You will want to call this home at $_________.

Your dreams can become a reality for $_________.

For a unique living experience, call. . .

Tastefully different at $_________.

Upscale living at $_________.

A home to be proud of $_________.

Your American dream realistically priced at $_________.

The home you deserve priced at $_________.

Spoil yourself for only $_________.

See it and you will own it at $_________.

Price at $_________. Isn't this your dream home?

An opportunity not to be missed at $_________.

Spacious and gracious at $_________.

A lot to like at $_________.

Destined to steal your heart at $_________.

It will steal your heart at $_________.

Treat yourself to the good life $_________.

Your search ends here $_________.

The good life awaits at $_________.

Simple elegance at $_________.

Make your dreams a reality $_________.

All your dreams are possible at $_________.

Packaged to go at $_________.

Rare offering at $_________.

Rare opportunity at $_________.

Don't miss this at $_________.

Overworked

Must see to appreciate $_________.

This wall-to-wall comfort can be yours at $_________.

Come over to the good life $_________.

Owners will relinquish for $_________.

Envision it yours $_________.

Exciting individuality at $________.

Your new home for $________.

Be the proud owner for $________.

A unique offering at $________.

It's going to be love at first sight $________.

Your future at $________.

Your dreams are possible $________.

Ready for you at $________.

Not to be overlooked at $________.

Make it yours $________.

Certain to please at $________.

An uncommon find $________.

Don't wish when you can own $________.

Sure to delight at $________.

Something for everyone at $________.

Waiting for you at $________.

Something special at $________.

A home for a happy tomorrow $________.

What more would you want $________.

Don't let this one get away $________.

One-of-a-kind offering at $________.

Outstanding at $________.

A very special home at $________.

You will get excited over this at $________.

Your dreams will come true for only $________.

You won't believe it till you own it $________.

Submit any offer $________.

The problem with such a request is that you are saying the owner will take less than list price. You will also invite low offers which will make a reasonable sale difficult. Before it is used you should explain the problems to the owners and get their permission.

Own now for $________.

Delightful at $________.

Grab the good life $________.

Become the happy owner for $________.

The home for a beautiful future $________.

Buy yourself a new life $________.

Discover peace of mind $________.

Discover the good life $________.

Discover a better life $________.

This is a dangerous closing because you are saying the price is not firm. Be sure you get the owners' permission before it is used.

Asking $_________.

Delightful living for $_________.

The home you have dreamed about $_________.

Offered at $_________.

This closing does not have the same connotation as asking.

Offered proudly at $_________.

Action Closings These closings encourage the reader to do something.

Pull up your van and move right in for $_________.

Do hurry at $_________.

Don't delay—call today $_________.

A must-see for the quality conscious $_________.

Make your move now at $_________.

It's your home at $_________.

Make this No. 1 on your must-see list $_________.

Buy it and love it $_________.

One visit and you will decide $_________.

You will reach for your checkbook when you see the price $_________.

No need for hesitation at $_________.

Don't wait till it's gone, act now $_________.

Worthy of your immediate consideration $_________.

Warrants your immediate attention at $_________.

Merits your prompt attention at $_________.

Definitely worth your immediate inspection $_________.

Let us tell you more today.

If this meets your needs, we recommend quick action.

If you've missed exceptional buys before, call this minute.

Call now. It's too good to miss.

Demands immediate attention at $_________.

Be the first to inspect this rare find $_________.

Your new home is only a phone call away $_________.

Make it yours for $_________.

Deserves your attention *now* $_________.

Have it all now for $_________.

See it today at $_________.

Consider the advantages, then act fast at $_________.

Your search has ended if you call today $_________.

Besides open houses, the only time to give an address is if the house has an exceptionally good exterior appearance. Whenever you include an address, you lose the opportunity to switch the buyers to property better meeting their needs if they are not impressed by a drive-by.

Drive by, then call to see $_________.

Inquire now at $_________.

See it, you will want it $_________.

You won't need a second look at $_________.

Be the first one to call at $_________.

You'd better start packing $_________.

One look will make you the owner $_________.

Seeing will be buying $_________.

Call today for a happy tomorrow $_________.

Hurry to own at $_________.

Reassurance of Value These closings reassure the reader of the property's value.

A great value at $_________.

An obvious value at $_________.

Realistically priced at $_________.

Competitively priced at $_________.

Well-priced at $_________.

Priced right at $_________.

Only $_________. And worth every penny.

Rock-bottom-priced at $_________.

Priced to sell at $_________.

Action-priced at $_________.

All the space-age luxuries at a down-to-earth price of $_________.

An excellent buy with the future in mind $_________.

Seems too good to be true at $_________.

Excitingly priced at $_________.

Solid value at $_________.

All this for only $_________.

Yours for only $_________.

Unmatchable at $_________.

Hard to believe at $_________.

A tempting value at $_________.

Value-packed at $_________.

Packed with value at $_________.

A must-see for the buyer who expects more $_________.

Unprecedented value at $_________.

An uncommon find at $_________.

An uncommonly fine home at $________.

The price is right at $________.

Offered at an amazingly reasonable $________.

Truly worth seeing and worth owning at $________.

Hard to believe at only $________.

Priced to move at $________.

Emphasizing Urgency These general closings emphasize urgency.

Won't be around long at $________.

This picture-book property can be yours today. It will be gone tomorrow $________.

If you wait, it will be too late $________.

Call now, for you are not the only one reading this ad $________.

Be first or be sorry at $________.

Completed Ads for General Homes

Here are a few examples of completed ads for general single-family homes where neither location, price, terms or special features are really strong.

Since the price seems attractive, it is mentioned in the heading.

If there were more than one bath, the ad should have said so.

If the garage is larger than a one-car garage, the ad should indicate it.

If special financing was available, it should have been covered.

This is a good ad for an older small home in an older area.

HEART CLUTCHER
$43,900

You will fall in love with this 3BR Spanish bungalow set amidst giant palms on a very special street in Covina. With luxury features such as a red tile roof and central air, the home also offers a separate garage, a delightful patio and your own orange and grapefruit trees. Call to see it and you will love it.

Clyde Realty **476-8200**

This attention-getting heading calls for action and is followed by a short ad that sets forth the desirable features.

This ad was written to get the reader to call for additional information.

STOP—CIRCLE—CALL

It's hard to believe, but you can find a classic 2BR expandable Cape Cod with a double garage on one of the finest west-side streets for only $79,500.

Clyde Realty 476-8200

This well-written ad is likely to result in a favorable reader response.

ONCE IN A WHILE

a home will come on the market that offers everything from location to condition and price. Look no further, for here it is. This 3BR and den, 2-bath brick traditional in delightful Edgerton is only 6 years old. On a quiet tree-lined street, it is walking distance from shopping, has a fully fenced garden-size yard and a double garage with an automatic opener. Don't be sorry, call now, as it won't last long at $84,500.

Clyde Realty 476-8200

While a little cute, this simple attention-getter heading ties in with the closing.

SIMON SAYS

Take a look at this exciting 6-year-old ranch set on a tree- and flower-covered site that's walking-close to shopping. There are all the amenities you wanted, including oak floors, cabinetry and woodwork, poured basement, economical natural gas heat, paved drive, full 2-car garage, as well as a perfect spot for a vegetable garden. Simon says look, then buy at $89,500.

Clyde Realty 476-8200

This nostalgia ad appeals to pleasant memories.

New England *adds distinction to* bungalow.

REMEMBER THE OLD NEIGHBORHOOD

of quiet tree-lined streets and children roller-skating on a summer afternoon? Well, you can come home again with this 3BR, 1½-bath New England bungalow. A full basement, 2-car garage, air-cond., family-size garden and 3 apple trees make good living easy at $67,500.

Clyde Realty **476-8200**

Family Homes

Love for others can be an extremely strong motivator. People will often spend for loved ones what they wouldn't consider spending for themselves. Ads can appeal to love of family and family responsibilities as well as family needs.

Headings Ad headings set the proper mood.

THE HOME YOUR FAMILY DESERVES

CHILDREN WANTED

FOR YOUR FAMILY

SOMETHING FOR THE FAMILY

ROOTS FOR YOUR FAMILY

3BR FAMILY HOME

This is much warmer than saying the house includes an in-law unit.

ROOM FOR GRANDMA

LOOKS LIKE HOME

People often feel that a new home in a different area will solve the problems they have.

A HAPPY HOME

WHAT PRICE HAPPINESS?

HAPPINESS FOR SALE

RECIPE FOR HAPPINESS

FAMILY IN MIND

A HILL FOR SLEDDING

WHAT YOU HAVE BEEN WORKING FOR

This ad is aimed at a child's dreams.

PRIVACY IS
a room of your very own in this...

LOTS OF TOTS

PUPPIES AND CHILDREN

BIRDS, BEES AND APPLE TREES

BACK TO SCHOOL

HORSES, DOGS AND KIDS

NEEDS LARGE FAMILY

WATCH YOUR FAMILY GROW
with room to spare in this...

DESIGNED FOR CHILDREN

A KID'S HOUSE

FOR THE GROWING FAMILY

4BR—NEEDS BOYS & GIRLS

YOU PROVIDE THE FAMILY

ROOM FOR THE FAMILY

LET THE KIDS OUT
A huge fenced child-safe yard comes with this...

HEIR CONDITIONED
Lots of room for the little ones with this...

The mention of a pony gives us a vision of happy children.

ROOM FOR A PONY
Kids, dogs and horses, too. Room for all in this...

GET SETTLED
before school starts in this...

WE'RE NOT KIDDING
Your kids will love this...

LET YOUR FAMILY GROW
in this...

This heading would be particularly appropriate for the Christmas season.

THE GIFT OF LOVE

NOT JUST A PLACE TO LIVE
It's a home for family love.

Large house

BIG FAMILY
The original owner of this...had 9 children.

FRIENDLY DOG
not included, but this 4BR family home has everything else.

THE AMERICAN DREAM
is alive and well in Sagewood Heights.

GO WHERE THE GROWING'S GOOD
Your family will love this. . .

TRIBE-SIZE YARD

ROOM TO ROMP

Body Copy Your ad body can also include family references.

Across from the park

1 block from the playground

For additional language on schools, see the Neighborhood *section of Chapter Two.*

Walking-close to grade school

In Kildare school district

Children's playhouse

Fenced play area

Completely fenced backyard

Additional language on roads can be found in Chapter Three.

On a quiet cul-de-sac

On a child-safe cul-de-sac

For a bedroom with bath

Teenager suite

Gramma's room or teen suite

Playroom

Rainy day playroom

Nursery

Nursery off master bedroom

Tribe-size backyard

Safety feature for small children

Fully fenced backyard

Child-safe fenced yard

Playground backyard

Room for swing set, sandbox and a gaggle of children

The backyard is just waiting for your children.

Room for bikes and trikes

A family-oriented community

A friendly family neighborhood

Fond memories are made in a home like this.

With the mellow warmth of a well-loved family home

This family charmer features. . .

Move before school starts.

A ranch home for you and your cowboys and cowgirls

This *18th-century colonial* reflects the time when the family home was the center of one's existence.

A much-loved home of the past for your family future

Trees for climbing

A place where children can still run free

If you're tired of driving the children to school, you will appreciate this. . . walking-close to. . .

Family-size yard

Older home	A place to raise your children in all the old ways

Fully fenced

The backyard is just waiting for a sandbox and swing.

The old *oak* tree in the backyard is the perfect place to hang your swing.

A boy and his dog will love bunking in their own rugged paneled bedroom.

Dormitory-size bedroom

Storybook nursery

Closings Closings, too, can evoke family feeling.

Lead your family to the good life $________.

A happy home for $________.

Family-priced at $________.

A spouse-pleaser at $________.

The home for your family $________.

For optimum family living $________.

An investment in your family at $________.

For a whole new life $________.

A very special family home at $________.

Just add your family $________.

All it needs is your family $________.

The best thing you can do for your family $________.

A real home to come home to $________.

A joy to come home to $________.

Makes coming home a pleasure $________.

A family investment in happiness $________.

A family investment for a lifetime of happiness $________.

A home that will secure your family's future $________.

Idyllic family living can be yours $_________.

Welcome home $_________.

Load up your family and see it today $_________.

Certain to please your family $_________.

No better way to show your family love $_________.

Ready for your family $_________.

Family-ready at $_________.

Waiting for your family's love $_________.

An investment in your family $_________.

Buy today and your family will thank you forever $_________.

An investment in your peace of mind $_________.

Completed Ads Stressing Family

These completed ads carry through the family theme in each of their elements.

This is an unusual but effective attention-getting heading that sets the mood of a pleasant childhood.

A large basement area is a rainy-day playroom.

The only thing missing in the ad is walking-close to grammar school.

BARE FEET WIGGLING

in the grass. Room for children to roam on this 1/2-acre wooded site. The pleasant 3BR family home was designed with children in mind. Besides the large family room, there is a huge rainy-day playroom in the finished basement. The oversized 2-car garage has plenty of room for bikes and trikes. Located on a child-safe cul-de-sac in Bayside, this is a very special family home at $97,500.

Clyde Realty **476-8200**

This heading is very powerful. Every parent who has felt his or her heart sink at the sound of brakes will appreciate this benefit.

Because parents spend a lot of time in the kitchen, being able to look out and see the children is a great reassurance.

NO SCREECHING BRAKES

on this child-safe cul-de-sac in beautiful Fox Point. The friendly 3BR, 1½-bath Cape Cod offers room to grow with an unfinished attic that's big enough for two additional rooms. The sun-filled kitchen opens to the large fenced play yard. Only two quiet blocks from the grade school, it's the perfect home for family living $86,800.

Clyde Realty 476-8200

While it is extremely difficult to write an ad that is cute as well as effective, it can be done. The following is an example:

Note that the benefits shown for children also are applicable to the grandparents.

TO GRANDMOTHER'S HOUSE

Your grandchildren will love to visit you in this delightful 2BR home in friendly Bay View. There's a real fireplace for toastin' marshmallows and poppin' corn, a dry basement perfect for playin', a huge workroom in the garage for tinkerin', a dozen bird houses just for watchin', 6 apple trees for pickin' and a sun-filled kitchen for pie-bakin'. This is the perfect home for family lovin' $69,500.

Clyde Realty 476-8200

The next ad, while cute, fails to really sell the benefits of the property. You cannot forget that the purpose of the ad is to invite inquiries.

TOO CUTE
This ad is probably a little too cute. It also fails to sell its benefits in a strong manner. It definitely is not a power ad.

RECIPE FOR HAPPINESS

Take 3BRs, add 2 baths and an oversized garage, place on a tribe-size lot and blend in a quiet tree-lined street in a choice south-side neighborhood, move in your family and you have happiness. It's ready for you at $79,000.

Clyde Realty 476-8200

A rewritten ad for the same house follows. While it does have a cute attention-getting heading, the rest of the ad sells the benefits of the house and creates a desire in the reader to know more about it.

Better

FRIENDLY DOG

Not included with this 3BR, 2-bath family home, but it has everything else—a quiet tree-shaded street in a choice south-side neighborhood, quality schools, a tribe-size yard just made for children, an oversize double garage and a house that will be the envy of your friends. Truly a very special family home at $79,000.

Clyde Realty 476-8200

The strong points about this property are probably location, price and terms. Very little is told about the house. If there were strong family features, they should have been mentioned. A good action closing.

CHILDREN'S CHAUFFEUR?

If you are tired of driving your children to school, this 3-bedroom, 2-bath brick traditional in Westview will be the answer to your dreams. Only a short walk on quiet streets to schools and park. Priced at $87,500 with a low down payment, you better load up the station wagon and see this one NOW.

Clyde Realty 476-8200

Open House Promotion

Some newspapers, such as the *Washington Post,* have special sections for open house property. In this situation, an open house ad differs from an ordinary ad only in that it includes the property address, days and hours of the open house and possibly directions to the property.

If your paper does not have an *Open House* section, your ad has to call attention to that on its own, usually by using it as a lead in large type.

OPEN HOUSE

OPEN HOUSE $49,500

OPEN HOUSE—BRENTWOOD

The fact that a home is being shown for the first time will attract some prospects because it indicates the house has not been previously rejected by other buyers who may be as picky as they are.

OPEN HOUSE—1ST SHOWING

OPEN HOUSE—1ST OFFERING

OPEN HOUSE—PREMIER SHOWING

OPEN HOUSE—FIRST PRESENTATION

Your ad naturally should indicate when the house will be open and its location.

OPEN HOUSE
Sat. & Sun. 1–4 P.M.
812 West Bradbury
(1 Block East of Clinton)

In summer when the days are longer, you might want to have longer open house hours.

You might want to include detailed directions if the house is difficult to find, or you could simply state:

Follow our arrows from the corner of Clinton and 8th Street.

Instead of saying *Open House,* all you really need is the word *Open*. Other alternatives are:

A good heading for a luxury home

OPEN FOR ADMIRATION

OPEN TO PUBLIC

COME BY 1–4

OPEN—COME BUY

Open house *should also be prominent in the ad or these headings are likely to be missed.*

DUSTY SHOES PREVIEW

COME AND APPRECIATE THIS

HEY LOOK US OVER
Open today 2–4

COME AND SEE
Sunday 2–4

VISIT 1–4

SEE TODAY 1–4

To add a personal touch to an open house ad, you can include above the firm name, *Your Hostess: Joan Clyde.*

Some brokers advertise *Champagne Opening* and serve champagne to the viewers. Others include *Wine and Cheese* in their ads hoping it will bring prospects. While free food and drink will certainly bring viewers, We strongly doubt their effectiveness in helping sales.

Many prospects take the papers and drive to look at the homes. When the homes don't "turn them on," they drive by without stopping.

Some effective language for your ads to get the *drive-byers* to stop includes:

Don't be a drive-byer—you won't believe the space and extras until you go inside this...

OPTICAL ILLUSION
It's much bigger than it looks.

COME INSIDE—YOU'LL BE SURPRISED
This house is only truly appreciated once you step inside.

DON'T DRIVE BY
Park your car and be delighted by what's inside...

OPEN HOUSE
LARGER THAN IT LOOKS
Don't judge a book by its cover. You will be pleasantly surprised when you enter this...

Additional language for open house ads includes:

A subheading under a Sunday Open House

NEVER ON SUNDAY
will you find a better value than this...

Load up the family and hurry over to...

Come visit us, you will be delighted and surprised.

Come see what elegant living is all about.

6 Large Homes, Small Homes, New Homes and Old Homes

Large Homes

There are people besides those with big families who want houses with more than three bedrooms. They might want them for guests, hobbies, storing collectibles or just for the feeling that larger is more prestigious than smaller. Whenever a home has more than three bedrooms, treat this as an important feature, preferably in the heading.

Headings In this case, the simplest headings are usually the best.

4BR NORTHRIDGE

If price is less than normally expected, it should also be featured. Larger families are often interested in economical housing.

4BR $49,500

4BR + *SITTING ROOM*

4 BR—COLONIAL

These are the most effective headings for large homes, but many brokers feel they show little imagination. They prefer what they consider to be more creative headings. The headings shown below are not as good as simple 4BR headings because they can easily be missed by readers looking specifically for four- or five-bedroom homes.

***10* ROOMS**

None of these headings has the immediate impact of simpler styles, at least on buyers who specifically want four or more bedrooms.

ROOM TO ROAM (10 OF THEM)

GREAT BIG HOUSE

LITTLE BITTY PRICE

Without 4BR *the ad could be missed by readers seeking large homes.*

SPACE ODYSSEY 4BR

ROOM FOR EVERYTHING

WHO'S LOOKING FOR A BIG HOUSE?

THE BIGGIE
6 bedrooms in this. . .

EASE THE SQUEEZE
This 4BR. . .

NEED SPACE?
AT AN AFFORDABLE PRICE

DON'T CRAMP YOUR STYLE

ELBOW ROOM

S-T-R-E-T-C-H-O-U-T

IT'S BIG

ROOM TO SPARE

NEED MORE SPACE?

ROOM TO BREATHE

LARGE AND NICE

BIG IS BEAUTIFUL

BIG FAMILY

ARE YOU A BIG FAMILY?

BIG FAMILY NEEDED
to fill the 6 bedrooms of this. . .

Applicable if separate guest suite or apartment

IN-LAW SOLUTION

L-A-R-G-E

H-U-G-E

THE BIG HOUSE

LARGE FAMILY WANTED
for this. . .

SPACED OUT
Huge 4BR home features. . .

A SMALL KINGDOM
is yours with this 5-bedroom *colonial* situated on an estate-size lot in. . .

Showing the 6BR *in the heading would have made a much more effective ad.*

LOTS OF FRIENDS?
Try this for size—6BR

Body Copy For large homes, your ad body might include:

This gives a reason for the sale.

Empty-nesters selling this lovely *10*-room ranch

Plenty of room for collectibles in this...

A whopping *3,000 sq. ft.* of living space in this...

You won't squeeze the children in this 9-room, 4-bedroom colonial.

Space abounds inside and out in this...

Mammoth rooms

Some people feel large homes are cold.

This home boasts over *2,500 sq. ft.*, yet it retains feelings of warmth and intimacy.

Embassy-size *colonial*

3000 square feet of magnificent space

The size of the rooms can be emphasized with language such as:

Rooms of grand proportions

Castle-size rooms

Dramatically proportioned *living room*

Magnificently proportioned

Texas-size rooms

Baronial-size rooms

Texas-size *family room*

Mammoth rooms

Family-size kitchen

Tribe-size kitchen

Closings You can tailor your closings for large homes with:

A lot of house for $_________.

A room for everyone at $_________.

Enjoy king-size comfort $_________.

A home for a real family $_________.

Your relief from claustrophobia $_________.

Expansive but not expensive at $_________.

An expansive home at the low, low price of $_________.

Completed Ads for Large Homes

Putting the elements together produces ads like these, some more effective than others.

The simple heading gets the message across.

4 KING-SIZE BEDROOMS

This bright and cheerful 3-bath colonial features a tribe-size country kitchen, living room with massive orchard stone fireplace, paneled den (or 5th bedroom), formal DR and a hobby-size 3-car garage. Set on an estate-size lot amidst ancient oaks, it's expansive but not expensive at $198,500.

Clyde Realty 476-8200

LESS EFFECTIVE
While cute, this ad could be easily overlooked by a prospect for a large home.

5 BR *added to the heading would make for a much stronger ad.*

ALL THE KIDS

will have their own bedrooms in this 5-bedroom, 3-bath home. A huge family room, formal dining room and country kitchen are just a few of the features that highlight this rare offering. Family-priced at $92,000 with a low-low down payment.

Clyde Realty 476-8200

LESS EFFECTIVE
The same comment as above applies to this ad. A much more effective heading would be, 5 BEDROOMS—HACIENDA HIGHLANDS.

Cute is fine if it conveys the message; in this case it really doesn't.

COMPANY COMING?

You will love the private guest suites in this 5BR rambling ranch. All the amenities for entertaining including wet bar, formal dining room, game room, pool and much, much more. Located in prestigious Hacienda Highlands $198,000.

Clyde Realty 476-8200

This ad has a good heading and action closing, and is aimed at buyers who want space at a reasonable cost. If exceptional financing were available, it should have been included. The ad is obviously for an older home. See the section in this chapter describing older homes in a positive manner.

6 BEDROOMS
$89,500

Room for the children, grandma and cousin Charlie, too, in this 11-room American traditional home set on a quiet tree-canopied street in Westview. There is an unfinished windowed attic that would make an ideal artist's studio. There are 2 full and 2 half-baths, a double garage and a full basement with a huge hobby or workroom area. If affordable space is what you need, call today or be sorry tomorrow.

Clyde Realty 476-8200

Small Homes

Homes having two bedrooms or less are generally more difficult to sell than larger homes. Often people want more space than they actually need. At times the only reason for wanting a three-bedroom home is that the buyer feels it will be easier to sell.

The word *small* has a negative connotation and should be avoided generally. However, you can use ad headings that make *small* a plus, rather than a negative.

Cottage *carries a connotation of small but cozy.*

ENCHANTED COTTAGE

SECLUDED COTTAGE

GRANDPA'S (OR GRANDMA'S) COTTAGE

WRITER'S COTTAGE

HANSEL & GRETHEL COTTAGE

A little too cute.

CUTE AND COZY

GINGERBREAD HOUSE

MINI-CHATEAU

LA PETITE MAISON

MAISONETTE

MINI-ESTATE

Your ad can appeal to the type of person you expect as a buyer with:

ATTENTION SINGLES

SINGLE'S DELIGHT

PROFESSIONAL COUPLE

ARTIST'S STUDIO/HOME

SINGLE'S HIDEAWAY

SINGLE'S PARADISE

SINGLE'S PAD

FOR THE SINGLE
who doesn't want a condo

BEGINNER'S LUCK
A cottage made for newlyweds

JUST MARRIED

RETIREE'S DELIGHT

HONEYMOON COTTAGE

RETIREMENT-SIZE

SOPHISTICATED ADULT HOME

For an expandable home heading consider:

LITTLE HOUSE
BUT ROOM TO GROW

E-X-P-A-N-D-A-B-L-E

EXPANDABLE BUNGALOW

ROOM TO GROW

ROOM TO E-X-P-A-N-D

IT IS EXPANDABLE
Cape Cod with *2* bedrooms and room for *2* more

Your ad body can include language such as:

A home for the mature adult who deserves a more luxurious environment

Designed for today's adult life-style

Unfinished attic would make an ideal studio or?

One large room

An open-concept living room/dining room/kitchen

This is much better than saying the house has two bedrooms, which might appear inadequate. Now the two bedrooms appear as more than what is needed.

Master suite plus guest room

Flexible floor plan with expansion possibilities

You will find magical charm in this fairy-tale cottage.

Completed Ads for Small Homes

This ad makes a one-bedroom home seem more than adequate.

ARTIST'S STUDIO

The window wall of the combination living room/studio catches the morning light. There is a delightful eat-in kitchen, and the oversized bedroom is loaded with closet space. A separate garage has possibilities for additional studio space or guest quarters. It's bound to sell quickly at $61,500.

Clyde Realty **476-8200**

This ad also makes two bedrooms seem more than enough.

ENCHANTED COTTAGE

Nestled in a wooded lot is this storybook cottage with a master suite, separate guest room and a spacious open-concept living room/dining room/kitchen with beamed cathedral ceiling and an orchard stone fireplace. A warm and cozy home you will be proud to own $63,900.

Clyde Realty **476-8200**

This ad is aimed at a single buyer or a couple. It makes two bedrooms, a small kitchen and a small patio seem very desirable. The persons responding to this ad will likely consider themselves sophisticated. A very similar ad could be used for condominium advertisements.

MINI-CHATEAU

Twin master suites with sumptuous baths, soaring ceilings in the living/dining area and a state-of-the-art European-inspired gallery kitchen combine to make this the perfect home for a very sophisticated life-style. Other amenities include a double garage and a very private patio screened by flowering shrubs for intimate entertaining or just relaxation. This very special home is available now at $129,500.

Clyde Realty 476-8200

New Homes

New homes are often advertised in the display ads rather than classifieds. Unfortunately, many prospective home buyers pay little attention to display advertising but concentrate their house hunting in the classified sections. New homes should also be advertised in the classified sections even though display ads are being used.

Headings Headings appropriate for new homes appeal to freshness and good condition.

BUILDER-FRESH

A BRAND-NEW CLASSIC

MUDDY-SHOES OPENING

A MODERN CLASSIC $69,500

NEW—WAITING FOR YOU

This home would not necessarily have to be new.

YOUNG & BEAUTIFUL

ONLY 3 LEFT

NEW IS BETTER

WHY BUY USED?
when you can own this brand-new. . .

BE THE FIRST OWNERS
of this. . .

Attention-getter

GEORGE WASHINGTON
would have loved to have slept in this new. . . but he was 200 years early.

NOBODY SLEPT HERE

Body Copy Your ad body could include information such as:

A future classic

Timeless quality and pride are yours with this new. . .

A new home with a dramatic flair

The name of the builder can add prestige.

Sumptner-built

One of the most exciting new homes we have seen

Never lived in

Be the first to live in this. . .

See why 9 of these new homes were sold in just 2 weeks.

We saved the trees.

A brand-new Victorian that captures ageless beauty

Opens a new era in elegant living

All the normal extras are standard features on this. . .

Still time to decorate to your individual taste

Still time to pick the colors and floor coverings for this. . .

You will smell the newness in this. . .

A rare opportunity to buy one of the *original furnished models* at. . .

A sparkling-new rendition of a *1760 English cottage*

Specific closings for new homes include:

Preconstruction priced at $________.

Price guaranteed for *30* days $________.

Under construction

Price guaranteed at $________.

Completed Ads for New Homes

This short but effective ad has an attention-getting heading.

WHY PAY

more for an older home when you can own a brand new 3BR, 2-bath, double-garage home on a family-size lot in Sunnyvale Estates for only $79,500? FHA and VA available.

Clyde Realty **476-8200**

MUDDY SHOES OPENING

They just finished hammering on this new 3BR, 2½-bath red brick custom French Regency home. Combining the elegant style of the past with all of the "I-want" modern features of today, it is situated on an estate-size wooded lot in prestigious Brookfield. Over 2,000 sq. ft. of luxurious living space. Excitingly priced at $178,000.

Clyde Realty 476-8200

This ad, with its attention-getting heading, has an emphasis on sleep. A great many people have trouble sleeping and will be intrigued by the ad.

NOBODY SLEPT HERE

because this 3BR, 2½-bath Mt. Vernon-inspired colonial is brand-new. Set on a heavily wooded acre in Pine Cove, this stately residence is highlighted by an impressive center staircase, massive fireplace, beamed family room, 3-car garage and all the luxury appointments and appliances that you ever dreamed of. The climate-controlled environment includes an electronic air cleaner for dust- and pollen-free living and untroubled sleep. A genuine sleeper at $249,500.

Clyde Realty 476-8200

The ad shows the advantages of a new home (choosing colors and so forth plus state-of-the-art amenities). The closing creates urgency and indicates the builder will likely raise the price. For additional language appropriate for new homes, see the Architecture *section in Chapter Three.*

NEW PILLARED COLONIAL

There is still time for you to reflect your personal tastes in the carpets, tile and colors for this new 3-bedroom, 2½-bath southern colonial home patterned after the noble houses of Virginia. Set in a select community of fine homes, it combines the allure of classic design with state-of-the-art amenities—a residence bound to be a legendary home of the future. Inspect NOW as the builder will only guarantee the price of $189,500 for the next 30 days.

Clyde Realty 476-8200

Old Homes

For many years we were on a new-home kick. Most people equated new with better. Today the pendulum is beginning to swing back and people are beginning to realize that older can be better. There is even an interest in building brand-new old-fashioned homes such as Victorians.

Besides people interested in financial savings, old homes are sought for their unique personality and charm. Older homes are a reminder of a grand past and provide a feeling of continuity in today's world.

Old should be sold as a positive feature. There can be real prestige in escaping the sameness of new homes to live in a place that has existed through several generations.

The *Architecture* section of Chapter Three contains a great deal of appropriate language applicable to older homes of particular architectural styles. Additional wording that can be used for ad headings or as part of the ad body for older homes includes:

LIVE IN HISTORY

OWN A BIT OF HISTORY

THE GRANDEUR OF YESTERDAY

STEP BACK IN TIME

This heading provides a pleasant mental picture.

GRANDMA'S HOUSE REVISITED

BRING BACK YESTERDAY

STEP INTO YESTERDAY

While this ad has sexual connotations, it is attention-getting.

LIKE THEM MATURE?

OUT OF THE OLD WEST

1790 CHARM
WITH 1990 CONVENIENCES

1790 ORIGIN—1990 CONVENIENCES

150 YEARS OF LOVING CARE

STEEPED IN HISTORY

Old-time beauty

Out of the past

A home with a history

A home with a past

Better than new

Minister's home

The old manse

Historic treasure

Reflections of the past

Turn back time

Weatherboard home

The best of the past

Historic register

Time will stand still in this...

FORGOTTEN BY TIME

Remember grandma's house

Nineteenth-century brownstone

Yesteryear's dream

Step back in history

Time stands still

Museum piece

Old-world charm abounds in this...

A GRAND OLD HOME
LOVINGLY MAINTAINED

YESTERYEAR'S ELEGANCE—TODAY'S COMFORT

LESS THAN $500 PER YEAR
200-YEAR-OLD COLONIAL—$96,000

AMERICANA FOR SALE

A BIT OF EARLY AMERICANA

YESTERDAY'S ELEGANCE—TODAY'S TREASURE

TIMELESS ELEGANCE

HEIRLOOM ESTATE

A LIVING LEGEND

NOSTALGIC SHOWPLACE

PRESERVED FROM YESTERYEAR

AGELESS BEAUTY

This phrase could be used for a large home built around 1920.

GATSBY'S PLACE

Circa *means approximately.*

CIRCA 1860

BUILT IN 1860

BETTER THAN NEW

LANDMARK

HISTORIC STONE COTTAGE

HISTORIC LANDMARK

AN OLDIE BUT GOODIE

A GOLDEN OLDIE

GEORGE WASHINGTON SLEPT HERE?
Well, he could have. This superb colonial was built in 1738.

DID GEORGE WASHINGTON SLEEP HERE?

GEORGE WASHINGTON COULD HAVE SLEPT HERE

GEORGE WASHINGTON WOULD HAVE LOVED TO HAVE SLEPT HERE

REVOLUTIONARY ERA

CHARM AND TRADITION

CENTURY OLD—YOUNG AT HEART

IT'S OLD ENOUGH TO VOTE BUT YOUNG AT HEART

ELIZABETHAN ERA

EDWARDIAN ERA

VICTORIAN ERA

HEIRLOOM VICTORIAN

YEARS OF LOVE AND DEVOTION
have been given to this. . .

A REAL FARM HOUSE

COUNTRY-STYLE HOME

19TH-CENTURY PERFECTION

ART COLLECTOR'S DREAM

TURN-OF-THE-CENTURY RANCH

OLD-WORLD CHARM

OLD-WORLD CRAFTSMANSHIP

A real attention-grabber

FIDDLER ON THE ROOF
This home has tradition.

A HOME TO CHERISH

CENTURY OLD—BRAND-NEW PRICE $_______.

HERITAGE SHOWCASE

TAKE A GIANT STEP BACK IN TIME

A CENTURY OF LOVE

A CENTURIAN

A CENTURY YOUNG

BICENTENNIAL

AN AMERICAN HERITAGE

AS OLD AS THE NATION

ANTIQUE TREASURE

ANTEBELLUM

Antebellum *carries a connotation of elegance and refers to the time before the Civil War.*

ANTEBELLUM BEAUTY

OLD CHARMER

TIMELESS BEAUTY

Restored Restored means returned to an original condition. The following could be used when a house has been restored or is restorable:

You will turn your clock back to 1760 when you move into this lovingly restored center-hall colonial.

Totally restored

Superbly restored

Exquisitely restored

Charmingly restored

Meticulously restored

Faithfully restored

Completely and beautifully restored

Completely restored to capture the aura of yesteryear

Appeals to purists

Completely and authentically restored

Restored to combine old-fashioned elegance with up-to-date amenities

Tastefully restored

Restored nostalgia

Restored to its former splendor

Lovingly restored

Restored with the antique lover in mind

Restored colonial

90% restored

Artistically restored to functional and aesthetic perfection

RESTORER'S DELIGHT

Painstakingly restored

Born-again *colonial*

Tastefully restored and updated to meet the living standards of the most discriminating

Restored with imagination and elegance

Museum-quality restoration

Restoration under way

Partially restored

Giving the name of the restorer adds desirability.

Restored by ________

Not yet restored

Restorer's treasure

Worthy of restoration

Ready for restoration

A masterpiece in need of restoration

Restorable

Restorable Colonial

An attention-getting heading where restoration is not necessary

FORGET ABOUT RESTORATION
This *federal colonial* has been meticulously maintained for all of its *150* years.

Remodeled *Remodeled* means changed. Normally it involves a modernization. The following can be used to indicate the property has been remodeled:

STUNNINGLY REMODELED

COMPLETELY REBUILT

BETTER THAN NEW

REMODELED WITH NEW EVERYTHING

ELEGANTLY MODERNIZED

Dramatically updated kitchen retains the charm of yesterday

Thoughtfully updated to combine the best of the old with the new

Refurbished with state-of-the-art conveniences

Updated systems

Refers to plumbing, electrical and heating systems.

New everything

With old-world detailing and modern amenities

19th-century elegance combined with 20th-century convenience

1889 farmhouse with *1989* interior combines antique charm with today's conveniences

Unobtrusive improvements include...

Renovated Renovation is repairing without necessarily restoring to a former state or making changes. The following can be used in ads to indicate renovation:

BORN AGAIN
completely renovated...

Totally renovated

Partially renovated

Completely rebuilt

Tastefully renovated

Handsomely renovated

The meticulous and imaginative renovation offers...

Masterfully renovated

Maintenance For any house that is not new, maintenance is important. Words that can be used to show a home has been kept up are:

Well-maintained

Meticulously maintained

Exquisitely maintained

Special Features Desirable special features should be covered in either the ad heading or body. Some of the special features likely to appeal to buyers of older homes are:

Established neighborhood

Prestige neighborhood

Realistic taxes

Low taxes

Old-fashioned window box

Gracious is an excellent adjective for older homes.

A place for your antiques. Nooks and crannies abound in this gracious Victorian.

Nooks and crannies provide room to display your treasured collectibles.

Rough-hewn beams

Hand-hewn beams

Massive fireplace

Butler's pantry

Heart pine floors

Crystal doorknobs

Solid brass hardware

Original hardware

Cupola topped by an antique weather vane

BEAMS—NOOKS AND CRANNIES

Dumbwaiter

Carriage house

Coach house

Artistic-minded people are often seekers of older homes.

Studio

Artist's loft

These create the image of a simpler time.

Original smoke house

Rocking-chair front porch

Large front porch

An ancient stone fence rings the garden.

Random-width floors

Root cellar

Wine cellar

Delightful gazebo

Bow windows

Classic lines

Massive brick chimneys

A strong plus for antique buffs

One-hundred-year-old furniture stays

The electrified gas lights reflect the gracious charm of this...

Original detailing intact

Plaster moldings

Crown moldings

This should be emphasized for an unrestored older home.

Sound structure

Solid oak floors

Solid walnut paneling

Handcrafted

Hand-carved

Inlaid hardwoods

Intricately crafted

Built by skilled artisans

Built by old-world craftspeople

Magnificent cupola

Dramatic floating staircase

Raised paneling

Sweeping staircase

Dramatic sweeping staircase

Elizabethan detailing

Pegged beams

Plantation shutters

Rock-solid

All original details in this...

Pegged-beam construction

Built in *1926* to endure for centuries

Filled with myths and tradition

Look back in time at this...

If the property has a special feature not consistent with what many buyers want, do not mention it in the ad. An ad for a 200-year-old restored colonial with aluminum siding will turn off prospective buyers who might have liked the place had they seen for themselves that the siding did not spoil its charm.

Other Body Copy Additional language for the body of old-house ads often makes use of the romance of the past.

Embodies the charm and romance of a bygone age

This garrison colonial has been admired since it was built in *1764*.

Reflects the pride of *4* generations of family ownership

. . . has been home to *6* generations

150 years in the same family

There is a growing revival of bed-and-breakfast inns. The income potential will be an attractive plus. The property could also be advertised under Business Opportunities.

Bed-and-breakfast potential

Inn potential

Over *3,500* sq. ft. of traditional charm

Enjoy the charm and warmth found only in older homes.

Looks like a farmhouse right out of Vermont

This turn-of-the-century 4-bedroom frame home looks like it belongs on an Iowa farm.

Gracious turn-of-the-century charm

Gracious old-world charm

1912 was a great year for classic homes.

A rich blend of tile, wood and stained glass

Built to endure

Its beauty has increased for *118* years.

Older homes have attics and artistic people are drawn to older homes.

The attic would be perfect for an artist's studio.

This home brings back classic memories of workmanship and pride.

A once-in-a-lifetime opportunity to secure a piece of America's heritage

A diorama of yesteryear

The *leaded-glass* doors enter into the gracious world of yesteryear.

Offering an elegance unobtainable in today's homes

8 generations have meticulously maintained this . . .

Exciting *1860* town house

Every room is filled with classic appointments.

A patina of love and care shines from this gentle reminder of the good full life of a long-ago time.

Offering the charm of yesteryear with the conveniences of tomorrow

Artfully proportioned and graciously maintained

Your chance to live in a legend

Reflects *200* years of loving care

Offering a quality of life that only the past can provide

A unique vestige of the past

An opportunity to live in the opulence that recalls the grandeur of ages past

Horse-drawn carriages and parasols recall the days when this . . . was young.

One of the finest specimens of *18th-century* architecture, carefully preserved so you can enjoy its future

. . . reflects a spectacular era in America's past

Reminiscent of the Gatsby era

You will step back in history as the owner of this. . .

For the special few who desire the ultimate in unabashed charm of *the early 1900s*

The elegance of yesterday can be yours for tomorrow.

Built in *1927* when quality counted

Built in the tradition of a bygone era

The opulence of yesterday refreshingly provides the perfect atmosphere for gracious entertaining and family living.

This *18th-century colonial* reflects the time when the family home was the center of one's existence.

A much-loved home of the past for your family future

Time-mellowed

Original (stained-glass windows/hardware/cabinetry)

Custom-built in 1908

This. . . echoes old-world charm.

Built in 1914, a vintage year for fine homes

You will be reminded of a way of life that has been all but forgotten.

The antique brick in this charming colonial was new when it was built in 1789.

This garrison colonial has been preserved, refurbished and enhanced throughout its 132-year existence.

A rare brownstone town house

Old-fashioned space and grace

Rich in history

You will be struck by the excitement and romance of the spectacular manor house.

A very gracious home from the past

The quality of a more gracious era is found in this. . .

Return to yesteryear with this. . .

With all of the gingerbread of the 1880s

All of the ornate goodies of the 1920s

It's like an autumn in New England when you first view this enchanting Cape Cod.

Built when fine craftsmanship was honored

Built when they knew how to build houses

Many families have been raised in this century-old beauty.

It truly represents the grandeur of the past with all the modern conveniences of tomorrow.

This classic offers a tour through yesteryear with the conveniences of tomorrow.

Captures the atmosphere of yesterday with the comforts of today

Shine up this older home and watch it sparkle.

Or you could mention old New England, the Spanish Southwest, old New Orleans, and so forth.

Reflects the charm of the antebellum South

Style and tradition are captured in this. . .

Registered with the National Register of Historic Places

Landmark-eligible

Possibly eligible for National Registry

If the home has had a well-known previous owner or even guest, it can be brought out.

Presidents and ambassadors have dined by candlelight in the richly appointed dining room.

You can tie the home into a historic fact to add to its prestige.

Completed 20 years before Arizona became a state

Closings The *Architecture* section of Chapter Three offers many ideas, but here are some especially effective examples for the older home:

Own this treasure of yesteryear $________.

Own a piece of history $________.

History can be yours $________.

Your chance to return to gracious living $________.

If you miss the charm of yesteryear, this is your chance to return to gracious living $________.

Enjoy old-time living for $________.

Live in a bit of history $________.

Living history at $________.

Awaiting creative renovation at $________.

Renovation-ready at $________.

Older homes can be economical to purchase.

Why buy a box when you can buy a real home $________.

A home with character $________.

Bring your antiques $________.

For a new life and an old life-style $________.

The romance of yesterday can be yours today $________.

This vintage estate can be yours for $________.

This heirloom is yours at $________.

Don't let time pass you by. The elegant past can be yours now at $________.

Best of all, an old-fashioned price of $________.

A preservationist's dream at $________.

Yesterday's treasure at $________.

Check the old-fashioned price $________.

Craftsmanship and individuality at the price of a tract home $________.

For a taste of yesterday $________.

Own a bit of Americana $________.

For the imaginative restorer $________.

A renovator's delight $________.

An antique lover's delight $________.

All systems new at $________.

Commuting close yet a century away $________.

Completed Ads for Old Homes

When you've put together all the parts that describe a particular older property, your completed ads may resemble these:

A TRUE HACIENDA

One hundred and fifty years of living have not diminished the classic beauty of this Spanish colonial hacienda. The ancient tile, intricately hand-carved beams, and colonnaded, enclosed courtyard with its fountains still echo the happy sounds of fiestas long ago. Situated on a prestigious 20+ acre ocean-view site, the home has been thoughtfully updated to combine the best of the old with the new. Offering 6+ bedrooms, 6 full baths, 2 half-baths and a dramatic but modern kitchen with tons of Mexican tile. Far more than just a grand and beautiful home, it is a part of our history. Proudly offered at $2,800,000.

Clyde Realty **476-8200**

If the setting or location were desirable, they should have been included in the ad.

100 YEARS BEHIND THE TIMES

This 1889 Victorian reflects the gracious, spacious and elegant living that has almost become forgotten. The 2½ baths, modern kitchen and systems were skillfully integrated into this 4BR home so as not to distract from its basic charm and quiet luxury. The values of yesteryear can be yours today at $97,600.

Clyde Realty 476-8200

This ad creates a desire in the reader to be the one to restore this treasure.

GEORGE WASHINGTON SLEPT HERE

Well, he could have, since there are 5 huge bedrooms in this Registry-eligible classic Greek revival manor built by master craftsmen in 1738. You will be struck by the feeling of excitement and romance that have been captured from another era and preserved for you in its wooded village site. While the crown moldings and intricate carvings are intact, the home is awaiting tasteful and authentic restoration which you can provide. A window into our past at $129,500.

Clyde Realty 476-8200

This is an attention-getting heading. If the location was not indicated by the newspaper ad category, it should have been mentioned in the ad body.

BORN AGAIN

This turn-of-the-century 3BR, 2-bath American traditional has been completely and thoughtfully revitalized with modern heating, air-conditioning, plumbing, wiring and a tile, copper and brick kitchen that will be the envy of your friends. Its basic charm is retained with the exquisite paneling and woodwork, high ceilings, formal dining room, enclosed sun porch and a separate garage and garden house. Set among towering trees and flowering shrubs, it's ready for your gracious living at $89,500.

Clyde Realty **476-8200**

This type of ad can give desirability to older city homes that have been abandoned by many people in favor of homes in the suburbs.

1914—A VINTAGE YEAR

for fine homes with high ceilings, intricately carved solid oak woodwork, leaded glass and a feeling of spaciousness for gracious living. This 3BR red brick traditional offers all these and more. Situated on a quiet tree-shaded street of fine homes, it also offers a formal dining room, eat-in kitchen, paneled shelf-lined library and a front parlor with a bow window and a window box. The two baths have claw-footed tubs, solid marble basins and brass fittings. The home has been fully insulated and the wiring, plumbing and heating systems have been modernized without sacrificing its charm. A home with real character for far less than the price of an ordinary home $69,500.

Clyde Realty **476-8200**

This ad for an older home is particularly aimed at family living rather than for entertaining or antique buffs.

THE BEST OF THE PAST

Built in 1892 when quality counted and the family home was the center of one's existence, this American colonial has been tastefully restored and updated to meet the living standards of the most discriminating. Featuring 3 bedrooms, 2 baths, den, dramatic floating staircase, two orchard stone fireplaces and lavish woodwork, this much-loved home of the past is ready for your family future. In a Williamsburg-like setting, this exceptional family residence is proudly offered at $189,500.

Clyde Realty 476-8200

7

Luxury Homes, Low-Priced Homes, Bargain Homes and Financing Terms

Luxury Homes

You should realize that *luxury* is a relative term. What you might regard as a comparatively ordinary home could well be perceived by others as the ultimate in luxury. Therefore, luxury ads work for a broad range of housing. The inclusion of the price in the ad will avoid unrealistic expectations by the readers.

When an area is synonymous with luxury, such as Beverly Hills or Fifth Avenue, the area should be included in your heading if it is not a separate category in the newspaper. You can then use what would normally be your heading as a subheading.

Headings Avoid trite headings. *Super deluxe* sounds like a burger, not a fine home. The following headings convey the image of a quality home:

PRESTIGIOUS PORTALS

THE GOOD LIFE

SO MUCH LUXURY

ONLY THE FINEST

SHEER ELEGANCE

OVERWHELMING

ONE OF THE GREATS

OPULENCE AND GRANDEUR

FAR FROM THE ORDINARY

ESTATE OF THE ART

BEAUTY AND THE BEST

ABSOLUTELY AWESOME

THE ULTIMATE RESIDENCE

RATED A 10

ON A SCALE OF 1 TO 10, THIS IS A DEFINITE 11

CONNOISSEUR'S CHOICE

TRÉS ELEGANT

PIÈCE DE RÉSISTANCE

Use of the term decorator *or reference to an interior decorator denotes quality.*

OOO-LA-LA
Decorator-furnished French Provincial

A GREAT HOUSE

THE ULTRA IN EXECUTIVE HOMES

DEFINITELY TOP DRAWER

This provides prestige appeal to some buyers who can now tell their friends that they own the house of a famous person.

(NAME OF FORMER OWNER) ESTATE

TOP OF THE LINE

PAMPER YOURSELF

SPOIL YOURSELF

CAESAR'S PALACE
offers fewer delights than this. . .

IF ONLY THE BEST IS FOR YOU
you will want to know about this. . .

Generally, mansion *is not a desirable term to use because it denotes a large and inefficient structure.*

MOGUL'S MANSION

This would be appropriate for a furnished home.

BRING YOUR OWN BUTLER
Everything else is included with this. . .

The broker who used this heading indicated she received an excellent response. The following lead is similar.

RICH
and not ashamed of it

FOR THE COUPLE
who have arrived and are not ashamed to let the world know

A little crude and that is what this ad might attract

HEY BIG SPENDER

Most likely to attract nouveau riche

MILLIONAIRE NEEDED

Subdued, obviously understated language can appeal to people who feel secure in their positions.

UNDERSTATED ELEGANCE

MUTED ELEGANCE

SUBDUED ELEGANCE

CONSERVATIVELY ELEGANT

COMFORTABLE ELEGANCE

EXECUTIVE PARADISE

CRÈME DE LA CRÈME

This would be a good heading for a Spanish-style home.

MAGNIFICO

PRIVATE ESTATE

SHOWPLACE

IT'S TIME TO MOVE UP

MOVE UP TO (NAME OF AREA)

MOVING ON UP
The good life will be yours with this. . .

ONLY THE BEST

Mentioning the name of the builder and architect tends to be a reassurance of quality.

THOROUGHBRED BY THOMAS BUILDERS
out of a design by Henry Wilcoxen

LAVISH ESTATE

THE ULTIMATE

LIFE-STYLE IN A HIGH STYLE

DOM PERIGNON
of fine estates—treat yourself to the best

PALATIAL ESTATE

A TOUCH OF ELEGANCE

AURA OF ELEGANCE

A TOUCH OF CLASS

EPITOME OF ELEGANCE

HOME EXTRAORDINAIRE

SHOW-OFF

OWN A SHOW-OFF

A SHOWCASE HOME

Rolls Royce

RR
the standard of excellence

THE STANDARD OF COMPARISON

SLEEK AND SOPHISTICATED

PRESTIGIOUS

SEARCHING FOR THE FINEST

JUST A LITTLE BETTER
than anything you have seen

MAGNIFICENT ESTATE

SUITED FOR ROYALTY

COUNTRY CHATEAU

LUXURY ON A GRAND SCALE

Many of the above headings can also be used within the ad body or as a closing that reassures the reader of excellence.

Body Copy You can also express luxury within the body of your ad with language similar to the following:

Great room *provides an image of old-world charm much better than* living room. *Be careful not to overuse it.*

Great room

Uncompromised quality

Built with uncompromising quality

A home that will exceed your expectations

An address to be envied

Uncommon luxury

Graciously elegant

Designed for lavish entertaining

Quiet elegance

The epitome of quality

An awesome list of amenities

Baronially proportioned rooms

Urban home

A metropolitan masterpiece

Beautiful, elegant and formal is this...

A myriad of exciting details

Magnificent in its scale and design

Thoughtfully planned to provide the ultimate life-style for those accustomed to the very best

A very special life-style is enhanced by...

Built for a life-style to be envied

Refined elegance

A home that mirrors your achievements

Reflecting the goals and ambitions of today's achievers

Providing an unexcelled quality of life

Reflecting the classic taste and subtle sophistication of the most discriminating buyer

Truly an unparalleled home

A charismatic blending of regal splendor with delicate charm

This phrase also could be used for an older home.

Magnificently alive with elaborate craftsmanship

Truly a feast for the senses

For the life-style you deserve

A home that echoes "achievement"

The unmistakable air of elegance is expressed eloquently in its. . .

The home for those who appreciate the fine art of living

Elegance personified

The epitome of elegant living

Exceptional detailing

A home that knows no compromise

In a private preserve for a fortunate few

What civilized living is all about

An ambassadorial residence

Superior appointments

Exquisitely appointed

Providing a new definition of elegance

A remarkable blend of authentic character and luxury amenities

Lavishly decorated

Dramatically combining the best traditional detailing with high-tech amenities to provide for the ultimate life-style

Designed for grand-style entertaining

All the appointments one would expect in a home of this caliber

Magnificent public rooms

All the amenities one demands in a home of this stature

Impeccable detail

Resplendent with magnificent details

Exceptional millwork

Crafted in the finest traditional manner

A level of craftsmanship that says "quality"

Superb construction rarely seen in homes today

Imported is a plus.

Built with stone from Tennessee

An architectural reference adds desirability.

Reminiscent of the style of Frank Lloyd Wright

Lush atrium

Foyer

Formal entry

Hot spa

Walnut-paneled library

> Library *carries a more prestigious image than* den. *If you refer to the room as a library, so will the buyers, and it will give them a sense of pride.*

Impressive dimensions

> *Much better than giving actual size*

Commodious rooms

Grand proportions

Baronial-proportioned rooms

A truly great house

While life is filled with compromises, you need compromise no more.

Just a step above anything you have seen

The look of prestige is captured magnificently in this stately . . .

Once in a rare while a home such as this will appear on the market.

Very seldom does such a home appear on the market.

Vaulted ceiling

> *A high ceiling*

Dual master suites

> *A much better image than two large bedrooms with baths*

Butler's pantry

> *More impressive than* pantry *alone*

Formal dining room

> *Much finer image than a plain dining room*

Billiard room

> *This certainly conveys a higher quality image than* game room *or* recreation room.

4,000 sq. ft. of sumptuous living space

The aura of comfort and excellence is evident throughout this . . .

Extensive use of marble and mirrors throughout

Imported wall coverings

> *This is far superior to saying the wallpaper was made in Taiwan.*

Stunningly decorated

Professionally decorated

Decorated by . . .

> *The name of the decorator adds appeal.*

Thoughtfully appointed

> *A little lower key, which appeals more to the very wealthy*

Meticulously appointed

The home is enhanced by . . .

Unrivaled in amenities

Remarkable amenities

Exquisite amenities throughout

Many sought-after amenities, including . . .

Features an enticing . . .

The degree of excellence is reflected in such outstanding features as . . .

. . . complements this . . .

Aesthetic touches include . . .

A gracious style of luxury that soon may no longer be available

Provides a new definition of elegance

Featured in (name of magazine or paper)

Offers the utmost in gracious living

Radiates pride of ownership

Offers country-club living at its finest

One of Akron's truly spectacular homes

A rare opportunity to own one of the fine homes of Fox Point

One of the area's most admired homes

The ambiance of this fine residence projects success.

Perfect for guest room or live-in

Exceptionally fine guest accommodations or servants' quarters

Ideal as a consulate or grand residence

Lavish appointments

A flair beyond the ordinary

Well beyond the ordinary

Enjoy the life-style others can only hope to match.

Has a snobbish appeal

You will be the envy of your friends owning this . . .

Many people actually buy to impress others.

This Georgian colonial will reflect your community status.

For the discriminating few

Aimed at newly wealthy

For the hostess who prefers gracious dining and entertaining

A more formal home

Suitable for entertaining on a grand scale

Room for courts and pool

This turns the absence of these amenities into a plus.

Truly a "world-class" residence

A feeling of royalty emanates from this beautiful estate.

A masterpiece of elegance

Magnificent is an understatement for this . . .

Closings Closings for luxury homes amplify the prestige appeal that the other parts of the ad have set up.

Discover the ultimate in prestigious living $________.

Treat yourself to something irresistible $________.

A truly handsome home offered at $________.

Offering a new dimension in gracious living at $________.

Most assuredly this magnificent residence could not be duplicated at its price of $________.

A very special home at $________.

Uncompromising quality at $________.

Don't miss your opportunity to enjoy the best that life has to offer $________.

An enviable estate at $________.

An unparalleled opportunity at $________.

For those who refuse to settle for less $________.

For a life-style to be envied $________.

Truly a residence in the grand style $________.

Call now for the good life $________.

This experience in gracious living can be yours at $________.

A one-of-a-kind masterpiece proudly offered at $________.

For the buyer who will not compromise, offered at $________.

Reward yourself with the home you deserve. Proudly offered at $________.

A home that speaks for itself. Proudly offered at $________.

Priced for the discerning buyer at $________.

Priced for the discriminating buyer at $________.

Truly the culmination of all your dreams, proudly offered at $________.

You can have it all for $________.

Call today to view this very special property $________.

The charm of luxurious living can be yours at $________.

An estate worthy of your inspection $________.

Definitely merits your inspection $________.

Offered to the discriminating buyer at $________.

Proudly offered at $________.

Truly impressive at $________.

Unexcelled at $________.

Own with pride for $________.

A home you will be proud of, offered at $________.

An investment in a better life $________.

An investment in living $________.

The ultimate statement of your success $________.

Get in on the good life $________.

Step up to the good life $________.

Don't wait to enjoy the good life $________.

The good life awaits you at $________.

Reward yourself with the good life $________.

If you've promised yourself the best in life, there is no better time than now to keep that promise. Offered proudly at $________.

You have worked hard for the good life. It's here now for you to enjoy $________.

The home you deserve $_________.

This is not the home for everyone, but if you are one of the few who can afford a truly spectacular residence you owe it to yourself to investigate now $_________.

Offering a truly enviable way of life $_________.

Available for the fortunate few at $_________.

It's time to turn dreams into reality $_________.

Pamper yourself $_________.

Spoil yourself $_________.

Your estate is ready $_________.

Unpretentious luxury at $_________.

A grand residence you will be proud to own $_________.

A very handsome estate offered at $_________.

For the estate of your future $_________.

Available for qualified buyers at $_________.

If you expect the very best, you won't be disappointed $_________.

An executive home with true executive comfort $_________.

An aristocratic home you will be proud of $_________.

All the amenities of gracious living at $_________.

Offers a new dimension to luxury living at $_________.

Discover a new definition of elegance $_________.

By request of the owner, this exquisite estate is priced for immediate sale $_________.

Priced in the upper $300s

While the price is not given, the reader knows the general price. Some brokers feel that not giving the price of expensive homes adds to their prestige in the same manner as a restaurant with an unpriced menu.

Completed Ads for Luxury Homes

THE ULTIMATE RESIDENCE

Once in a rare while a home such as this will appear on the market. From the long tree-canopied drive of 100-year-old red paving stones to its slate roof and copper gutters, you will see that nothing has been spared as to the quality of this 4BR, 4½-bath, brick French Regency situated on the choicest site in Holmby Hills. It offers every imaginable luxury including illuminated tennis court, pool, spa and cabana and even a 9-hole putting green. A home definitely worthy of your inspection. Proudly offered at $2,650,000.

Clyde Realty 476-8200

IF YOU DIDN'T CARE WHAT IT COST

this would surely be the house for you. An ivy-covered English Tudor home featuring 6 bedrooms and 6 full baths plus a powder room. From its leaded-glass windows to its solid walnut-paneled library that opens onto the rose garden, it exudes the kind of quality possible for just a very few. A truly handsome estate at $480,000.

Clyde Realty 476-8200

WORLD-CLASS RESIDENCE

This 5-acre wooded estate centers on a 12-room Georgian colonial with 3½ baths. Exquisite amenities include pool, championship tennis court and a 4-car heated garage. While life is often filled with compromises, you need compromise no more. Own with pride at $520,000.

Clyde Realty 476-8200

When the home was owned by a well-known family, the name can be used as an effective heading.

Many brokers prefer giving price ranges on higher-priced homes rather than exact dollars.

THE FALK ESTATE

This is not the home for everyone, but if you are one of the very few who can afford a truly spectacular residence you owe it to yourself to view the 12 rooms of this Italianate architectural masterpiece in its formal garden setting. The ultimate in truly gracious living, offered in the mid $400s.

Clyde Realty **476-8200**

This ad paints a verbal picture of a luxurious way of life and should have a positive effect upon the readers it is aimed at.

ONE OF THE GREATS

Magnificent in design and scale, this 12-room English country estate is resplendent with superb detailing. Cloistered behind massive stone walls and set amidst acres of sweeping lawns and towering trees, this ultimate residence will provide the life-style sought by those accustomed to the very best. Included are all of the amenities one would expect of a home of this caliber: court, pool, spa, greenhouse and formal gardens. We proudly offer this estate, which speaks so eloquently for itself, at $2,400,000.

Clyde Realty **476-8200**

This attention-getting heading gives no clue to the property. Such a heading should be used only if the newspaper area category covers only better homes.

Financing is important to many luxury-home buyers.

WE ARE PROUD

to offer one of the great homes of Westchester. Set on the highest point, this 4BR, 4½-bath authentic French chateau offers a commanding view of the valley. Everything you ever dreamed of is right here, including a rockscaped garden enhanced by a delightful patio, pool, spa and cabana. If you promised yourself the best in life, there is no better time than now to keep that promise. $580,000 with advantageous owner financing.

Clyde Realty **476-8200**

The Owner and the Image

A home's previous owner can make a difference in how prospective buyers see its worth: When President Reagan's California home was placed on the market, it received unusual interest and sold at a high premium.

A particular owner can help you sell a property, but never advertise any information about a seller without permission.

Headings Ads for quality homes can be headed based upon the owner's occupation, social status, character or fame.

A reader would probably correctly assume that the home was built of the finest materials.

BUILT BY A LUMBERYARD OWNER
For his own personal residence

LUMBERYARD OWNER'S HOME

Again, this will convey a quality-constructed home.

BUILDER'S DREAM HOME

ORIGINAL BUILDER'S OWN HOME

EXTRAVAGANT BUILDER
must sell his own home featuring the finest of appointments

CARPENTER'S HOME
Featuring the finest in cabinetry

This gives the impression that nothing was spared.

MILLIONAIRE'S HIDEAWAY

This gives the impression it is better than most homes.

DOCTOR'S HOME

FORMER BUILDING INSPECTOR
built this home for his family to the most demanding specifications

Architects, interior designers and artist owners convey the image that the house is well built and well appointed.

ARCHITECT OWNER

ARCHITECT'S OWN HOME

ARCHITECT'S DREAM HOME

ARCHITECT'S PRIVATE DREAM HOME

ARTIST OWNER

ARTIST'S DREAM HOME

A famous owner or former owner adds desirability.

THE THOMAS KLYDE ESTATE

ERROL FLYNN'S HOME

If a well-known person currently lives in a home, this should not be advertised without that person's specific approval. Many celebrities are concerned about theft, kidnapping and invasion of privacy, and therefore would not want the location of their residence widely circulated.

Body Copy

Owned by a renowned interior designer

Built with care for his own family by a craftsman-builder

The original owner-builder was a true craftsman.

Owner/craftsman designed and built this...

These convey the impression that no expense was spared

Built by a doctor for his family

Physician selling his...

Owner's pride shows throughout this...

Closings Ad closings could give owner information such as:

Retiring owner will turn this paradise over to you for $________.

Out-of-state owner will let go for $________.

Millionaire owner says sell at $________.

Excellent closing for a builder's own home

See the difference that pride makes $________.

Additional owner features can be found later in this chapter under *Bargain Homes.*

Completed Ads Stressing Owner's Image

DEVELOPER'S HOME

Built to demanding specifications for the developer's family use, this exciting 3BR, 2½-bath French Regency home offers every conceivable luxury. Situated on a huge professionally landscaped corner lot in Morningside, it is available for the first time at $179,000.

Clyde Realty **476-8200**

A seller who does not want to leave can add desirability to a quality home.

PHYSICIAN'S HOME— WESTWOOD

The doctor who built this home has taken a position as Chief of Surgery in another state and reluctantly has placed it on the market. Sited on an estate-size lot, no expense was spared in the construction of this 4-bedroom, 3½-bath residence. The professionally landscaped grounds are enhanced by a championship tennis court, pool and hot spa. Interior amenities include Jacuzzi baths, soaring ceilings, walnut-paneled library, solarium and much more. One look and you will realize why the owner loves it so. First time offered at $670,000.

Clyde Realty 476-8200

CARPENTER'S DREAM HOME

Built by an old-world-trained carpenter for his own family, this 3BR, 2-bath center-hall colonial with attached 2-car garage on a wooded oversized lot is truly an exceptional home. The fine craftsmanship is evidenced by the matched walnut paneling and built-in bookcases in the den, the intricate spindled staircase, the built-in china cabinet in the formal dining room and the gleaming solid cherry cabinetry in the country kitchen. One look and you will realize that it's a step above the ordinary at $169,500.

Clyde Realty 476-8200

Low-Priced Homes

Headings Headings for lower-priced homes may emphasize a special feature or that the home is a fixer-upper. Generally, however, you will want the heading to make the point that the home is economical. This can be done with any heading by simply adding the price. Some examples of headings specifically aimed at lower-priced homes include:

HERITAGE VICTORIAN $69,500

BUDGET BALANCER $47,500

GREAT LIVING ON A BUDGET $59,500

BUDGET PLEASER $42,800

QUALITY ON A BUDGET $159,700

THE PRICE IS NICE—$32,800

THE PRICE IS RIGHT $39,500

START SMART $39,500

A FIRST HOME $36,500

STARTER HOME $39,500

FOR THE NEW FAMILY $42,000

START OUT HERE $43,600

ONE WAY OUT
of the rental trap is to buy this. . .

PRICED LIKE A CONDO $49,500
but no condo fees here

NOT A FIXER $79,500

LOWEST PRICE IN GREENWOOD $67,500

TAKE THE LANDLORD
off your payroll with this. . .

EZ ON THE EYES
EZ ON THE BUDGET $74,500

DOLLAR STRETCHER
Lots for less with this. . .

ELEGANTLY AFFORDABLE

AFFORDABLE LUXURY $39,500

Luxury *is, of course, a relative term.*

EASY TO OWN AT $39,500

NIFTY AND THRIFTY $68,500

BIG HOUSE—SMALL MONEY

LIVE HIGH FOR LESS

BUY LOW—LIVE HIGH

LOVE AT PURSE SIGHT

FITS THE PURSE $39,500

CASTLE ON A BUDGET—$75,000

WALLET WATCHER—$42,500

SPEND LESS—RECEIVE MORE

SEE WHAT $79,900 BUYS

GIVEAWAY! WELL, ALMOST

AN OLD TIME PRICE TAG—$37,500

ATTENTION TENANTS
Why rent when you can buy this...

RENTER'S REBELLION

TENANT'S REVENGE $39,500

TELL YOUR LANDLORD "GOOD-BYE"

WANTED—UNHAPPY RENTERS

"ADIOS" LANDLORD

GOOD-BYE LANDLORD—HELLO HOMEOWNER

BREAK THE RENT HABIT

THE RENT BUSTER $59,500

TIRED OF PAYING RENT?

TIRED OF RENT RECEIPTS?

DON'T RENT
when you can own $39,500

RENTING?
What for, when you can buy this... for only $________.

Additional ad language as well as completed ads appealing to renters will be found further on in this chapter under financing.

The following headings carry the connotation of an inexpensive house but don't really say so. We believe they are too subtle to be effective.

All these ads fail to clearly state the low price and so probably won't work very well.

COZY BUNGALOW

LITTLE YELLOW HOUSE

ENCHANTED COTTAGE

BEGINNING OR RETIRING

SOUND 4-ROOM COTTAGE

This was intended to mean $50,000, but the reader could also assume it means 50 years.

UNDER 50
But not quite a 10

Body Copy The low-price theme can be carried through in the ad body.

An inexpensive home in an expensive neighborhood

This 3BR home will fit your family and your pocketbook.

Payments less than rent

Your good taste and wallet will agree that this 3BR north-side beauty warrants prompt action.

Build up equity, not rent receipts.

Closings Closings, too, can specifically relate that the property is low-priced.

Low price *is a relative term.*

See what $_________ buys.

Easy on your pocketbook $_________.

Easy to own at $_________.

Won't leave you house-poor at $_________.

First-time-buyer-priced at $_________.

Priced to break the rent habit at $_________.

Affordable elegance at $_________.

An affordable life-style at only $_________.

Stretch your dollars at $_________.

Sensibly priced at $_________.

Low-priced homes are not necessarily bargain-priced. If they are, see the next section, *Bargain Homes.*

Keep in mind that, while people want *inexpensive,* they never want *cheap.* Better words are *affordable, inexpensive* or *realistically priced.*

Completed Ads Stressing Low Price

This ad and the following tell very little about the house. The purpose isn't to sell features but to get the reader to make a phone call.

ESCAPE THE LANDLORD

Finally, a home you can afford to own. A great 3BR west-side home with a low, low down payment and monthly payments you won't believe. Call now for details on this $39,500 budget pleaser.

Clyde Realty **476-8200**

LOVE YOUR LANDLORD?

If you want to make your landlord happy, then stay where you are. If not, call today to let us show you how easy it can be to become the owners of a lovely 3BR, 2-bath north-side rambler set on an oversized corner lot. It's priced to break the rent habit at $59,500.

Clyde Realty 476-8200

An attention-getting heading for renters

WALLET WATCHER $39,500

Don't let rising housing prices pass you by. This could be your last chance to own a 3-bedroom Cape Cod at a realistic price. A great place with a desired location, 2-car garage, full basement and fenced yard. Make your move now.

Clyde Realty 476-8200

Attention-getting heading

This ad gives a reason for the buyer to justify the purchase of an economical home.

WHY BE HOUSE-POOR

This charming 3BR traditional on a quiet tree-lined west-side street is the ideal home for your family. Enhanced by mature landscaping, economical gas heat, solid oak woodwork and a 2-car garage, it won't leave your wallet empty each month at $62,500.

Clyde Realty 476-8200

Short and to the point with an action closing

NOT A MISPRINT $69,500

If you want a 3-bedroom home in the Adams school district with a low-low down payment, then hurry and call.

Clyde Realty 476-8200

Bargain Homes

Everyone loves a bargain. Any ad that offers a bargain—or implies the possibility of one—will get an exceptional response. Then why doesn't everybody use a bargain ad? There are two reasons to be selective in choosing this type of appeal. First, the promise of a bargain has to be fulfilled; an agent who advertises a nonexistent bargain ends up merely advertising his or her own unreliability.

Equally important, the bargain ad tells prospective buyers that the seller will accept less than fair market value for the property. The result will be harder negotiations and lower offers than when more positive ads are used.

There are times when the need for a quick sale makes it worthwhile for an owner to offer and accept price concessions. Keep in mind, however, that the agent has a fiduciary duty to try to get the best price for the owner. When circumstances seem to demand the use of bargain advertising, it is essential to explain your plan and its probable effects to the owner, and get his or her permission to go ahead. You also need the owner's specific permission to reveal personal information about the reason for selling or the owner's need for a quick sale.

The same requirement for disclosure and permission applies to the use of any language suggesting that a price is not firm. *Asking $________* or *Submit all offers* tells the prospective buyer that the stated price is for negotiation and the seller really expects to get less.

Where the circumstances call for a bargain ad and the owner understands and agrees, you can use this section to write an ad that makes the fullest use of the pulling power of the bargain.

Headings A bargain heading can get attention without mentioning the seller's motivation, which may be included in the ad body.

HYSTERICAL OWNER

INSANE SELLER

HOT & DESPERATE

This heading has a possible sexual connotation that may not be appreciated by all readers.

DESPERATE

SUCH A DEAL

WHAT A DEAL

MEET A BARGAIN

SOS

SOS
Their ship is sinking and the sellers must bail out now.

H-E-L-P

ANXIOUS OWNER

MOTIVATED OWNER

DISTRESS SALE

THE ROPE HAS PULLED TIGHT
Owner must sell this . . .

A little cute, but a good heading for a smaller newspaper

CATCH A FALLING PRICE TAG

A little overworked

LAST CHANCE

SOMEBODY'S DREAM—YOUR OPPORTUNITY

NAIL BITING OWNER
must sell now . . .

NEED AN OFFER

PANIC-PRICED

OWNER DESPERATE

OWNER ORDERS IMMEDIATE SALE

EMERGENCY

CAN YOU MOVE FAST?

FORCED SALE

BARGAIN 4BR

A feature can also be included in the heading.

COOL POOL AND HOT FOR AN OFFER

BARGAIN TIME

Bargains don't have to be low-priced.

AN EXPENSIVE BARGAIN—$200,000

BARGAIN HUNTERS

UNBELIEVABLE PRICE

THE BARGAIN OF INDIAN WELLS

If the ad is repeated the next day, it should read 48 hours. *The body of the ad should include the reason for the 72 hours.*

JUST 72 HOURS TO SELL

SUPER BUY
Underpriced at $80,000

EXCITING VALUE AT $80,000

$40,000 BUYS A HOME

WOW! WHAT A VALUE

IMMEDIATE SALE REQUIRED

YESTERDAY'S PRICE

A CRACKERJACK
The surprise is the price.

WAS IT YOU
who said you wanted a bargain? Then read on about this...

SOUNDS TOO LOW—$69,500
Don't be fooled. This is a really motivated seller.

Many of these headings can also be used to close the ad.

Crude headings or statements in an ad can turn off buyers. Never indicate that a property is *cheap*; this carries a connotation of poor quality. Also, you should generally avoid the word *steal*. While buyers are delighted with bargains, many righteous buyers will be turned off by an offer to make them thieves.

Foreclosure A specific financial difficulty is foreclosure or threat of foreclosure. While foreclosure could be shown in the body of an ad that uses another heading, it is such a strong reason for sale that, with the owner's permission, it should be shown in a heading.

FORECLOSURE

FORECLOSURE SALE

NEAR FORECLOSURE

You must have the owner's permission to disclose any facts about him or her.

STOP FORECLOSURE

BEAT FORECLOSURE SALE

BEFORE FORECLOSURE

FORECLOSURE PENDING

LAST CHANCE BEFORE FORECLOSURE

LENDER FORCES SALE

BEAT THE SHERIFF

Even after foreclosure, property that is being resold by a lender means a bargain to many people. In many cases they are right, as lenders often want out of a property-ownership role, and so are willing to make concessions in price or terms or both in order to move property. The following ad headings can be used for lender-owned property:

BANK SAYS SELL

LENDER WANTS SALE NOW

LENDER SAYS SELL

LENDER ORDERS SALE

REPO

BANK REPO

LENDER-OWNED

This heading can also be used where the owner stopped the foreclosure.

OUT OF FORECLOSURE

FOR SALE BY LENDER

This heading is appropriate when the foreclosure was by a seller who foreclosed on a purchase-money loan.

OWNER GOT IT BACK

GOVERNMENT-OWNED HOME

For FHA or VA foreclosure

GOVERNMENT FORECLOSURE

FHA SAYS SELL

Estate Sale Most people believe that bargains are possible in estate sales. Therefore, the following can be productively used as headings or within the ad body:

ESTATE SALE

ESTATE CLEARANCE

HEIRS SAY SELL

HEIRS SELLING

ESTATE SETTLEMENT

ESTATE SETTLEMENT PROMPTS SALE

ESTATE SETTLEMENT REQUIRES QUICK SALE

PRICED TO SETTLE ESTATE

PROBATE SALE

PROBATE-ORDERED SALE

HEIRS WANT OUT

HEIRS WANT CASH NOW

If the heirs are from out of the area, a statement such as *Out-of-town heir orders sale* becomes an even stronger indication of a bargain.

Builders A builder's inventory can be advertised in a manner that indicates a bargain.

BUILDER'S CLOSEOUT

BUILDER'S LIQUIDATION

BUILDER'S FINAL SELLOUT

MODEL SELLOUT

LIQUIDATION

ONLY 14 LEFT

BUILDER'S TRADE-IN

DESPERATE BUILDER

BUILDER SOS

BUILDER SACRIFICE

BUILDER MUST SELL

Other Reasons There are many reasons for sale that indicate a probable bargain. These reasons, after obtaining the owner's permission, can be covered in either the ad body or with headings.

WARNING
Advertising information about the owners without their express permission could be a violation of your agency trust and could subject you to legal liability.

HOMESICK
Owner wants to return to Chicago

OWNER MOVING EAST

LEAVING USA

OWNER TRANSFERRED

EXECUTIVE TRANSFER

TRANSFER FORCES SALE

ABSENTEE OWNER WANTS OUT

ABSENTEE OWNER MUST SELL

FOREIGN OWNER SAYS SELL

PARTNERSHIP DISSOLUTION FORCES SALE

PARTNERS SAY SELL

PARTNERS ANXIOUS

DIVORCE SALE

DIVORCE FORCES SALE

TRUST SALE

BANKRUPTCY FORCES SALE

BANKRUPTCY SALE

OWNER BANKRUPT

NEAR-BANKRUPTCY SALE

ATTORNEY ORDERS SALE

COURT-ORDERED SALE

CORPORATE OWNER MUST SELL

CORPORATE OWNER ORDERS SALE

UNLOAD IT
The corporate owner wants it sold.

Surplus *implies a bargain.*

SURPLUS DISPOSAL
Corporate board of directors has declared this...
as surplus and ordered an immediate sale.

EXCESS PROPERTY
Corporation orders sale of excess real estate

The ad body should indicate the specific reason.

TO BE ABANDONED

This heading is likely to give the reader the idea that the sale price won't be that important, so a bargain is possible.

MILLIONAIRE SAYS SELL

IT'S BACK ON THE MARKET AGAIN

PLAY IT AGAIN, SAM
It's back on the market, but not for long. This...

SELLER BLUE
Sale fell through

WHOOPS!
Desperate owner thought (he/she) sold (his/her) house and purchased another, then the sale fell through.

SALE FAILED

COLLAPSED SALE

FELL OUT OF ESCROW

SALE FELL THROUGH

BUYER BACKED OUT

ORPHANED
(Mamma/Poppa) left to get married.

HYSTERICAL OWNER
has two houses—must sell one

DOUBLE TROUBLE
Owner has 2 houses and must sell one.

TWO HOMES—ONE SPOUSE

1 HUSBAND—1 WIFE—2 HOUSES
Must sell this...

CAN YOU AFFORD
2 house payments? Neither can the owner of this...

ONE HOUSE TOO MANY

OWNER PINCHED
Mortgage note due, so must sell

This doesn't really give a reason but it can be effective in the ad body.

VERY SIMPLY—OWNER NEEDS THE CASH

You don't really have to be specific about the exact reason for sale. The headings above referring to foreign owners, absentee owners and corporate owners really give no reason for sale, yet they create the appearance of a forced sale.

The idea of a bargain can be communicated in any ad by a statement in the body such as *Unfortunate circumstances necessitate immediate sale.* This statement is effective and allows an owner privacy as to personal problems.

Below Cost If a property is being sold below its cost or reproduction cost, a heading such as one of the following could be used:

BELOW COST

BELOW BUILDER'S COST

BELOW REPRODUCTION COST

BELOW APPRAISAL

PRICED UNDER APPRAISAL

THEIR LOSS—YOUR GAIN

You can also cover the below-cost aspect in the body of your ad or as a closing with words such as:

Priced at a fraction of its reproduction cost

Can't be duplicated for its price of $_________.

Owners are forced to sell far below their purchase price.

Priced below appraisal at $_________.

Appraised at $_________. But priced at $_________.

Below *FHA* appraisal

Price Reductions Price reductions do not necessarily mean bargains, but most prospective buyers view a price reduction as an opportunity to save. The following headings reinforce that belief:

DOWN TO YOUR PRICE

NOW AT YOUR PRICE

REDUCED FOR ACTION

PRICE DRASTICALLY REDUCED

SUBSTANTIAL REDUCTION

REDUCED $20,000

REDUCED AGAIN

LAST REDUCTION

FINAL REDUCTION

BELOW '83 SALE PRICE

$10,000 BELOW LAST SALE PRICE

2ND PRICE REDUCTION

While this heading does not necessarily promise a bargain, it does give that impression.

Closings Closings for bargain ads should end with a final assurance of value.

Panic-priced at $________.

Priced for immediate sale at $________.

Must be sold within 10 days $________.

Must be sold today $________.

This is an excellent closing for an open house ad.

Your last chance at $________.

Opportunity won't knock again at $________.

Must-sell-priced at $________.

Offered on a first-come-first-served basis at $________.

Unbelievable value for your dollar at $________.

Compare—then hurry to buy at $________.

Grab your checkbook—only $________.

Start packing—it's priced at $________.

Liquidation priced at $________.

Yours for the price of an ordinary home $________.

Excellent for a luxury home

The clincher is the price $________.

Full-price offers only $________.

Priced firm at $________.

These statements give the impression that the property has already been priced as low as possible.

Sale price of $________ is subject to court approval.

This gives the impression that the price set may be too low.

Makes cents at $________.

At this price you better act quick $________.

You will think it's too good to be true $________.

Don't miss this at $________.

Too good to last at $_________.

Nothing like it at this price $_________.

Won't last long at $_________.

Call for fast action at $_________.

Priced to go at $_________.

Priced for quick sale $_________.

For the alert buyer $_________.

Hurry at $_________.

"Pinch-me" priced at $_________.

Action priced at $_________.

Destined for quick sale at $_________.

WARNING—This closing indicates the price asked is not firm.

Let's talk $_________.

Talk about value $_________.

Priced at less than the replacement value of the home alone $_________.

Take advantage of the reduced price of $_________.

Priced below replacement cost $_________.

Priced below market at $_________.

Priced below appraisal at $_________.

Quick action wanted at $_________.

Auction-priced at $_________.

Bound to sell quickly at $_________.

Challenges comparison at $_________.

Even the price is beautiful $_________.

Speculator-priced at $_________.

Completed Ads for Bargain Homes

This heading and lead can be used whenever there is a corporate owner.

SURPLUS DISPOSAL

Corporate board of directors has declared this executive retreat as surplus and ordered an immediate sale. The 9-room, 4BR, 3-bath French Regency home is situated on a 1/2-acre professionally landscaped site in Sunrise Estates. No expense was spared in its construction and meticulous maintenance. Your chance to obtain a one-of-a-kind estate at the price of an ordinary home. $268,000.

Clyde Realty 476-8200

AGAIN—Have the owner's permission before revealing any personal data.

DIVORCE SALE

Almost new 1,800-sq.-ft., 3BR, 2-bath colonial ranch in Morningside Estates has been ordered sold immediately. Situated on an oversized wooded lot, it has a family room with fireplace, full basement, paved circular drive, attached 2½-car garage with automatic opener and a great deal more. It's MUST-SELL-priced at $119,500.

Clyde Realty 476-8200

This two-line heading could be very effective during a summer hot spell.

This ad is really a teaser. Just enough information is given to perk the reader's interest with the possibility of a bargain.

A HOT BARGAIN ON A COLD HOUSE

Central air is just one of the luxury features in this 3BR brick ranch on a double lot in desirable Falcon Cove. The court has ordered an immediate sale, so it's your opportunity at just $87,500.

Clyde Realty 476-8200

STOP FORECLOSURE

Owner about to lose this Shamrock model 2BR, 2-bath condo in Morningside. Special features of this rare end unit include upgraded all-wool carpeting, custom drapes, decorating and wall coverings, all in muted earth tones. Auction priced at $79,300.

Clyde Realty 476-8200

Advertising a sale in a style similar to that used in public announcements can be extremely effective for a lender foreclosure!

Show the name of the owner.

PUBLIC ANNOUNCEMENT

The following described property is offered for immediate sale by order of Amalgamated Savings and Loan.

NORTHRIDGE COLONIAL

3BR, 2½-bath, 3-car garage on choice site. Property in excellent condition. Attractive terms to qualified buyer. Offered on a first-come-first-served basis at $139,500.

Clyde Realty 476-8200

First-come-first-served *is an excellent motivator—no one wants to see a bargain go to someone else.*

A similar announcement style can be used whenever a sale is pursuant to a court order related to bankruptcy, divorce, partnership dissolution, estate sales and so forth:

PUBLIC ANNOUNCEMENT

Pursuant to the order of the Superior Court of the County of Riverside, the following described property is hereby offered for immediate sale:

Financing Terms

Regulation Z (Truth-in-Lending) applies where individuals or businesses are offering or extending credit. If an ad includes specific credit information such as precise down payment, dollar amount of finance charges, monthly payment or the period of the loan, then the ad must also include:

Amount or percentage of down payment
Terms of repayment
Annual percentage rate (APR)

Advertising "no down payment" or the use of the annual percentage rate does not trigger the above full ad disclosure requirement.

The requirements may apply where the seller has agreed to provide specific credit to a buyer. While the act often seems to be ignored by advertisers, we recommend you either comply or avoid credit specifics when subject to the act. Including all of the required information in a classified ad will likely result in a cumbersome ad that lacks impact.

If your ad is subject to regulation disclosure requirements, a statement similar to the following would be required:

> *Full price $98,000, down payment $16,000, monthly payments $971.60 P & I on $82,000. 30-year loan at 14% (14½% APR).*

It is our interpretation that assumptions of existing loans at the original interest rate do not require disclosure of all the terms when one term is given, because the seller is not extending or arranging credit. Despite requests for clarification, the Federal Trade Commission has failed to specifically address this issue. However, the Truth-in-Lending Act does require full disclosure before the assumption takes place.

During January 1983, the Federal Trade Commission started a pilot Real Estate Credit Compliance Project in which they examined display advertising in 16 cities. They found that only 13 percent of the advertising met legal requirements. The FTC claims to have increased that rate to 84 percent through letters and calls to advertisers.

Though the FTC study did not examine classified advertising, a quick look at the Sunday papers suggests that the compliance rate in this medium is little better. Despite the widespread abuse, I strongly recommend that you fully comply with the regulations—any convenience you gain by taking shortcuts will be more than made up for by loss of reputation, the possibility of enforcement action and the potential for legal liability. For a free copy of the booklet *Regulation Z: Truth in Lending,* write to the Federal Trade Commission, Washington, DC 20580.

Prior to advertising, it is important to either have an agreement with the owner as to owner financing or to fully understand available alternative financing. Many buyers view total price as secondary to the amount of the down payment, monthly payment and/or interest rates.

It isn't just low-cost-home buyers who are interested in terms. Luxury homes with low down payments will attract far more prospective buyers than those requiring a normal down payment. Therefore, whenever you have a property with better-than-average terms, be sure your ad reflects this advantage.

Assumable Loans Ad headings that indicate a loan can be assumed:

ASSUMABLE 7%

ASSUMABLE LOAN

VA-ASSUMABLE

ASSUME VA LOAN

ASSUME 7% VA

When the interest rate of the assumable loan is quite low, it should be included in the heading.

FHA-ASSUMABLE

ASSUME FHA LOAN

ASSUME 8% LOAN

$8,730—TAKE OVER

You might want to emphasize a fixed-term rate, but don't mention adjustable rate loans in your ads. They can be an immediate turnoff for people who don't understand them.

ASSUME 8% LOAN—NONESCALATING

PAY DOWN TO 7½% LOAN

SUPER ASSUMPTION

SUPER ASSUMABLE LOAN

HIGH & LOW
High assumable loan—low down payment

ASSUMABLE & BEAUTIFUL

ENDANGERED SPECIES
10% assumable loan

IT'S BACK
8.7% interest. Assume this. . .

ASSUMABLE-ATTRACTIVE
and just reduced

These ads have a strong appeal for people who were turned down for other loans because of low income.

CAN'T QUALIFY?
Assume loan—no qualifying

NO QUALIFYING

NO CREDIT CHECK

BEEN REJECTED FOR A LOAN?
No qualifying—assume 10% FHA

Owner Financing Owners are often flexible when they agree to finance. Buyers know that owners usually will carry back a loan at an interest rate less than the market. Owner financing can be covered in the heading, the ad body or as a closing statement.

That a property is free and clear indicates to a buyer that the owner has more room to negotiate.

FREE & CLEAR
Owner willing to finance buyer

These headings can also be used for assumable loans.

OWNER FINANCING

BELOW-MARKET FINANCING

OLD-FASHIONED INTEREST
Owner financing well below market rate

This could be used as a heading where there is a deferred down payment.

BUY NOW—PAY LATER

This wording can also be used when you have a variety of conventional loans available.

OWNER WILL TAKE 2ND

UNPRECEDENTED FINANCING

FLEXIBLE TERMS

FLEXIBLE FINANCING

OWC *means* owner will carry, *but should be avoided since first-time buyers and less-sophisticated buyers might not know what it means.*

OWC

These can be used for a closing. You must have the owner's permission before you use language such as this because it invites offers far below the market rate.

NAME YOUR OWN TERMS

SUBMIT TERMS

Other Financing The following headings can be used for new financing as well as assumable and owner financing. Keep in mind that stating the specific terms for new financing triggers the full disclosure requirements of the Truth-in-Lending Law.

Since these ads are suggestions and not stated rates, the Truth-in-Lending advertising requirements do not apply regardless of the type of financing. You should obtain the owner's permission before you suggest a down payment or terms.

LESS THAN $3,000 DOWN

DO YOU HAVE $1,000 DOWN PAYMENT?

CAN YOU AFFORD $500/MONTH?

FIXED RATE 9%

OLD FASHIONED FINANCING

DOWN-TO-EARTH FINANCING

TRY $5,000 DOWN

EASY TO BUY

NO MONEY
or very little cash to pay down?

NO MONEY DOWN?

ZERO DOWN?

Attention-attractor for possible no-money-down situation

A PENNY DOWN?

TALK ABOUT TERMS

LET'S MAKE A DEAL

HARDLY ANYTHING DOWN

Zero interest is increasingly available for short-term loans carried by a seller or where a seller buys down the interest rate from the lender.

ZERO INTEREST?

POSSIBLE 10% FINANCING

8% INTEREST?
It's possible on this . . .

NO-DOWN VA

LOW-DOWN FHA

VA-FHA BUYERS

For Renters Ads featuring attractive terms have great appeal to renters.

GOOD-BYE LANDLORD

WHY RENT

ESCAPE FROM THE LANDLORD

Because interest is a deductible expense, even though a house payment might be more than rent, the tax benefits could reduce it below rent levels.

LANDLORDS HATE US
because we are offering this . . . with almost nothing down and a monthly payment that works out to be less than rent.

Body Copy Statements for the ad body regarding financing include:

Large, no-qualifying assumable loan

Large assumable loan

Owner financing available

Owner will finance qualified buyer

8% assumable loan

Nonescalating long-term assumable loan

Owner owns free and clear

Indicates possibility of excellent owner financing

Owner will accept mobile home for down payment

This can be an excellent approach.

Seller pays points and closing costs

Seller pays all settlement costs

Structured financing to meet your needs

Fixed-rate 8% assumable loan

8½% nonescalating assumable loan

Liberal owner financing

Owner will subordinate

Where an owner will allow purchaser to place a priority encumbrance on the property

Exceptional owner financing

Creative financing available

Locked-in interest rate

Owner will carry total loan after down payment

Payments like rent

30-year assumable amortized mortgage

Count your savings with below-market owner financing.

Unusually generous owner financing available

Long-term owner financing available

Long-term low-interest owner financing

If you earn $300 per week, you can afford this . . .

Excellent statement for duplex

Payments less than $300 after collecting rents from your tenant(s)

Even when you have no advantage in financing, you can appear to have an advantage with:

Financing has been arranged.

Financing available

Closings The following ad closings emphasize financing:

You won't believe the financing $_________.

Ask how we can tailor the financing to your needs $_________.

Low down to qualified buyer. Full price only $_________.

Financing customized to your needs $_________.

Call about the fantastic terms $_________.

Have the owner's permission before you advertise this.

Bring your creative offers $_________.

Bring your checkbook—the down payment is less than $_________.

Ask about the low-low down payment.

Unbelievable financing $_________.

Move in with almost nothing down. Full price only $_________.

Offered with extraordinary financial arrangements at $_________.

Discount Some ads give the price and terms and then add *Discount for cash*. This may attract cash buyers but turns off the buyer who must finance. Offering a discount for cash is really telling the buyer who must finance, "Because you can't pay cash, I will make you pay more." The net effect is likely to be negative.

Completed Ads Stressing Financing Terms

SELLER WANTS $2,000

and you can take over the 9% loan on this newer 3BR, brick split-level located on an estate-size wooded lot in Meadowbrook. Full price only $67,000.

Clyde Realty 476-8200

GREAT TERMS ARE YOURS

Owner will carry balance at a below-market interest rate after a reasonable down payment. Like-new 3BR, 2-bath colonial ranch near the hospital. One look and you will buy at $89,900.

Clyde Realty 476-8200

This unusual heading is an attention-getter. The price is not given. To the readers this ad is aimed at, the monthly payment—not the price—is important. Because specific terms are not given, the Trust-in-Lending Act does not apply.

CRAZY CLYDE

plunks down more money in rent each month than it would cost to buy this 3BR, well-cared-for rambler on the desirable north side. Low, low down payment and less than $500 per month.

Clyde Realty 476-8200

This ad doesn't give a price or monthly payment. It was written to get the veteran to call.

VIETNAM VETERAN

Let the government guarantee your home. This sensational 3BR, 2-bath hillside ranch has everything you could want in a family home at a low price. Best of all, you are eligible for a no-money-down, low-monthly-payment VA loan.

Clyde Realty 476-8200

Very little is told about this house. The ad sells the idea that the readers could be owners.

The price is not given, but it is not important to the buyers to whom this ad is targeted. This ad sells terms.

RENTERS ARISE

Break the landlord's bondage. With less than $2,000 down, you can be the owner of this 3BR, 1½-bath ranch that offers better living than any rental could. Total monthly payments of less than $500 will build equity in your own home. Call today to bid your landlord farewell.

Clyde Realty 476-8200

If the terms are for new or seller financing, then the ad would likely have to comply with the full disclosure provisions of Truth-in-Lending.

LET YOUR TENANT PAY

for this quality brick duplex on prestigious Washington Circle. Each unit has 3BR, 1½ baths, stone fireplace, formal dining room, central air and double garage. With $8,000 down, after collecting your rents the total monthly payment is only $376.

Clyde Realty 476-8200

Attention-getting heading

The price is not included, nor is the down payment. The ad is selling a low monthly payment and is written to encourage calls for more particulars.

The ad is for an older home (attic, established neighborhood). It probably has a single-car garage and one bath.

CAN YOU AFFORD $300 FOR RENT

If so, you can be the owner of a great 3BR home on a huge fenced lot in an established north-side family neighborhood. Walking-close to schools and shopping, the home boasts a full basement, storage attic, attached garage and a garden that will be the envy of your friends. It's not going to last long so call NOW for details.

Clyde Realty 476-8200

8 Vacation Homes, Mobile Homes, Condominiums and Timeshares

We are all very concerned with the quality of our lives. After meeting our basic needs, we think of ways to enhance our life-styles and leisure time. Second homes help by providing an escape from an otherwise very dull existence.

Large newspapers usually list second homes under headings such as *Vacation Homes, Lake Property, Mountain Property,* and so forth.

Besides the ideas listed in this chapter for vacation homes, you should also check Chapter Ten for language applicable to country property and Chapter Three for language dealing with trees.

Vacation Homes

Headings Ad headings can sell the second home as a place to get away to.

NORTHWOODS RETREAT

DESERT RETREAT

MOUNTAIN RETREAT

FAMILY RETREAT

Large property

CORPORATE RETREAT

WEEKEND RETREAT

For a small cottage

SINGLE'S HIDEAWAY

ARTIST'S HIDEAWAY

LOVERS' HIDEAWAY

LOST IN THE WOODS

BE A DROPOUT
The perfect place to drop out from the hectic and dirty city life

COUNTRY ESCAPE

ESCAPE KIT

ESCAPE TO. . .

ESCAPE THE RAT RACE

YOUR SHANGRI-LA

SHANGRI-LA

HIDE OUT

GET AWAY FROM IT ALL

REFUGE

YOUR REFUGE

YOUR QUIET PLACE

CHAIRMAN OF THE BORED
Here's your chance to get away from it all.

GETAWAY HOUSE

THE GREAT GETAWAY

RETREAT
to this. . .

WEEKEND "STEAL-AWAY"

YOUR SANCTUARY

ARTIST'S SANCTUARY

Here are some other appeals:

SKI *MT. BALDY*

CHALET IN THE WOODS

CHALET IN THE FOREST

4-SEASONS CHALET

NORTHWOODS CHALET

AFFORDABLE CHALET $39,500

Log home

LINCOLN WOULD HAVE LOVED IT

MOUNTAIN CHALET

EASY TO REACH BUT HARD TO LEAVE

JUST FOR FUN

YOUR PLACE IN THE SUN

FOR WEEKENDS OR WEEKS ON END

Could also be used as a closing

FUN FORTY

40 acres

YOU HAVE EARNED IT

COUNTRY QUIET

SPORTSPERSON'S HAVEN

YOUR HOME ON THE RANGE

WOODCUTTER'S COTTAGE

Cottage *gives a positive image to a smaller home.*

MOUNTAIN LODGE

Lodge *is much more prestigious-sounding than* cabin.

NORTHWOODS LODGE

THINK SUNSHINE

BUY THE SUN

BASK IN THE WINTER SUN

YOUR PLACE IN THE FUN

CITY NERVES
Just what the doctor ordered

LOWER YOUR BLOOD PRESSURE
You will forget your cares at this...

Body Copy The ad body should sell the home's special desirable features and benefits.

Start a family tradition with this extended family-size summer home.

Enjoy those lazy days of summer in this...

Every day will be a holiday at this charming *lakefront cottage.*

The place for your weekend getaway

Where winter is just a memory

For a second home in the Sunbelt

Slow down the tempo of your life.

The place for a relaxing country weekend

An experience with nature for weekends or a lifetime

An unbelievable wooded hideaway

On 8 acres tucked away from civilization

Loaded with peace and quiet

This 2-bedroom modern cabin is located less than 1 hour's drive from downtown.

You will feel at peace with nature in this...

Rocking-chair front porch for summer enjoyment

Located in a 4-seasons vacationland

Unique rustic atmosphere

Storage building for your boat and snowmobile

Present owners feed the deer during the winter

Winterized cottage — *Winterized means the cottage is heated and its plumbing is protected.*

Sleeps 8 — *Small cottages often have beds in the living room and on the porch. Showing the number who can sleep there indicates it can handle visitors.*

Sleeping porch
Sleeping loft
Bunkhouse — *Shows areas can be used for sleeping*

Wood-burning stove — *Adds nostalgia*

Swiss-style chalet

A-frame

A-frame with sleeping loft

Constructed of lodgepole pine logs

Solid log construction

Lodgepole log home

Full log construction
Constructed of 10″ logs — *Log construction has a strong appeal due to "natural" and "strength" connotations.*

Screened porch

Screened gazebo

Fully insulated for winter use

3-season home — *Means it is not winterized*

4-season home — *Means it is winterized*

Simplicity with a flair

Roaming deer and curious raccoons will visit you at this. . .

Closings Besides the closings shown under other categories elsewhere in this book, the following closings would be appropriate for second homes:

Your escape kit $________.

Your own hideout at $________.

Plan your escape now $________.

The good life can be yours $________.

Grab the gusto $________.

Active fun living for $________.

Everything you have always wanted $________.

Everything you want in a vacation home $________.

Your place to unwind $________.

Your relief valve from city life $________.

An exciting hideaway at $________.

The antidote for city blues $________.

For your family $________.

Your escape from the commonplace $________.

Offering a lot of fun for only $________.

Your hideaway for only $________.

Awaits your pleasure at $________.

Your retirement home or 4-season retreat $________.

You can make this your place in the sun for $________.

Your place in the fun $________.

Your getaway for weekends or weeks on end $________.

Make this your escape hatch from the city $________.

Your place in the sun for $________.

Hideaway here for $________.

Peace and contentment for $________.

For the fun-seeker $________.

Bring your (fishing pole/tennis racket/golf clubs) $________.

Many second homes are purchased by retirees who live in them year-round. Closings specifically for retirees would be:

A great place to retire $________.

Pension-priced at $________.

Let your retirement be for living $________.

Completed Ads for Vacation Homes

This ad makes a virtue out of the lack of modern conveniences. It can be extremely appealing to many. To understand its effectiveness, close your eyes and imagine the mental picture that this ad conveys.

MOUNTAIN ESCAPE $32,000

A picture-book full-log home set in a sun-filled clearing overlooking a mountain stream can be your weekend escape from city life. Featuring a massive stone fireplace, this 1BR home also has a huge open sleeping loft above the great room. Amenities include a mammoth cast-iron cookstove with water from your own iron pump by the sink and convenience facilities just up the path. Best of all, there is no phone. This is your chance to slow down and enjoy.

Clyde Realty 476-8200

This ad sells a way of life.

The closing gives an assurance of value.

PALM SPRINGS HIDEAWAY

Escape the smog and enjoy healthful weekends and vacations in the sun. Tennis, golf and swimming will be yours to enjoy with this newer decorator-furnished 2BR, 2-bath Southend hacienda. Featured are window walls for indoor-outdoor living, cathedral ceilings and a red tile roof. The pool area is surrounded by an oasis of palms and citrus and the block wall insures you absolute privacy. Offering so much more for less than the price of a condo. $119,000.

Clyde Realty 476-8200

This ad sells the image of the good life.

TENSION RELIEVER—WRIGHTWOOD

Escape city drudgery for weekends or weeks on end. Modern mountain lodge features 3 bedrooms, sleeping loft and a massive stone fireplace. Set on a huge wooded acre, it is only minutes away from the golf course and a great trout stream. It's your antidote for city blues. Take it at $87,500.

Clyde Realty 476-8200

Farm homes with several acres are very popular vacation and retirement homes for city dwellers. This simple heading was prepared to set forth the major attractive features of this particular property.

HOME, BARN AND APPLE TREES

Less than 3 hours from NYC are 2 acres of pastoral splendor. Set amidst century-old oaks, the 8-room brick farmhouse has been fully modernized. You will delight at the nooks, crannies, high ceilings and original detailing. Included is your own apple orchard and an ancient barn that would make a great studio or? Your relief valve from city life. $189,500.

Clyde Realty 476-8200

This is an ad for a second home that is aimed at being the primary residence for a retiree. Benefits are low cost, low taxes, low heating costs, close to facilities and a quiet, simple, safe life. The mental picture painted by this ad is very appealing.

RETIRE TO THE NORTH

You will live royally on your pension in this newer 2BR northwoods chalet that's only 15 minutes from Iron River. This is a low-tax 4-season recreation area offering all the modern conveniences at down-to-earth prices. This exceptional home on a pine-studded acre just 1/2 mile from a boat landing boasts a full walk-out basement that would make an ideal workshop or recreation room, economical wood/gas central heat, a massive fireplace in the paneled living room, a large garage and a fantastic view. The price can't be beat at $49,900.

Clyde Realty 476-8200

Water-Related Homes

Unless your newspaper has a special category for lake, river or beach property, your ad heading should announce the water location.

If the body of water is well known and desirable, it should be specifically named in your heading even when your newspaper has a separate heading for water-related property.

CEDAR LAKE—3BR

CEDAR LAKE—$79,800

CEDAR LAKE—YEAR-ROUND HOME

HUDSON RIVER VIEW

Other headings don't mention specific places but make clear the property's nearness to the water.

ON THE WATER

MARINER'S SANCTUARY

THE SOUND OF SURF

ON THE PERFECT LAKE

AT WATER'S EDGE

100′ OF LAKEFRONT

SPLASH AND FISH

FISH AND FLOAT RIVER

CREEK-FRONT DAZZLER

RIVERFRONT SANCTUARY

DOWN BY THE RIVERSIDE

BY A WATERFALL

WATER WATER EVERYWHERE

WISHIN' YOU WERE FISHIN'?

FISH OFF YOUR DOCK

FISH-FILLED POND

FISH-FILLED CREEK

Attention-getters for river front property

BE A TOM SAWYER

FOR THE TOM SAWYER IN YOU

SAILBOAT WATER

ATTENTION: SAILBOAT ENTHUSIASTS

WALK ON WATER
just off the deck of this. . .

BY THE OLD MILL POND

WALK TO BEACH $79,500

STROLL ON THE SAND

STROLL ON THE BEACH

WALK ON THE SAND

ON THE SAND

OCEAN BREEZE

ON THE BEACH

BLUE WATER—WHITE SAILS

RIVER MYSTIQUE

BEACHCOMBER

BEACH RETREAT

BEACH HOUSE $89,500

A PLACE ON THE BEACH
at a price within reach

BEAUTY AND THE BEACH

BY THE SEA—BUY THE SEA

BUY THE SEA

ON THE WATERFRONT

SERENITY ON THE WATER

½ MILE OF RIVER FRONTAGE

LAKEFRONT SHANGRI-LA

FISH AND GAME HAVEN

YOUR OWN PRIVATE LAKE

In describing a large but relatively unknown lake, include the size of the lake with language such as:

200′ of choice sand frontage on 820-acre Lake Gerald

Descriptive words for water-related property ads include:

Commanding waterfront site

100′ perfect lake frontage

100′ of frontage on a good fishing lake

100′ of the finest beach

Lawn to water's edge

Practically in the water

White sand beach

White sets a positive mental picture.

Gradual sand beach

Gentle wading beach

Parents with small children fear sharp drop-offs.

High and dry 3BR home on the banks of . . .

Reduces fear of floods

Spring-fed lake

For those who appreciate the beauty and serenity of waterside living

Overlooking the tranquil waters of . . .

Babbling brook

A babbling brook runs merrily at your doorstep.

You will go to sleep with the gentle sound of the *babbling brook.*

Only a short stroll to catch the waves

Listen to the surf and watch the waves from this . . .

Sandy beaches await you at this . . .

Watch the reflections of the changing seasons in the tranquil waters of *Lake Ojibwa.*

These phrases provide the image of clean water.

Crystal-clear spring-fed lake

Sparkling spring-fed lake

Offers a captivating blend of golf, tennis and beautiful beaches

Enjoy the tranquility of wide waters and quiet beaches.

Promenade on a spectacular stretch of white sand beach.

On the sandy shores of. . .

This shows the property is not on the beach but close. Walk to Beach *would be closer yet.*

Bike to beach

Walk to fishing dock

2 miles to trout stream

Swim and fish in your own backyard.

Swimmin'-Fishin' lake

Beside a meandering stream

Meandering stream flows through. . .

Cool mountain stream

Lazy fish-filled river

A peninsula is desirable for both privacy and summer breezes.

Peninsula setting

Ice-cold flowing spring

Clear mountain stream

Rainbow trout abound in the sparkling stream crossing this 14-acre tract.

30′ dock

30′ dock with electric hoist

Boat house with electric hoist

This means the boat house is built over the water.

Wet boat house

Boat hoist

Covered dock

Permanent pier

Fish off your own dock

Fish off your own pier

Beach privileges

Private mooring

Mooring rights

Beach rights

Promenade

Waterfront esplanade

Enjoy the waterfront esplanade

Steps from the sand

Steps from the beach

Spring-fed waters

Crystal waters

Dock and davits

Heavy-duty davits

Beach access

Dedicated beach access

Seawall

Protective docking

Deep-water dock

200′ of bulkhead frontage

These are important for big-boat owners.

Protected anchorage

In protected cove

The gentle sound of rushing water will lull you to sleep in this. . .

Listen to the nearby creek

Means a right-of-way to the water

Your southwest view of the sunset over the water is unsurpassed.

Lake access

An exclusive right-of-way to the water

Private lake access

Storage building for your boats

Closings for water-related properties sum up the temptations.

Make every day a vacation for $________.

Bring your boat $________.

For lake living at its best $________.

One of the last remaining oceanfront sites $________.

Live by the lake for $________.

First-cabin living for $________.

For the discriminating yachtsperson $________.

For the discriminating sailor $________.

Completed Ads for Water-Related Property

The first two ads are for undeveloped land and set a very appealing mental picture.

WALDEN POND

Your very own pond to enjoy nature in all its seasons on this idyllic 8-acre wooded site less than 1 hour from the city. The ideal setting for a very special hideaway. It's your opportunity at $19,800.

Clyde Realty **476-8200**

WATERS RUSH

over a rocky stream and through this quiet valley. A sunlit glade provides the idyllic setting for your dream home. Six acres of tranquility less than 30 minutes from the square. Perfection and contentment can be yours for $39,500.

Clyde Realty **476-8200**

This ad emphasizes there is plenty of room for company.

LAKE ST. ANDREW

Nestled amidst towering pines on 200′ of choice sandy shoreline is the home of your dreams. This modern 2-bedroom bungalow features a huge sleeping porch as well as a bunkroom in the garage to accommodate your guests. Fully furnished, including pier and boat. The owner financing will help you start a family tradition. $79,900.

Clyde Realty **476-8200**

This property is water-related but not on the water.

Mentioning the possibility of income is likely to evoke interest in many readers.

GONE FISHIN'

It could be you as the owner of this 9-acre wooded tract just minutes away from the beach and boat landing. Older 2-bedroom home has full basement and attached 2-car garage. The 24′ × 60′ barn could be converted to workshop or profitable boat storage. Bring your imagination and your fishin' pole. Full price only $67,500.

Clyde Realty **476-8200**

This ad sells a mood and tells very little about the house itself.

POUNDING SURF

is at your front door as the owner of this picture-book oceanfront natural-wood-shingled Cape Cod. Features 2 bedrooms plus a huge studio or sleeping loft and a native stone fireplace to add warmth on those chilly mornings. Miles of sand beaches for barefoot walking are just waiting for you. $120,000.

Clyde Realty 476-8200

This ad also sells the mood rather than the house. It was written to bring an emotional response.

BY THE OLD MILL POND

The gentle sound of rushing water will lull you to sleep each night in this orchard stone and cedar 8-room home that blends into the rocky shore of an historic mill pond near Riverdale. An ideal setting for the writer or artist who is inspired by beauty and an ambiance of contentment. An unusual opportunity at $79,000.

Clyde Realty 476-8200

This heading is all right if the property is advertised under a newspaper category for waterfront property. If not, it would be too subtle. Better headings would then be FISH-FILLED RIVER *or* RIVERFRONT HOME. *The ad body would then read* You would love living on this. . .

TOM SAWYER

would have loved living on this lazy fish-filled river. The sweeping green lawn, studded with giant hickory, slopes gently to the sandy shore where there is a 2-slip boat house, mooring dock and a sunset fishing deck cantilevered over the water. The 4-season home has 3 bedrooms, 1½ baths, a huge glassed and screened sleeping porch and an incomparable river view. There is a 2-car garage and a separate storage building that could easily be converted to a studio. This home is completely furnished—including boats, motors and riding mower. This can easily be your family's vacation home with special owner financing and a low price of $87,500. Call:

Clyde Realty 476-8200

Mobile Homes

Because of this cost advantage, mobile homes have become the choice of an increasing segment of our population. Today's mobile homes are not really mobile, though, since they are often joined together and set on concrete foundations, making their movement both difficult and expensive.

Some people use the term *modular home* for *mobile home.* They are not the same. A modular home is not built to be moved after it is erected; a mobile home can be moved on its own chassis. Use of the term *modular housing* for mobile homes is unfair.

The mobile home industry prefers *manufactured home* or *manufactured housing* to the *mobile home* designation. Mobile homes are not truly mobile; plus, people in the industry believe *mobile home* has acquired a negative connotation.

Location is no less important a feature for mobile homes than it is for conventional single-family residences. A desirable park will sell a mobile home much as a desirable neighborhood will sell a conventional home. The name of the park could be a strong factor to mention in an ad, as could its newness or its high Woodall Rating (a system of rating parks, with five stars being the highest).

Headings These headings feature location:

These give the park and the size of unit.

EAST VIEW—TRIPLE-WIDE

EAST VIEW—24′ × 60′

Use these headings if the name of the park is not well known.

5-STAR PARK

TRIPLE WIDE—5-STAR PARK

NEW 5-STAR PARK

5★ PARK

CHOICE MIDDLETOWN LOCATION

General headings for mobile home ads include:

MOBILE CASTLE

LIVE IN A PARK

COST LESS

MOBILE HOMES REALLY COST LESS

Body Copy If parks have separate adult and family sections, the location of the coach should be covered in the ad body with:

Located in the family section of one of the area's most desirable parks

If the park allows small pets, you should be sure to cover it with:

Small pets permitted

Location within the park could also be important.

Near recreation area

Steps away from the pool

Walk to the community center.

On the 9th fairway

Choice corner lot for spacious privacy

For old parks you can use *established park* to give what otherwise could be a negative feature a positive image. For older or less desirable parks with lower-than-average rent, emphasize the lower cost.

REASONABLE RENT

SPACE RENT ONLY $100/MONTH

LOWEST RENT IN AREA

LOW PARK RENT

BARGAIN LEASE

3-YEAR LEASE AT $120/MONTH

Lenders as well as buyers often evaluate mobile homes based upon book value. If you are offering a mobile home at less than retail book value, you might state:

Offered below blue book

Offered below NADA book value

The size of the mobile home is very important and should be either in the heading or in the ad body.

Give actual dimensions

24′ × 60′

28′ × 48′—3BR

DOUBLE-WIDE

TRIPLE-WIDE

SUPER DOUBLE-WIDE

WIDE—WIDE—DOUBLE-WIDE

For newer mobile homes you would want to give the year of the coach.

1984 Coachman Deluxe

Advertising the year of older coaches, on the other hand, may produce an undeserved negative response to an excellent home. Let prospective buyers see the coach and then make up their minds.

If the coach is of a prestigious make or is a luxury model, then the make and model should be in the ad.

24′ × 60′ Coachman

Top-of-the-line Coachman

Award-winning Presidential model

Upgraded Winston model

Saratoga Deluxe with stone fireplace

If the park has more than customary recreational facilities, they should be covered.

Pool, sauna and a lot more

Golf membership is included.

T-off for free

Country-club living features golf and tennis.

Other general plus factors for mobile homes:

10′ × 40′ aluminum awning

10′ × 30′ covered deck

8′ × 10′ storage shed

Former display model

Full skirting

If the lot is oversized, say so.

On a 65′ × 100′ lot

Paved drive

Paved double drive

We now have many mobile homes sold with the lot. If the lot is included, say so.

Comes with your own lot

Home & lot

No more rent

You own coach and lot

NEVER A RENT INCREASE
because you own the lot on this...

OWN YOUR OWN LOT

For closings appropriate for mobile home ads, see the section in Chapter Five, *Family Homes.*

Completed Ads for Mobile Homes

This is an attention-getting heading.

The ad is aimed at prospective buyers not fully sold on the idea of living in a mobile home.

YOU WON'T BELIEVE IT

It really is a mobile home but you would never know from its colonial clapboard siding or spacious sun-filled interior. Set on a quiet paved street in the nicest 5-star adult park in Sunnydale, the 2BR and den home features over 1,500 sq. ft. of air-conditioned, luxurious, carefree comfort. Amenities include 2 full baths, quality appliances, a huge covered deck for relaxation, 2-car carport plus a storage building. Better than new, it's priced to please at only $42,000.

Clyde Realty 476-8200

This is probably an older model.

24′ × 60′ GREAT LAKES

Deluxe 2-bath model features a huge master suite plus a completely separate guest suite and paneled den. You can move it or leave it in quiet Westside Park. NADA-book-priced at $18,600. Seller's price for quick sale $16,500. Call us about the great financing available.

Clyde Realty 476-8200

This ad really sells terms and price. Neither the age nor make of the coach are given nor are they really important to the buyers toward whom this ad is aimed.

24′ WIDE—$12,000

Over 1,100 sq. ft. in this super-clean 1½-bath, 3BR model. Set up with full skirting in a small family park. After a low-low down payment, your total monthly payment including park rent will be less than an apartment rental. Call now for a deal you don't want to miss.

Clyde Realty 476-8200

OWN YOUR OWN LOT

behind guarded gates in the friendly community of Palm Greens. The triple-wide, 1950 SF home features 3BR, 2½ baths and comes completely and exquisitely furnished. There is a double carport, oversized storage shed, delightful plantings and a huge screened veranda for relaxation or entertaining. On an extra-large lot on a quiet cul-de-sac, it is walking-close to the clubhouse. This is a better-than-new opportunity not to be missed. At $87,500 you better call quickly.

Clyde Realty **476-8200**

Condominiums

Since most newspapers now list condominiums under a separate *Condos* heading, it may not be necessary to repeat that the property is a condo. Condo buyers generally know what they're looking for, so if your local newspapers don't have separate condo headings, your heading should make it clear.

CONDO—MORNINGSIDE

2BR CONDO—$69,500

CONDO—CONDO—CONDO

CONDOMAXIMUM

CHAMPAGNE CONDOMINIUM
at a most reasonable price

LOFT—CONDOMINIUM

If your newspaper category heading indicates condominiums, your ad heading can be an attention-getter.

NO GRASS TO CUT

TAN ON THE 14′ BALCONY

SELL THE LAWN MOWER

NO MOWING—NO TRIMMING—NO SHOVELING

PICK OF THE LITTER
The best corner unit in the best building in the best block of Bayside

PLEASURE-ORIENTED
No work, just pure enjoyment with this...

EMPTY-NESTERS
It's time to worry about yourself.

CAR-FREE

KISS YOUR CAR GOOD-BYE
walk to everything from this...

FOR CAR-FREE LIVING

BROWN THUMB
Someone else tends to your yard at...

Upper floor in high rise

MOVE ON UP
to this...

HALFWAY TO HEAVEN

THE HEIGHT OF LUXURY

If your unit is in a well-known desirable area or development, headings should emphasize this.

MORNINGSIDE—2BR—2 BATH

Include the price in heading if it is a strong feature.

MORNINGSIDE—$77,000

When new units are still being sold

SUNRISE RESALE—$88,000

While the general rules for writing ads for condominiums are the same as for homes, condominiums do have different features that can help focus your ads.

End unit

Means more privacy

Impressive end unit

Means separate building

Free-standing unit

Less noise and better view

Top-floor unit

More window space and greater privacy

Corner Unit

At last, a corner unit

Elevator building

HI-RISE

Two or three stories

MID-RISE
Built as a condo—not a conversion

ONE-STORY CONDO

First floor

GARDEN UNIT

Swim & Tennis club membership included

Health spa membership included

Valet parking

Off-street parking

Party room in recreation center

Sleeping balcony

Very private patio

Very private balcony

Maintenance-free

Rental service available

Full-time resident manager

Golf, tennis, pool and more

Most units are upgraded to some extent.

Upgraded unit

Upgraded appliances

The addition of the model name adds desirability.

Upgraded Shaugnessy model

Sought-after Shaugnessy model

A hard-to-find Shaugnessy model

If the assessment fees appear low, they should be emphasized.

Monthly assessment only $52

Low monthly assessment

Low condo fee includes everything

Maintenance fee includes heat

Close to clubhouse

Close to pool

Indoor/outdoor pool

Close to courts

An exciting alternative to apartment living

Upgraded beyond belief

A condominium that gives you the privacy of a single-family home

Designed with the emphasis on privacy

A resort-style life-style with big city sophistication

Sophisticated yet so comfortable

Dine on your private balcony with a panoramic view of. . .

18 windows welcome the sunshine in this immaculate corner unit.

Country-club amenities

For a uniquely comfortable urban life-style

Villa-style

Garden unit

Free from the burden of maintenance

Concierge services

Full concierge services

Flower-bedecked *courtyard*

Monitored security

Canopied entry

Never a rent increase

Strategic location

High-rise unit

High in the clouds

Fantasy villa

Association fees only $_________.

Low association fees

All the amenities of a fine resort

More than just a new place to live, it's a whole new way of living.

Resort environment

Manicured greenbelt

Soundproofed walls

Elevator building

Doorman

Denotes quality of construction

Prewar building

Full-service building

You won't have to whisper in this soundproofed...

Whisper no more—fully soundproofed building

More than just a place to live, it's a world of fun and leisure.

Health spa for residents

While most single-family home closings are applicable for condominiums, the following closings are particularly suitable:

Offering a life of quiet sophistication at $_________.

For comfort and uncomplicated living $_________.

The closest thing to carefree living $_________.

Condominium convenience with the privacy of a single-family home for $_________.

Easy living at $_________.

For the opportunity of a life-style $_________.

If you have a large number of condos for sale, a two-column ad such as the following can be very effective because it shows you deal in condos.

WE HAVE CONDOS

Complex	Bedrooms/Baths	Price	
RIDGECREST	2/2	$125,000	F
SKYVIEW	1/1	72,000	UNF
SUNSHINE ESTATES	2/2	106,000	F
MORNINGSIDE	2/2	107,500	UNF
MARINER'S WALK	2/2½	158,000	F
STONE HAVEN	2/2	199,500	F
HILLTOP	1/1	62,500	F
THE RIVIERA	1/1	64,000	UNF
SKYVIEW	2+/1¾	69,900	UNF
COUNTRY CLUB ESTATES	1/1	86,000	UNF
MOUNTAINVIEW	1/1	92,000	F
MOUNTAINVIEW	2/2	147,500	F
RIDGECREST	2/2	115,000	F
NORTHGATE	2/2	199,500	UNF
WESTGATE	2/2	119,000	UNF
RIDGECREST	3/2	119,500	F
MARINER'S WALK	2/2	139,000	F
GOLFVIEW	2/2	139,500	F
MISSION WAY	2/2	139,900	F
MISSION WAY	2/2	239,500	F
MARINER'S WALK	3/2	144,900	UNF
RANCHO PARK	2/2	149,000	UNF
CANYON ESTATES	2/2½	165,000	UNF
HILLSIDE	2/2	395,000	F
CANYON ESTATES	2/2½	495,000	F
INDIAN WELLS	2/2+	275,000	UNF
VISTA POINT	3/2½	319,000	UNF
VISTA POINT	3/3	395,000	F

Clyde Realty **476-8200**

Completed Ads for Condominiums

This ad should be used only where the newspaper category is Condominium. *A superior heading would have been* RIDGECREST. Unusual circumstances *gives the impression this is a very special opportunity.*

JOIN

the discerning people who have discovered the good life at Ridgecrest. Unusual circumstances allow us to offer this sought-after 3BR, 2-bath Ambassador model on the greenbelt close to clubhouse and courts. Bound to sell quickly at $99,500.

Clyde Realty **476-8200**

This ad was prepared for the same condo unit as prior ad. Different features were emphasized. A few more lines of type create a much more effective ad. This ad sells the "sizzle" as well as the "steak."

RIDGECREST

"Upgraded beyond belief" describes this much-sought-after but seldom available 2BR, 2-bath Ambassador model. With the choicest greenbelt location you will enjoy magnificent vistas through the one-way walls of glass. You will want to dine and entertain on your very private flower-bedecked patio. With top-of-the-line appliances, it is truly a rare offering at $99,500.

Clyde Realty **476-8200**

This ad makes this Oxford model appear very desirable.

MORNINGSIDE—$94,000

At last—a 2BR, 2-bath Oxford model priced under $100,000. This rare end unit is only steps away from the pool and hot spa yet offers the privacy of a single-family home. With below-market owner financing, you better call now.

Clyde Realty **476-8200**

You must be very discreet with sexually suggestive ads.

In several states, condominium associations can't discriminate against children.

X-RATED CONDOMINIUM

- Mirrored master bedroom
- Sensuous double shower
- Very private hot spa
- Romantic fireplace

This 2BR, 2-bath corner unit in Morningside assures you maximum privacy.
FOR ADULTS ONLY $77,400

Clyde Realty **476-8200**

Cooperatives and Planned Unit Developments

Cooperatives should be advertised like condos with the only difference being the substitution of *cooperative* for *condominium*.

In many states there are Planned Unit Developments (PUDs). These are similar to condominiums, except that the individual unit owner owns the land under the unit, while the common areas are owned in common. As far as buyers are concerned, they are still condominiums with homeowner associations and assessment fees. An attempt to differentiate is likely to confuse. You would generally advertise PUDs as you would condominiums but add *and you own the land.*

Timeshares

Timeshare developers generally ignore classified advertising in favor of large display ads, billboards, radio, television and direct-mail advertising. They are missing a good thing because the classified section can be an extremely effective method of advertising timeshares, not only for developers but for resales by brokers as well.

People buy timeshares for the same reasons they buy second homes: They are seeking greater enjoyment from their lives. Headings, closings and body copy found in the *Vacation Homes* and *Water-Related Homes* sections earlier in this chapter may also be applicable to timeshares.

Timeshares are most effective when they are advertised under an applicable *Vacation Homes* category. Even if your local paper has a timeshare category, consider advertising under *Vacation Homes* as well.

You should make sure that a reader will not be deceived into believing you are advertising something other than a shared ownership. As in any advertisement, stress the virtues that you believe the property will offer to its purchaser.

Completed Ads for Timeshares

This heading is a real attention-getter.

Many timeshares have exchange privileges.

The one-or two-week price of a timeshare seems very low.

HAWAII IN MINNESOTA

Spend 2 weeks each and every summer in your own luxury 2-bedroom unit on the shores of Island Lake. Of course it includes your own boat for fishing or waterskiing. Enjoy tennis on your own courts or golf on your own course. Or, for a change of pace, you can exchange for 2 weeks at Kona Bay on the Island of Oahu. Best of all, it is yours forever at only $19,900.

Clyde Realty 476-8200

LAKE TOMAHAWK

You want your own cottage for 2 weeks, so why pay for 52? Lovely 2-bedroom chalet fully furnished with dock and boat on a choice sand beach. Now available on a shared-ownership plan. You will vacation in style and the full one-time price is only $8,000.

Clyde Realty 476-8200

The price for the lowest-cost time period is quoted. The desirability of the time slot will affect the price.

TAHOE HOLIDAY

Spend two weeks every year in your own fabulous 3BR, 3½-bath Lake Tahoe chalet. By day, enjoy water and mountain sports, golf and tennis. By night there are the legendary shows, casinos and restaurants of Lake Tahoe. Through a special shared-ownership plan, this millionaire's vacation can be yours for as low as $16,500. For a sample of what the good life is all about, call

Clyde Realty 476-8200

9 Negative Advertising and Fixer-Uppers

Most potential home buyers desire a dream home in picture-perfect condition, just waiting for them to move in: a home that looks straight out of *Better Homes and Gardens.* Therefore, we write most ads in a very positive manner, making the property seem as desirable as possible.

However, one group of buyers is looking for just the opposite. The less picture-perfect a house is, the more they want it. *Dilapidated* and *abandoned* are not dirty words to these buyers. Negative ad fans don't follow the same drummer as the majority.

Roy Brooks

A legendary London, England real estate agent, Roy Brooks, developed a cult-like following of readers of his real estate ads in the 1950s and 1960s. He became a master of the adverse ad. He thoroughly trashed property in a manner that was completely unique. His extreme negativism resulted in queues of customers awaiting an opportunity to see and buy properties he had just denigrated. Mr. Brooks has been credited with single-handedly causing the renovation of the crumbling neighborhoods of Pimlico and Chelsea by luring back well-to-do buyers.

A great deal of the allure of Mr. Brooks's ads seemed to be that they didn't try to sell a property's virtues. People reacted positively because he came across not only as a fair and honest agent but a fun person as well. Some quotes from Mr. Brooks's ads:

> *Space for garage—if you can grub up the roots of an old oak tree;*
>
> *Not the poshest part of. . . but what can you expect for $________ ;*
>
> *Library all of eight feet square suitable for erudite dwarf;*
>
> *Has almost luxury bathroom with removable ladder to secret sunbathing roof garden;*

> *Seedy family house, two rooms in basement. Decor peeling, faded, floral and flyblown. If you are too late to secure this gem, we have a spare along the road more derelict. A lightly built member of our staff negotiated the basement stair but Mr. Halstead went crashing through.*

Roy Brooks also made fun of his clients by describing them as a *hedonist of 19, redheaded sculptress* and *former Harvard lecturer turned tycoon in ladies' underwear.* A classic example of one of his reasons for a sale reads, *One of the big pots in chamber music, leader of a famous quartet, taking up suburban residence with former girl viola pupil, sacrifices excitingly newly built mews residence.*

Advertising in a Roy Brooks vein is likely to be very rewarding. When Mr. Brooks took over writing the ads for his father's firm in the 1950s, he almost immediately tripled the business. The reason, according to Mr. Brooks: "There have been so many lies about housing that if you simply tell the truth you get a disproportionate response." However, before you denigrate a property or give out personal information about an owner, you should make certain the owner approves of your advertising. American owners might not be as understanding as English owners.

The following are a few of Roy Brooks' completed ads:

BROTHEL IN PIMLICO

WANTED: Someone with taste, means and a stomach strong enough to buy this erstwhile house of ill-repute in Pimlico. It is untouched by the 20th Century as far as convenience for even the basic human decencies is concerned. Although it reeks of damp or worse, the plaster is coming off the walls and daylight peeps through a hole in the roof, it is still habitable judging by the bed of rags, fag ends and empty bottles in one corner. Plenty of scope for the socially aspiring to express their decorative taste and get their abode in 'The Glossy' and nothing to stop them putting Westminster on their notepaper. 10 rather unpleasant rooms with slimy backyard. £4,650 Freehold. Tarted up these houses make £15,000.

Roy Brooks

FASHIONABLE CHELSEA,

Lamont Rd. Do not be misled by the trim exterior of this modest Period Res. with its dirty broken windows; all is not well with the inside. The decor of the 9 rooms, some of which hangs inelegantly from the walls, is revolting. Not entirely devoid of plumbing, there is a pathetic kitchen & 1 cold tap. No bathrm., of course, but Chelsea has excellent public baths. Rain sadly drips through the ceiling on to the oilcloth. The pock-marked basement flr. indicates a thriving community of woodworm; otherwise there is not much wrong with the property. In the tiny back garden an Anderson shelter squats waiting . . . . Lse. 40 yrs? G.R. £50. SACRIFICE £6,750.

Roy Brooks

CHELSEA IS FASHIONABLE,

that is why it attracts predatory business men, with their awful wives & poorer envious detractors. All being slowly poisoned by the filthy effluvia of Lots Road Power Station, the Gas Works & a strong whiff from Battersea Power Station (it was only when they found that its corrosive fumes were attacking the fabric of London's ancient buildings that they did a partial filtration). One of my friends in this road (Limterston St.) a successful but still happy architect, loves the place. *"On Saturday afternoon,"* he says, *"I take a bus to Peter Jones & stroll back looking at the shops, the pretty girls. . . ."* This horror has 8 rooms, 2 thrown into one rm. about 32ft., with chimney-piece blood red painted marble & leprous yellow tiles, old shallow sink & coal fuel copper. The coal seems, recently, to have been removed from the bath itself. Upstairs the decor is fairly new, clean and in execrable taste. The oilcloth strikes a jarring note throughout. A small patch of earth behind. Lse. abt. 40 yrs. G.R. £60. ONLY £6,850. KEY OFFICE but tread with caution on the rotten basement boards.

Roy Brooks

FASHIONABLE CHELSEA.

Fine 8 rm. house. 2 bathrms. Consent to let rms. (Estimated income £1,500 p.a. plus owner's suite; 3 gd. rms.) £3,000 spent bringing up to her own high standards by friend of Royalty. (Trekked 800 miles on horseback with 100 bearers & baby brother in meat safe to make African camp for Edward, Prince of Wales. & took *"elevenses"*—stewed duck served in chamber-pot, with Great Queen Magui, aged 102: 13 husbands—2 thrown by herself to the crocodiles, & who had tin of sardines & Golden Syrup on the table to show how English she was . . .) Lse. 10 yrs. Thought renewable. G.R. only £20 p.a. £7,995, try ANY offer.

Roy Brooks

£5,995 FHLD! Broken-down Battersea Bargain. Erected at end of long reign of increasingly warped moral & aesthetic values, it's what you expect—hideous; redeemed only by the integrity of the plebs who built it—well. Originally a one skiv Victorian middle class fmly res, it'll probably be snapped up by one of the new Communications Elite, who'll tart it up & flog it for 15 thou. 3 normal-sized bedrms & a 4th for an undemanding dwarf lodger, Bathrm. Big dble drawing rm. B'fast rm & kit. Nature has fought back in the gdn—& won. Call Sun 3–5 at 21 Surrey Lane, S.W.11. then Brooks.

Roy Brooks

Fixer-Uppers

The most common negative ads are for fixer-uppers. Before you advertise any property as a fixer-upper, obtain the seller's permission if you don't want to face an outraged owner whose most valued possession has been publicly denigrated.

The two primary motivators for fixer-upper buyers are probably self-realization and savings. We all need the feeling of positive accomplishment, but not everyone can attain it through jobs that might offer few challenges and little personal satisfaction. The purchase of an undesirable property, on the other hand, presents a well-defined set of problems that can be overcome. Working with their hands allows people to feel they have some control over their destiny, rather than being controlled by it. People who have personally transformed their homes are likely to receive far more enjoyment from them than do those who have simply purchased a product to meet their needs.

Savings is another positive attraction for fixer-upper buyers. Everyone loves a bargain, and a creative person can transform his or her efforts into a property of far greater value than the sum of the purchase price and materials. Because of the initial price savings, fixer-uppers are often the one way for buyers with limited resources to have the kind of home they really want.

Some handypersons even reap cash profits by fixing up and selling property. Fixer-uppers have spawned a class of gypsy entrepreneurs who buy, move in, fix and sell as a way of life. They profit because they are able to visualize the effects that their labor and material will have on a property.

In the last few years interest in fixer-upper homes has increased because of seminars on profiting from these properties. Like Mr. Brooks, many brokers actually try to make a property sound worse than it is. Then the prospect gets a sense of discovery by realizing the property can be repaired with much less work than the broker indicated. Unethical brokers may even advertise "fixer-uppers" that don't need any work done.

The following terms are often used to describe actual fixer-uppers, but are also used to deceive:

> *Deserted*—A deserted house carries the connotation of disrepair and neglect, though all it really means is that the owners have left it.
>
> *Abandoned*—This term carries the same connotation as *deserted* and can be used interchangeably.

A home in need of some repair but not really a fixer-upper can be described with a simple yet effective heading.

This heading will attract fixer-upper buyers.

SEMI-FIXER-UPPER

Preferred headings for fixer-upper ads would be:

It's simple and it says it all.

FIXER-UPPER

If the price is right, it can be placed effectively in the heading.

FIXER-UPPER $27,000

These headings are effective because they include a positive feature as well as the fact that the property is a fixer-upper.

3BR FIXER-UPPER

FIXER WITH VIEW

FIXER-UPPER—SOUTH-SIDE

ENGLISH—FIXER-UPPER

FIXER-UPPER—COLONIAL

While FIRE DAMAGED *is an excellent heading for fixer-uppers, don't use* flood damaged *because the ad would indicate the property is prone to floods. This would turn off buyers before they had an honest opportunity to evaluate the property.*

FIRE DAMAGED

FIX-N-SAVE

These simple ad headings are excellent but many brokers are not satisfied with simple. The following headings are more imaginative.

Both of these headings indicate the possibility of profit.

SWEEP & REAP

WEED IT AND REAP

Rambling *gives the impression that the house is a long ranch home.*

RAMBLING WRECK

PANIC BUTTON

ABANDONED . . .

Will appeal to the artistic

ABANDONED ARTIST'S CHALET

IT'S A LEMON

Include the price in the heading if it appears unusually low.

HANDYPERSON'S SPECIAL—$29,500

DIAMOND IN THE ROUGH

A GEM IN THE ROUGH

Prewar *carries the connotation of a quality structure.*

PREWAR WRECK

For a larger home

MAGNIFICENT WRECK

A SHAMBLES

DEMOLITION DERBY

BIT OF A MESS

EXECUTIVE—FIXER

WORST HOUSE—BEST STREET

THE WORST-LOOKING HOUSE

PATCH, PAINT & PROFIT

PEELING-PAINT SPECIAL

LEAKING-ROOF SPECIAL

This is probably too subtle for many readers.

HENRY HIGGINS
needed to transform this . . .

TOOLBOX SPECIAL

BRING YOUR TOOLBOX

BRING YOUR PAINTBRUSH

FIX OR TEAR DOWN

JUST A LITTLE SPIT AND POLISH

BRING YOUR HAMMER

PAINTBRUSH NEEDED

These three headings also can be effective if used instead as closings before the price.

NEEDS LOVE

NEEDS TLC

NEEDS LABOR OF LOVE

NEEDS A FACE-LIFT

DUMPY DUPLEX

NEED A TURKEY?

TURKEY OF THE YEAR

UGLY DUCKLING
But could be a swan . . .

HARDY REHABBERS ONLY

FORGOTTEN COTTAGE
It hasn't been lived in for over_________years.

FIXER-UPPER POSSIBILITIES
But it's going to take a lot of work

While this heading would have a positive appeal to fairly literate readers, it is liable to go over the heads of many.

PYGMALION
What can you do to improve this . . .

IN TERRIBLE CONDITION
but this. . . is structurally sound

A TON OF COSMETICS
will be needed to make this. . . presentable.

EL DUMPO

NEGLECTED

For a large house

NEGLECTED GIANT

NEGLECTED RANCH

NEGLECTED—OH! YES!

DILAPIDATED

DILAPIDATED COLONIAL

NEEDS EVERYTHING

The ad body should then read, I'd fix this . . .

IF I HAD A HAMMER

Using this heading the body could read, To transform this ugly duckling into a swan.

MAGICIAN WANTED

High-class *indicates a luxury home.*

You can cover the architectural style, such as Colonial ruin.

HIGH-CLASS DISASTER

SPANISH RUIN

Bad Images The following headings are used frequently, but we recommend strongly against their use. We feel they don't create the proper image, even for a fixer-upper.

Buyers don't mind cleaning but don't like dirt.

DIRTY DOG

DIRTY AS SIN

People want bargains but don't want to be thieves.

STEAL AND FIX

While you want it clear that the property needs a great deal of work, you also want to convey that the structure is basically sound. Seldom is a home not structurally sound, but for your protection you should ask the owner to have a termite and structural inspection. The body of your ad can convey this with:

Before you use the term quality, *you should make certain it applies.*

Quality construction in need of cosmetic surgery

Needs cosmetic repair

The structure is sound

Old but sound

Solid construction

Brick and masonry convey an image of strength. They can be used in a heading such as BRICK RUIN.

Brick

Solid masonry

You might also want to indicate the property can be lived in while the buyer makes repairs:

Presently livable

Barely livable

Livable but. . .

Body Copy Language for the ad body includes:

Make no mistake—there is work to be done.

Needs a few bushels of nails and barrels of paint

Loaded with potential but needs a barrel of paint

Bring your paintbrush and a flair for decorating.

A little spit and polish should dramatically increase the value of this . . .

This makes a good close.

Bring your imagination and some elbow grease.

You can bring this abandoned home back to life.

You can breathe new life into this. . .

A neglected beauty awaiting a Prince Charming

Every fixer-upper-buyer looks for potential.

Lots of potential

Every buyer thinks he or she is the person who can give it.

Needs tender loving care

Describing a room as a possible studio is a definite plus. Fixer-upper-buyers often have an artistic flair.

Possible artist's studio

This. . .home boasts 3BR and 2 baths. What it doesn't boast about is its horrible condition.

Wear your old clothes and bring along aspirin

Overgrown yard and garden

This is a positive image for green thumb buyers.

A jungle of overgrown shrubs and trees

It looks like it fought in World War III and was the loser.

Basically sound structure

Sturdy *colonial*

Be sure it is before you say it

Structurally sound

We scraped the bottom of the barrel to come up with this . . .

A sound structure but badly in need of cosmetic surgery

Closings Some possible closings for fixer-upper ads include:

Bring your hammer $________.

Bring along your toolbox $________.

Toolbox special at $________.

A diamond in the rough for $________.

Bring your imagination $________.

You can make this something special $________.

Hammer-swinger priced at $________.

Awaiting your imagination $________.

A gem in the rough at $________.

Bring your own good taste $________.

You can bring it back to life $________.

The negative works when it comes to fixer-uppers.

Not for the timid $________.

Not for timid souls $________.

Exciting potential for $________.

For the couple who are not afraid of hard work $________.

Quaint it ain't but it's yours at $________.

A little hard work will awaken this sleeping beauty $________.

Touch-up special at $________.

For the creative rehabber $________.

Get on your overalls and do your thing $________.

For ambitious buyers at $________.

Bring your tools and imagination $________.

Trade your work for dollars and save big at $________.

Additional closings appropriate for fixer-upper ads can be found in Chapter Seven in the *Bargain Homes* section.

Completed Ads for Fixer-Uppers

After a negative heading, this ad comes on strongly positive, then leads into the problem.

The type of people interested in fixer-uppers often have artistic talent.

Most people think they are good decorators.

NEGLECTED RETREAT

Nestled on a hillside acre amidst towering trees, this potential artist's hideaway offers old-world charm and craftsmanship in its hardwood floors, beamed ceiling, leaded glass and massive fireplaces. All 8 rooms show the ravages of time and neglect. If redecorating is your thing and you want to start from scratch, this home will make you ecstatic. Bring your color charts. $89,500

Clyde Realty **476-8200**

This heading is attention-getting, but a simple FIXER-UPPER *would have been more effective.*

The ad includes some positive descriptions, describes the problems and suggests a savings possibility. Include the area if it is a desirable one.

IT'S A LEMON

This 3BR, 2-bath rambler has been neglected beyond belief. It's the eyesore of Morningside Heights. If you are willing to start your cleanup with a shovel, this could be your opportunity to save big. $59,000

Clyde Realty **476-8200**

Note how this ad does include strong positive points with 4 bedroom, Morningside Heights, brick *and* colonial.

FIXER-UPPER— 4 BEDROOMS

Murphy's Law says, "Whatever can go wrong will go wrong." This home proves Murphy was right. Just about everything in this Morningside Heights brick colonial that could conceivably break is broken. Toolbox special at $73,500.

Clyde Realty **476-8200**

The reason for the sale explains the condition of the property and the possibility of a bargain. Fixer-uppers don't have to be low-priced.

HIGH-CLASS DISASTER

Just foreclosed and looks it. Sure it needs work, but the price reflects it. You will be getting a 3,400-sq.-ft., 4BR, 3-bath brick executive home in exclusive Morningside Heights for only $180,000.

Clyde Realty 476-8200

Weak Headings The following ads are well written but fail to indicate in their headings they are for fixer-upper properties. In a small-town paper, where every ad is likely to be read, they can be effective, but when they are in competition with perhaps hundreds of other properties, they are likely to be overlooked by fixer-upper buyers.

While the heading is attention-getting, a far more effective ad would be:

FIXER-UPPER
This home auditioned for the Gong Show and lost. . .

THE GONG SHOW

This home auditioned and lost. It has all of the proper parts, 3BR, den, 2½ baths, fireplace and even a decent neighborhood, but one look and you will understand why the owners left it. Disaster priced at $89,500.

Clyde Realty 476-8200

While this heading does not indicate it is a fixer-upper, it attracts the attention of the group it is aimed at.

It tells very little about the house other than what it lacks, but it does set a very positive image. A fixer-upper ad aimed at a particular trade can be extremely productive, as the house will be half-sold before it is shown.

ELECTRICIAN'S DREAM HOUSE

Actually the 19th-century wiring in this two-story colonial home belongs in a museum. If you know your AC from your DC, this property is for you. The house is set back from the street on a spacious lawn. The garage was originally a carriage house and has a storeroom, hobby room or studio above. The house is spic and span and ready to move into, but bring your own electricity. You won't be shocked by the price of $49,800.

Clyde Realty 476-8200

This ad, in the style of Roy Brooks, certainly has an attention-getting heading. While this ad tears down the house, it is really only referring to the decor. The ad also indicates a bargain is possible. Such an ad can be expected to have a positive effect on a great many readers. Be prepared for the calls.

BAWDY HOUSE

Garish decor that a madam would love but a Mrs. would loath. If you have bad taste, this 3BR, 2-bath Nantucket colonial is probably your dream home. We would love to get rid of it and it's priced accordingly at $87,500.

Clyde Realty 476-8200

The heading is not very strong. A better one would be FIXER-UPPER—CLEANER-UPPER. *The ad body is as negative as possible and should be effective for a perverse buyer. While* cheap *should not be used normally in an ad, this is an unusual exception.*

WANT TO CLEAN UP?

If so, we have a house that looks as if it hasn't seen soap or polish since it was built in 1927. It's rumored that under the generations of grime, you will find an 8-room house that has all of the things you would expect, including a huge sun-room and two fireplaces. Not for the faint-hearted, but it is Dirt Cheap at $47,500.

Clyde Realty 476-8200

This negative approach will excite true fixer-upper buyers. It is an excellent heading for smaller papers.

AFRAID OF HARD WORK?

Then don't read this ad. This solid brick home offers 3BR, 2 baths and a choice location. While it could be the best home on the block, make no mistake, it's a genuine mess. If you are a dynamo with a paintbrush, you will save big at $89,500.

Clyde Realty 476-8200

Major surgery *should have been added to the ad body and a heading used which more clearly indicates it's a fixer-upper.*

Good action closing with humor

MAJOR SURGERY

is needed to save this 3BR, 2-bath senior citizen. It shows every one of its 85 years. Recuperation is possible, but it's going to require imagination and tender care. Better hurry, because when we say "it may not last long," we really mean it. $69,500.

Clyde Realty **476-8200**

Outbuildings If the property has outbuildings in rough shape, you can indicate they can be saved by:

Salvageable barn

Salvageable garage

Salvageable guest house

If an outbuilding is really beyond repair, you can make this a plus:

The ramshackle barn will provide you with tons of beams and boards for paneling, rebuilding or?

Unfinished Homes In the same category as fixer-uppers are unfinished homes. Your headings for these could be:

NEEDS FINISHING

NEEDS FINISHING TOUCHES

YOU FINISH

SHELL HOME

ADD YOUR OWN TOUCH

Besides covering size and features, your ad should emphasize:

The hard work has been done.

You could also turn the fact that the house is unfinished from a negative to a positive feature by a statement such as:

Finish to reflect your own tastes.

Other Negative Ads

A twist on the usual ad is the seemingly negative ad, used to get attention by telling the reader not to do something. A great many of us are perverse. Telling us not to do something ensures it will be done. Many years ago a popular song told children not to put beans in their ears. The result was that hundreds of children had to go to doctors to have beans removed from their ears.

This human trait can help call attention to properties that don't have many features to emphasize.

NOT FOR YOU
You don't need this . . .

DON'T READ THIS AD
unless you are interested in a great investment.

DON'T READ THIS AD
unless you are ready to save *$10,000.*

NOT YOUR BASIC HOUSE
If you want a house just like your friends, this is not for you.

DON'T LOOK AT THIS AD
unless you are a serious buyer.

DON'T BUY A HOUSE
unless you have seen Stonehaven.

PROCRASTINATORS
This is your chance to miss buying the home you always dreamed of.

WANT TO BE SORRY?
Then fail to check on this too-good-to-be-true . . .

An attention-getting heading

MASOCHISTS
If you enjoy hurting yourself, don't see this . . .

Here is a completed negative ad:

ATTENTION SKEPTICS

Don't believe us. Check this out for yourself. You know it isn't possible for a quality brick, 3-bedroom, 2-bath ranch on one-half acre in Westwood to be purchased for only $78,500.

Clyde Realty **476-8200**

Though not really negative, many ads for quality homes play down positive features. These ads appeal to people with a great deal of self-assurance.

UNPRETENTIOUS QUALITY

JUST A HINT OF ELEGANCE

UNASSUMING GRANDEUR

MUTED ELEGANCE

10 Country Homes, Horse Property, Farms, Land and Lots

Country Homes

Many people are willing to commute great distances in order to live in a country setting. They willingly sacrifice convenience and urban excitement in order to take their families out of cities where life often appears to be smothered by dirt, crime and lack of privacy. In addition, retirees in increasing numbers are choosing rural living for economic reasons as well as a desire to return to a simpler life-style. Many newspapers have special categories for country home ads, although some combine them with resort or farm properties.

Headings Potential buyers of rural homes will respond to headings like these:

This creates a very positive image.

ON A COUNTRY LANE

JUST A TOUCH OF COUNTRY

COUNTRY ACRE

TOWN-CLOSE—COUNTRY-FRESH

PASTORAL PERFECTION

COUNTRY MAGIC $59,500

BIRD-WATCHER'S PARADISE

ONE OF A KIND—COUNTRY FIND

WHERE HAWKS SOAR HIGH
and the air is crisp and clean

A NEW WAY OF LIFE—COUNTRY-STYLE

ACRE OF DELIGHT

GOD'S HALF ACRE

HEAVEN'S ACRE

The word estate *gives an impression of quality.*

COUNTRY ARISTOCRAT'S ESTATE

ESTATE IN THE COUNTRY

WHERE THE LIVIN' IS EASY

NOT JUST FOR THE BIRDS

COUNTRY LIVING WITH ROOM FOR THE KIDS, DOGS AND HORSES TOO

DOWN A WINDING ROAD
Near the village of...

Attention-getter

PINECONES & CHIPMUNKS
Country living...

EXECUTIVE LIVING IN THE COUNTRY

CUSTOMIZED COUNTRY

QUALITY BUILT & COUNTRY QUIET

COUNTRY QUIET FOR SALE

HASSLE-FREE COUNTRY LIFE

A FRIENDLY LIFE-STYLE

CITY CONVENIENCES AND COUNTRY CHARM

A PLACE WITH SPACE

Ideal if it has a big garden

WANT SELF-SUFFICIENCY?

COMMUTER'S DREAM

COMMUTER'S PRIDE

REFUGE FROM THE CITY

Body Copy Your ad body might include language such as:

Simplicity with a flair

Endowed with country charm

Calendar-scene estate features...

You will discover the joy of country life with this...

Picture the tranquil setting of this...

Charming countrified home

Old-fashioned country home

Everything you need for country living

The freedom-seeking family will appreciate this...

Your haven from metropolitan living

A happy alternative to metropolitan living

No need to worry about the septic system because it has metropolitan water and sewer.

Atlanta phone

Your nearest neighbors are squirrels and a family of raccoons.

The charm is country and so is the quiet.

Situated on a shaded 100′ lot along a country lane

Secluded yet 20 minutes from town

Exciting mini-estate features country living with city flair

Brings city convenience to the country

Combines country charm with city conveniences

Enjoy the simple pleasure of American rural life combined with big-city conveniences.

The country is right outside your door.

Only a short drive to town

Health reasons have a strong appeal to many.

You will enjoy breathing clean air.

Your family will enjoy breathing clean air.

Small storage building could be converted to your guest house

Blends harmoniously with the peaceful country surroundings

See the material under *Farms* later in this chapter for additional descriptive language.

Closings Closings for country home ads include:

Leave the city lights behind $_________.

For an uncramped life-style $_________.

For a simpler life $_________.

Most people regard country living as the ideal setting for raising children.

Do it for your children $_________.

Old-fashioned country living can be yours at $_________.

Enjoy the country life for $_________.

Answer nature's call $_________.

Tranquility can be yours $_________.

Enjoy matchless country beauty at $_________.

More than a home, it's a whole new life-style $_________.

The best of two worlds for $_________.

Country living as it should be $_________.

The country place to be $_________.

For the family who wants to get away from it all, but not too far $_________.

This is country living at its best $_________.

Enjoy the security of country living for $_________.

Completed Ads for Country Homes

While this ad says very little about the house itself, it sells an image of a way of life.

ARTISTS, WRITERS AND LOVERS

Thoreau and Muir would have loved the seclusion of this 6-room stone cottage nestled on a wooded 2-acre site. Hidden from view yet freeway-close to town, it offers today's conveniences coupled with the quiet life of long ago. If you are seeking a peaceful place, prepare yourself for your dream fulfillment $94,500.

Clyde Realty 476-8200

This attention-getting heading for a country home is targeted at the commuter.

Notice how this ad gives the reader a feeling of ownership.

The ad makes 40 minutes seem a small price to pay.

IS IT WORTH THE DRIVE?

to come home to an almost-new clapboard, double-chimney, 3BR, 2-bath colonial set back among the trees in woods that belong to you. The home features a paved drive, 2½-car garage with workroom, family room and full basement. It offers all of today's conveniences including central air combined with a country charm that has almost been forgotten. The patio off the sun-drenched kitchen will be your favorite spot for relaxation as you watch the squirrels gather hickory nuts and acorns from your trees. There can be no better place than this to raise a strong family. If you feel this is worth a 40-minute drive from the city, it can all be yours at $158,500.

Clyde Realty 476-8200

This ad tells very little about the house, which is probably an older home. The ad does a good job of selling small-town living in a few words.

IN A QUIET VILLAGE

Cows graze across the quiet lane from this very pleasant 3BR American traditional. Walking-close to schools and general store, the home features a huge garden, family orchard, a small barn and plenty of room for a family to grow. While commuting-close, it's still small-town priced at $68,500.

Clyde Realty 476-8200

Attention-getting heading

DON'T NEED A COUNTRY GIRL

City girls will love this almost-new raised brick ranch set in a wooded acre overlooking a sparkling stream. The 1½ sumptuous baths, orchard stone fireplace, gleaming hardwood floors, country kitchen with all of the built-ins, redwood deck and 2-car garage provide city conveniences combined with country charm. The school bus stops at the door and the Civic Center is only 1 hour away. Living as it should be can be yours at $84,500.

Clyde Realty 476-8200

This ad appeals to retirees and creates a positive image with rocking-chair-ready front porch *and* dining room suitable for family reunions *as well as the references to a workroom, hobbies and gardening. If the publication were running a great many ads for country property, then a better heading would be* RETIRE TO THE COUNTRY *to get the attention of the particular group the ad is aimed at.*

COUNTRY ADDICTION

One look at this brick farmhouse framed by flowering dogwoods and you will be hooked on country life. The two-story home features 3 or 4 bedrooms, an old-fashioned front parlor, large living room, a dining room suitable for family reunions, a real country kitchen and a rocking-chair-ready front porch. There is also a garage with separate workshop and a huge red barn for animals, hobby use, studio or? The 3-acre site includes the perfect sunny spot for your garden. It is easy to enjoy the country life at only $87,500.

Clyde Realty 476-8200

Horse Property

Close-in property zoned for horses will attract horse people like a lodestone. To many buyers, a good place for their horses is even more important than the people house that goes with the property.

Some newspapers have special categories for horse property. In this case there is no need to repeat it in your heading. Cover other attractive features instead. When your local papers don't have such categories, the heading becomes the place to announce that horses can be kept on the property. This is done fairly simply.

A HORSE OF COURSE

HORSE PROPERTY

HORSE COUNTRY

HORSE SENSE

WHOA THAR

WHOA NELLIE

MAKE YOUR HORSE HAPPY

A PLACE TO HANG YOUR SPURS

HORSING AROUND

GREAT PLACE FOR HORSES

HORSE PEOPLE

HORSE LOVERS

HORSE-LOVER'S DELIGHT

GET A HORSE
or several to fill the 4-stall barn.

HEY COWBOY/COWGIRL
There is room on this range to keep several horses.

HOLD YOUR HORSES
in the three corrals that go with this. . .

HORSE, COW OR CAMEL

EQUESTRIANS

EQUESTRIAN ESTATE

EQUESTRIAN CENTER

EQUESTRIAN ENCHANTER

ZONED FOR ANIMALS

KIDS AND KRITTERS

ANIMAL HOUSE
Room for your horse, cow, pigs and a gaggle of geese with this. . .

HORSES, DOGS AND KIDS

BRING YOUR HORSE

HORSE RANCH

Horse buyers perk up when they see such features as:

In many areas, the number of acres determines how many horses can be kept.

ZONED FOR 6 HORSES

TRAINING RING

RIDING ARENA

LIGHTED RIDING ARENA

PIPE CORRAL

2 CORRALS

HORSE WALKER

Perimeter and cross-fencing

Fenced and cross-fenced

This creates a very positive image.

Thousands (or hundreds) of feet of white board fencing surround this elegant. . .

HORSE BARN

RED BARN

Horse barn with Dutch doors

Horse barn with tack room

Tack room with shower

If no stalls in barn

Barn has space for 6 double box stalls

6 box stalls

2 double stalls

Adjoins miles of bridle trails

This means there are trails within the area.

Access to miles of riding trails

2 acres of alfalfa

2 acres of pasture

Watered pasture

Paddocks with accommodations for *brood mares*

Closings for horse-related properties could include:

Put your brand on this spread for $_________.

The ideal buy for serious equestrians $_________.

It makes horse sense at $_________.

The perfect spot to hang your spurs at $_________.

For horses and children this is the place at $_________.

A place for happy horses and people too $_________.

Completed Ads for Horse Property

Though cute, it does convey a very positive image.

If in a Horse *classification, this heading might be effective; if not, it might be overlooked by a horse owner.*

MIGHTY PURTY SPREAD

Raise horses, dogs and kids on this 5-acre fenced and cross-fenced ranch. Features a young 3BR, 2-bath city-style home that any country girl or boy would love. Two corrals, 4-stall horse barn with tack room and lots more. About $10,000 down should put your brand on the ranch. Full price $98,500. Call "Tex" Johnson at:

Clyde Realty 476-8200

This attention-getting heading tells the reader it's a horse property.

If the house had more than one bath, it would have been mentioned.

GET A HORSE

and ponies or even a cow to fill the 4-stall red barn. Nestled on 10 fenced park-like acres sprinkled with giant oaks, the 3BR traditional ranch home is enhanced by hardwood floors and a native stone fireplace. Extras include a 30′ × 30′ garage/workshop and a family orchard with apple, pear, plum and peach trees. Less than an hour to the city, it's your opportunity to return to old values and real family living. Excellent owner financing available and priced to move fast at $169,500.

Clyde Realty 476-8200

Attention-getting heading

FOR A HAPPY HORSE

Just a small spread, but it can be yours. 2½ acres, 2 fenced pastures, corral, 2-stall horse barn with tack room and a ranch house you will be proud of. 3BR, 2 baths, massive stone fireplace, loads of wood paneling and a 2-car garage with a separate workroom. It's a place for happy horses and people too. Yours at $87,500 with low-down owner financing available.

Clyde Realty 476-8200

This is a real attention-getting heading.

HORSE MANURE

Plenty of room for that and horses too with the prettiest 20-acre spread this side of the Rio Grande. An almost-new 4BR, 2½-bath ramblin' ranch with central air sits on a knoll overlooking the lush fields that are fenced and cross-fenced with thousands of feet of white board fencing. The western-style barn has 4 double stalls, 2 single stalls plus a tack room with its own shower. The perfect spot to hang your spurs at $170,000.

Clyde Realty 476-8200

A simple but very effective heading. This ad is structured to invite further inquiry. Very little is said about the house.

HORSE RANCH $169,500

Spread over 8 rolling acres only 30 minutes from the Beltline is the ranch that dreams are made of. The cedar and river rock main house has all the features you would expect in the perfect ranch house. Outbuildings include a gambrel-roofed red horse barn, equipment shed and workshop. An RV hookup for your traveling friends, corrals and western fencing make this the ranch to be envied. If you want happy horses and a happy family too, call now and ask about the exceptional financing available.

Clyde Realty 476-8200

Farms

Ads should, of course, be directed at the group of people that you believe will supply a buyer for a particular property. The market for farm property may be divided into several such groupings:

Independent professional farmers are looking for farms that are producing or can produce crops to pay off indebtedness and make a profit. Because of the huge costs to enter farming, increases in productivity and foreign competition, this group has been declining in number.

While some *investors* hope to make a profit on large-scale operations, most investors hold farms for appreciation and the tax shelter for the farm income provided by depreciation of improvements and orchards.

Gentleman farmers might be interested in appreciation and tax advantages, but they are also farm operators, usually with hired help. They usually buy or build well-maintained showplace farms. Gentleman farmers usually live full- or part-time on their farms, and pride of ownership is of extreme importance. They may want an operation they can be proud of more than they want profit. Of course, they expect their losses to shelter the profit from other investments.

Hobby, part-time and *retirement farmers* are usually retirees and people with other income using smaller farms to escape to a way of life. Often a desire for a simpler life or self-sufficiency motivates these buyers, who may have little or no farming background.

For the Farmer

Headings that appeal to real farmers include:

Generally, the size should be in the heading, as this is of prime importance to real farmers.

A FARMER'S FARM—400 ACRES

FAMILY FARM—120 ACRES

Use price in the heading if it appears quite reasonable.

FAMILY FARM—$190,000

REAL FARMERS—*400* ACRES

Repeating the word farm *is not necessary if under a farm heading.*

***400* ACRES—$190,000**

CATTLE RANCH—*1,400* ACRES

Two crops per year

DOUBLE CROPPER—*160* ACRES

A good attention-getter

STOP LOOKING—START MILKING

Grade A *is very important; it determines the price paid for milk.*

GRADE A DAIRY FARM—*120* ACRES

IT'S ALL GRADE A—*120* ACRES

IRRIGATED ALFALFA FARM—*640* ACRES

SEA OF GRASS
940-acre cattle ranch

DAIRYMAN'S PRIDE—*100* ACRES

STOCKMAN'S PRIDE—*620* ACRES

Can use CROP *as heading*

***400* ACRES OF ALFALFA**

Attention-getting headings

BEEF UP YOUR INCOME
320-acre cattle ranch

FOR THE BIRDS
Outstanding poultry ranch

WHO SAYS MONEY DOESN'T GROW ON TREES?
90-acre apple orchard

Attention-getting when low per-acre cost

LESS THAN *$800* PER ACRE

DIVERSIFIED FARM—*800* ACRES

Low-price farm could also put price in heading

FARMIN', BARGAIN—*120* ACRES

HIGH-PRODUCING SOYBEAN FARM

A WORKING FARM

***160*-ACRE WORKING FARM**

***1,320*-ACRE WORKING RANCH**

While every farm buyer is interested in total acreage, real farmers are particularly interested in the breakdown of the acreage as well.

100 acres in government program

90% tillable

800 deeded acres

40 acres under plow

60-acre pasture

160 tillable acres

10-acre tobacco allotment

7,000-lb. tobacco allotment

40-acre peanut allotment

240-acre tillable—balance pasture

10-acre woodlot

90 acres currently in alfalfa

Leased grazing rights in *3,000* acres

BLM lease for *3,000* additional acres

A real farmer will know BLM stands for Bureau of Land Management.

The capacity of the land can also be shown as:

Pasture for *120* cows

Will carry *120* cow units

Capacity for *600* feeder pigs

120 bushels of corn per acre reported last year

Said to be one of the best-producing farms in the area

A self-sustaining cattle operation capable of carrying *1,200* cattle units

Pasture can be described as:

Improved pasture

This means some leveling and planting of grasses.

Unimproved pasture

Means no leveling or planting

Natural pasture

Native pasture

These two descriptions mean the same as unimproved *but have a more favorable connotation.*

An adjective appropriate to pasture is *lush*: *lush improved pasture*. For nonfarmers, *parklike pasture* gives an extremely favorable impression.

Water is, of course, important for all farming. Real farmers want it for stock and irrigation. You can cover water with statements such as:

3 wells

Artesian well

Nonfarmers love artesian wells because they see them as giving something for nothing.

Drip irrigation

Overhead irrigation

Includes ample water rights

4″ drilled well

Natural spring

Year-round flowing river

Seasonal stream

½ mile of river frontage

Irrigation lines

240 acres irrigated and tiled

Irrigation water allotment

Creek could be used for irrigation

Creek presently used for irrigation

4 ponds

Land is well watered

Blessed with abundant water

Types of soil vary across the nation and even on the same farm. Soil types should be ascertained and included in ads aimed at real farmers with language such as:

90 acres silt loam

90 acres productive silt loam

90 acres deep loam

90 acres productive bottomland

90 acres fertile bottom

90 acres rich loam

The general topography is important and can be expressed as:

Gently rolling

Level to gently rolling

100 rolling acres

Easy rolling terrain

Bottomland

Flatland

Accessibility is very important, especially for dairy farms whose milk is picked up daily.

Paved road

County highway

All-weather road

Treated gravel road

On county-maintained road

½ mile of road frontage

½ mile off state highway

3 miles to town

3 miles to progressive town

Buildings are, of course, important. When the house is better than normally expected, it should be covered in detail. When buildings are larger than normal-size, that should be included:

30′ × 120′ machine shed

40′ × 100′ pole barn

80-stanchion barn

40′ × 100′ open-loft barn

11-room house

6 silos

4 Harvestor silos

Brand name for particularly desirable metal silo

Three *60,000*-bu grain bins

Modern *7*-room house

In many parts of the country, modern *means inside plumbing when used in a farm ad.*

42-stall barn

Some other features that could be of importance to real farmers:

If there is a gas well on property

Free gas

Milking parlor

Automatic feeders

Automatic barn cleaner

Family orchard

138 apple trees

Thriving fruit orchard

Fenced and cross-fenced

This could mean income.

Gravel pit on property

Price and terms are, of course, important and should be covered as in any ad.

Closings appropriate for real farmers include:

Farm with pride $________.

A farm with a future $________.

Farmer's choice at $________.

Rancher's choice at $________.

For the family with vision $________.

Insure your future now $________.

One of the finest farms we have seen $________.

A wise family investment $________.

For your family's sake $________.

For the agribusinessperson $________.

Make no mistake, this is a working ranch at $________.

Farm Investors

For farm ads targeted toward investors, you could use headings such as:

180-ACRE TAX CROP

TAX FARM

FARM NOW—DEVELOP LATER

FARM—IN THE PATH OF PROGRESS

$90,000 DEPRECIATION

Other factors of particular interest to investors:

Owner will lease back

Lessee available

$300,000 of depreciable assets

½ mineral rights

Development possibilities

Subdivision possibilities

Closings appropriate for investors include:

Exciting potential at $________.

You will reach for your checkbook when you see the price $________.

Investment-priced at $________.

Investor-priced at $________.

Impressive at $________.

For the investor with vision $________.

The ultimate tax shelter $________.

Tax-errific at $________.

Ask us about the tax benefits $________.

Gentlemen Farmers

The true gentleman farmer wants the feeling of pride that ownership gives, in addition to tax benefits. Because the gentleman farmer will generally live on the farm either weekends or full time, *big-city* conveniences and living standards are important. The gentleman farmer generally does not want to rough it. The gentleman farmer likes exotic animals, unusual crops and a showplace operation. He is willing to pay for these indulgences with a loss or break-even operation, though some large operations do turn out to be profitmakers. The gentleman farmer usually buys out of emotion but tries to justify it as an investment. Examples of ad headings that appeal to gentlemen farmers:

YOUR OWN EMPIRE *800* ACRES

YOUR OWN WORLD *800* ACRES

FAMILY SHOWPLACE

A SHOWPLACE—*800* ACRES

BE A COUNTRY SQUIRE

COUNTRY SQUIRE

HISTORIC FARM

STORYBOOK FARM *90* ACRES

STORYBOOK RANCH

HILLTOP FARM

HILLTOP RANCH

GENTLEMAN'S FARM

GENTLEMAN'S RANCH

FARM WITH PRIDE *$250,000*

PASTORAL PERFECTION *120* ACRES

SPLENDOR IN THE GRASS

WEEKEND FARM

For ranches and farms with a landing strip

FLYING COWBOY/COWGIRL RANCH

FLYING FARMER

The name of the farm can be used, especially if it sounds picturesque.

CEDARBURG FARM

Water frontage for recreation is a strong selling point to gentlemen farmers.

LAKESIDE FARM—*90* ACRES

RIVER RANCH—*90* ACRES

The name of the family who settled the farm adds individuality and desirability.

KNUTSON FAMILY HOMESTEAD—*160* ACRES

EXECUTIVE'S FARM

BE LORD OR LADY OF THE MANOR

***900*-ACRE EMPIRE**

Ideal for a big house and acreage

START A DYNASTY ON THIS . . .

Appeals to nostalgia and western buffs

SHADES OF THE OLD WEST

OLD WEST RANCH
Zane Grey would have felt at home on this 1,200-acre working ranch.

OUT OF THE PAGES OF ZANE GREY

BE THE MONARCH OF THE RANGE

THE OLD WEST IS ALIVE AND WELL
on this__________.

THE OLD WEST STILL EXISTS

PICTURE-POSTCARD FARM

CURRIER & IVES FARM

Use the ranch name if it is colorful.

BAR-T RANCH

The farm house should be emphasized in the ad in the same manner as you would advertise any comparable home.

Any historical significance of the property will be important to the gentleman farmer as an additional cause for pride.

The abstract of title could give you some excellent advertising ideas.

The historic Knutson farm established by a federal land grant in 1837

Manor house built in 1837

In the same family since 1843

If held by one family for a long time

This is the first time this farm has been on the market in 140 years.

If a former owner was well known

Formerly owned by ________

Keep in mind that the gentleman farmer may be less interested in production than esthetics. Features that would only mildly interest real farmers could clinch a sale with a gentleman farmer. Language likely to interest gentlemen farmers includes:

These descriptions carry an attractive image.

Dutch barn

Old red barn

Easy management is a strong plus for gentleman farmers as well as investors.

Complete cattle-working facilities were specifically designed for easy management.

Possible landing strip

Miles of white board fencing

Just the place for purebred cattle and thoroughbred horses

Farm pond stocked with bass

Bass-stocked pond

Trout-filled stream

With abundance of wildlife

Professional management available

Closings suitable for gentleman farmer ads:

Makes country living irresistible $________.

Be the master of your own domain $________.

Be a land baron (or baroness) for $________.

Be a country squire $________.

The life of a country squire is yours at $________.

An appeal to reason

Buy the entire farm for less than the price of a city home $________.

Custom country comfort for $________.

Quality country living for $________.

Move up to country pleasure $________.

Farm in style $________.

Pamper yourself $________.

Enjoy country life for $________.

The good life awaits you $________.

For the blue-jeans executive $________.

An outstanding agricultural estate $________.

Treat yourself to the good life $________.

Enjoy pastoral perfection for $________.

Make your dreams a reality $________.

The best in country living $________.

The best in town and country living can be yours at $________.

Create your estate $________.

Your own private world $________.

Make your life come alive $________.

Hobby, Part-Time and Retirement Farmers

These farmers usually buy smaller farms that are not expected to provide a full family income when conventional farming techniques are used with conventional crops. Hobby farms are usually purchased by city dwellers for a variety of reasons, including:

A better place to raise a family
Escape from city crime and grime
Escape from a job
Escape from stress
A desire for self-sufficiency
A desire for a simpler life
A desire to work with the hands

These farms can be advertised under *Farm* headings or under headings for *Home and Acreage,* if available in your newspaper.

Headings Ad headings designed to reach this group of buyers use more emotional language than is found in the previous categories.

MOTHER EARTH FARM *20* ACRES

SELF-SUFFICIENCY FARM

SELF-SUFFICIENCY AND MORE

BE SELF-SUFFICIENT—*40* ACRES

***40* ACRES AND INDEPENDENCE**

SELF-SUFFICIENCY RETREAT

BACK TO BASICS

BACK TO THE FARM—*40* ACRES

THE GOOD EARTH

BACK TO YOUR ROOTS

FIND YOUR ROOTS

CORNUCOPIA HOBBY FARM—*10* ACRES

YOUR OWN CORNUCOPIA

THAT COUNTRY FEELING

HARVEST THE GOOD LIFE

Farms where artificial fertilizers and insecticides have not *been used are attractive to many people.*

ORGANIC FARM

ORGANIC ORCHARD

This heading carries an image of a clean and neat small farm.

GRANDMA'S FARM

A FARM FOR YOUR FAMILY—*40* ACRES

GREEN & GRASSY *40* ACRES

ACRES OF DELIGHT

HEIGH-HO THE DAIRY-O

VEST-POCKET FARM

CHICKENS & DUCKS

Gives a pleasant image

WINDMILL FARM

FAMILY HOMESTEAD

BEGINNER'S FARM—*40* ACRES

Include the price in the heading if it appears reasonable.

STARTER FARM—$69,500

FARMIN' BARGIN—$69,500

If there are peach trees

A PEACHY PLACE

MINI-FARM—MAXI-VALUE

FARMETTE—10 ACRES

RANCHETTE—10 ACRES

HOBBY FARM

WEEKEND FARMER

Sets a positive image

A LITTLE RED BARN

COUNTRY CHARMER

Attention-getting heading

NUTS
and fruit trees in the orchard

Provides a pleasant, nostalgic image

FROM CURRIER & IVES

A rough farm

PIONEER FARM

Water frontage is important.

You can use a fixer-upper-type ad for these farms. See Chapter Nine.

RIVER FARM—10 ACRES

ABANDONED HILLTOP FARM

FORGOTTEN FARM

WOODSY FARM

THAT COUNTRY FEELING

RETIREMENT FARM 60 ACRES

OLD TIME FARM

FARMLET 20 ACRES

MINI-FARM 20 ACRES

OLD RED BARN
included with this. . .

WOBBLY BARN

A QUIET COUNTRY FEELING

MAKE HAY
and a variety of crops on this. . .

TAKE TO THE COUNTRY

JUST A BASIC FARM—20 ACRES

GO COUNTRY-STYLE

BARN SIDING
You also get the whole barn with this. . .

Body Copy The house should be described as you would a comparable home. However, an older farm house can be given a positive image with words such as:

Traditional farm home

Old-time farm home

For older homes without plumbing, you could state:

Solid 5-room home needs modernization

Comfortable home needs modernizing

For older barns you can state:

Hayloft barn

Old stone barn

Gambrel barn

Massive barn

Solid barn of hand-hewn timbers

Solid barns

Usable barn

Barn needs attention

Ancient barn built of hand-hewn timbers

Old-time barn

Weathered barn

Additional positive features that could appeal to small farm buyers:

On country lane

On quiet country lane

On quaint country lane

Windmill-powered well

Offering pastoral tranquility

Country living at its tranquil best

Pond site

Hydropower is a strong feature for some buyers.

Hydropower possibilities

BE ENERGY SUFFICIENT
Possible water generator site

Possible dam site for lake and hydropower

Surrounded by acres of gently rolling hills

Walk to fishing

Your own fishing pond

Spring-fed pond

Abundance of wildlife

Live in your own wildlife preserve

Enough mature timber to build several homes

Contains marketable timber

Woodlot will meet your heating needs

Woodlot contains ash, hickory, walnut and oak

Whenever equipment is included, stress this fact.

Full complement of modern well-maintained equipment

Easy drive to . . .

Closings Effective ad closings for these small farms sum up the appeal of country living.

More than just a place to live, it's a new way of life $________.

Have room to live $________.

Ideal for the energetic couple $________.

Declare your independence $________.

Your piece of paradise for $________.

For the rugged individualist $________.

It will give your life a purpose $________.

Not just a home, it's a new way of life $________.

Live off the land $________.

For the family who craves self-sufficiency $________.

Be your own boss $________.

Country contentment for $________.

Let this land work for you $________.

Break away from the city $________.

Your chance for a better way of life $________.

A place to find yourself $________.

For your family's sake $________.

Bring this abandoned farm back to life $________.

Get back to the land for $________.

Back to country basics for $________.

The perfect retirement farm $________.

Escape from city life for $________.

Your escape kit from city life $________.

An investment in your family's future $________.

Plant your roots here $________.

Your ticket to country living $________.

Escape to the country $________.

Escape to the simple life $________.

For a new way of family life $________.

A family investment at $________.

Start a whole new life $________.

Retiring owner will turn paradise over to you for $________.

Peace of mind for $________.

Room to breathe $________.

Leave city life behind for $________.

Completed Ads For Various Farms

This attention-getting heading is aimed at farmers interested in cattle.

If there is new financing, Truth-in-Lending advertising requirements would have to be considered.

BEEF FACTORY

This 1,280-acre spread will carry 840 cattle units. Fenced and cross-fenced, it has ample water with a natural flowing spring, 3 ponds and 2 wells. A fine set of buildings including two modern homes. A real family ranch at $750,000 with $150,000 down.

Clyde Realty 476-8200

A fixer-upper heading also would have been appropriate.

This ad is targeted at a family seeking a simpler life and willing to work. The ad waves a challenge in front of the reader.

CAN YOU MEASURE UP?

This abandoned 60-acre farm needs a pioneer family willing to carve out a family homestead with their own hands. Solid 6-room home needs modernization, fields need clearing and fences mending. Good well and outbuildings. Set in a picturesque valley at the end of a country lane. Your chance for a better life with very little down, $60,000 full price.

Clyde Realty 476-8200

This gentleman farmer ad paints an idyllic picture and places the reader in an ownership role.

ARMCHAIR FARMER —300 ACRES

Separate home for your tenant while you watch the crops grow from the veranda of the century-old 12-room colonial manor house that has been completely renovated to provide the ultimate in fine living combined with the charm of yesteryear. 160 acres tillable, balance in native pasture and woodlot. In the evening you will see deer crossing your meadow to drink at the trout stream that crosses your property. Offering everything you deserve, including tax benefits at $340,000.

Clyde Realty 476-8200

This ad sells benefits to the investor.

Inviting the accountant flatters the would-be buyer and gives the investment an air of seriousness and quality.

TAX FARM

This picturesque 80-acre foothill farm stands in the logical path of progress. Until you are ready to develop it, you can expect a yearly crop of significant tax benefits. Come in now and bring your accountant along. The price: $160,000 with flexible owner financing.

Clyde Realty 476-8200

This heading is aimed at real farmers.

Farm ads for real farmers provide more facts than images.

320 ACRES—
GRADE A DAIRY

This real-farmer's farm has 200 tillable acres of deep loam, 80 acres in improved pasture and the balance in unimproved wooded pasture. There is ample water with 3 wells and two ponds. The excellent set of buildings includes a 9-room brick home only 7 years old, a brand-new machine shed, modern milking parlor, 2 large barns, 3 Harvester silos and much more. One look and you will want to start farming at $350,000 with owner financing available.

Clyde Realty 476-8200

The name of the farm adds desirability.

This ad sets a mood and gives strong features for the nonfarmer. It ends with tax benefits to allow the buyer to justify the purchase.

BE A COUNTRY SQUIRE

We are proud to offer the historic 640-acre Hilltop Farm near Westchester that has been in the same family for over 150 years. A stately Victorian home with all of the modern amenities reigns over the beautiful countryside. Miles of white wood fencing, a 3-acre pond stocked with huge bass and a mouth-watering family orchard are just a few of the features that will delight you. There are two additional homes ideal for tenants and/or guest houses. Generations of family pride show in this farm. Offering the successful executive country living at its best plus interesting tax benefits, at $700,000 with negotiable terms to a strong buyer.

Clyde Realty **476-8200**

Undeveloped Land

Undeveloped or raw acreage includes everything from forests to deserts. It is land that has not been subdivided into small parcels for homes or businesses, nor has it been improved. Undeveloped land is normally sold by the acre at a much lower price than smaller subdivided parcels.

You should keep in mind that every parcel of land is valuable to someone at some price. The desire to own land is very strong in many people and fills a basic security need. You will see that people buy raw land for a number of reasons. Much of the language used for farms is also applicable to undeveloped land.

Subdividers Ads can be written to appeal to subdividers with headings such as:

SUBDIVISION POTENTIAL—40 ACRES

SUBDIVIDERS—PRIME 40

40 ACRES—200 LOTS

40 ACRES—SUBDIVISION-READY

160 ACRES—FUTURE CITY

40 ACRES—WASHINGTON COUNTY

Location is very important for subdividers.

SUBDIVIDE
this 160-acre parcel.

40 ACRES WITH A FUTURE

$4,200 PER LOT
will be your total land cost on this 40-acre parcel suitable for 160 lots.

For a large parcel

ATTENTION—CITY BUILDERS

This heading is an attention-grabber for a large property requiring substantial cash.

BIG BOYS AND GIRLS ONLY
320-ACRES—SUBDIVISION-READY

Subdividers are very interested in availability of utilities. Your ad body can include this information:

All utilities available

Natural gas available

Sewer line within 1/4 mile

Additional items of interest for subdividers include:

Engineering work completed for. . .

Some engineering work completed

Completed feasibility study for. . .

Zoned R3

Master-planned for town houses

Gently rolling

Avoids the monotony of a flat parcel without the great expenses associated with steep slopes

Favorable percolation tests

For septic systems

Beech and oak-covered

A wooded parcel is highly desirable. Subdividers try to leave as many trees as feasible to aid sales.

Some specific closings for land aimed at subdividers:

Development-ready at $________.

Prime for development at $________.

Ready to go at $________.

Waiting for development at $________.

Make this a new city for $________.

Less than $3,800 per lot at $187,000.

Investors Many buyers of raw land buy for appreciation in value, not for their own use. The following can be used in ad headings or within the ad body to appeal to investors:

FUTURE CITY

IN PATH OF PROGRESS

IN PATH OF DEVELOPMENT

IN PATH OF ANNEXATION

ANNEXATION-READY

CENTER OF BOOMING ANTELOPE VALLEY
Squeezed between the rapidly expanding communities of Lancaster and Palmdale

Not presently zoned commercial

FUTURE COMMERCIAL POTENTIAL

Mention a financially desirable use.

POSSIBLE FUTURE RV PARK

POSSIBLE RV-PARK SITE

FUTURE SHOPPING CENTER?

FUTURE INDUSTRIAL PARK?

Investors love profit or income from any source, so even the possibility of profit should be included.

All mineral and gas rights included

Mineral rights included

Includes 50% of mineral and gas rights

Potential for subdividing

Subdivision possibilities

Parcel split possible

An impressive investment

Exciting potential

Includes leased mineral rights

Agricultural lease available

Specific closings for investor ads include:

Invest in the future $________.

Own the good earth $________.

For your future $________.

For a secure future $________.

For the investor with vision $________.

Exciting potential at $________.

Outdoor People Many prospective buyers for undeveloped property consider themselves outdoor people. They like the idea of owning a piece of the wild.

YOUR OWN WILDERNESS—40 ACRES

YOUR WILDERNESS DOMAIN

YOUR OWN FOREST PRESERVE

YOUR OWN PRIVATE PRESERVE

ROUGH AND READY

WILD CRITTERS ABOUND
on this 40-acre paradise.

NATURE-BUFFS' DELIGHT—10 ACRES

HUNTING REFUGE—80 ACRES

YOUR OWN GAME REFUGE

OUTDOORSPERSON'S PARADISE

BIRD-WATCHER'S PARADISE

DUCK-HUNTER'S PARADISE

DUCK-HUNTER'S HAPPINESS

HUNTER'S—40

NATURE'S—40

UNDISTURBED 40

ACRES OF ACRES

A TERRIFIC 10

IT'S A 10

LAND LOTS OF LAND

TAKE 5

$90 PER ACRE

WILDERNESS FOR SALE

FOR LAND'S SAKE

THIS IS THE FOREST PRIMEVAL

AH WILDERNESS—40 ACRES

FISHERMAN'S PARADISE

HIGH 40 ACRES

Indicates land is not swampy or flood-prone

BE A HOMESTEADER—40 ACRES

WILD & WONDERFUL—40 ACRES

NATURE KNOCKS

CALL OF THE WILD

40 ACRES OF FUN

40 WOODED ACRES TO EXPLORE

YOUR PRIVATE CAMPGROUND

Wilderness trails for riding or hiking

Unspoiled splendor

Spring-fed pond

Fishing pond

Trout stream

RV hookup

12 undulating hilltop acres

Meandering trout stream

Sparkling trout stream

Creek with swimming hole

Possible dam site for your own lake

Deer and bear sighted on property

Wild critters abound on this 40-acre wilderness.

Presently home to deer, quail and pheasant

You will feed the deer in your own backyard.

Enjoy camping, fishing and swimming now and build later.

With a great swimmin' hole

Located in the center of a hunting and fishing paradise

Tying in a parcel to the historical past makes the parcel more desirable to many buyers.

Old logging trail crosses property

On the old Tucson-to-Phoenix stage line

You might find arrowheads along the sparkling creek crossing this . . .

It hasn't changed at all since Geronimo roamed this valley.

Carve your homestead out of the wilderness.

Just 80 minutes from ________

Commuting distance

Some large timber

Marketable timber

Timber could be marketed

Timber has not been cut in over 80 years

See Chapter Three for additional references to trees and Chapter Eight for water-related parcels.

Closings for outdoor-people ads could include:

Answer the call of the wilderness $________.

For decades of family fun $________.

You can be a Daniel Boone $________.

Be a pioneer for $________.

Nature lovers, call now $________.

Insure your wilderness vacations $________.

Own a piece of America's past $________.

Escapists There are growing numbers of escapists who, for various reasons, want isolation. The following headings will particularly appeal to them:

CREATE YOUR OWN RETREAT—10 ACRES

10 ACRES OF SECLUSION

FOR THE PIONEER

A FORGOTTEN VALLEY

RETURN TO BASICS—40 ACRES

BACK TO BASICS

CREATE YOUR OWN WORLD

ESCAPE SITE

Survivalists For survivalists, similar features attract attention:

Absolute seclusion from the outside world

Enough timber to build and heat your home forever

Timber, fish and game—everything you need is here.

Possible hydropower site

Additional acreage available

Closings used for outdoors people are also appropriate for escapists and survivalists. In addition you could use:

A safe refuge $67,500.

Insure your future $47,800.

A place for tomorrow $71,500.

Home Sites Many buyers of undeveloped acreage intend to use it now or in the future as a primary or secondary residence for other than escapist reasons.

Ads appealing to such buyers can use many of the headings listed earlier in this chapter under *Outdoor People,* as well as lot headings from the next section and second-home approaches from Chapter Eight.

Special points targeted at such buyers include:

Several good homesites

Shaded building site

Choice homesite

Terrific building site

All the natural stone and timber on the property to build your dream home

Favorable percolation test

Power and phone available

Utilities available

Completed Ads for Undeveloped Land

Available *does not mean presently at the parcel. It means they can be brought to it.*

This ad starts the developer thinking like an owner in naming the development.

The price per lot shows as a low desirable figure. The total price would be less than $16,000 per acre or less than $640,000 for the parcel.

40 ACRES—160 LOTS

A development-ready parcel with water, sewer and natural gas available in the highly desirable Orchard Creek area. Over 100 giant oaks will provide a distinctive theme for your development. Best of all, your total land cost will be less than $4,000 per lot.

Clyde Realty 476-8200

Attention-getting heading

And Will was absolutely right.

This is a strong ad for an investor.

WILL ROGERS SAID:

"To make money in real estate, find out where the people are going and get there first." This 40-acre parcel south of the city is in the natural path of tremendous future growth. Insure your future at the raw-land price of only $78,000 with excellent owner financing.

Clyde Realty 476-8200

CAMP OUT WITH NATURE—$16,000

Fill your family weekends with fun and adventure on your own 10-acre wilderness tract less than 2 hours from the city. Ride or hike the wilderness trails. Rough it or build a cabin with native timber from your own property. An investment in your family with very little down.

Clyde Realty 476-8200

This ad will appeal to outdoor people, escapists and survivalists.

$20,000 ESCAPE KIT

14 timbered acres to build the hideaway you always dreamed about. This hillside tract boasts a year-round natural spring and has access to an all-weather road. Escape before it's too late.

Clyde Realty 476-8200

Lots

Lots are subdivided parcels generally intended for a single structure. They are usually buildable now or buildable after bringing in available utilities. Lots generally have access to existing streets.

In newspapers where lots are listed in the same advertising category as undeveloped land, it will be necessary to identify your parcel as a lot in the ad heading.

Location Normally lots are in one or more separate categories. In larger areas lots will be divided by their locations, such as north-side or south-side. If the newspaper heading indicates that a lot is in a desirable area, it is unnecessary and wasteful to repeat this in your ad heading or body.

If the location of a lot is not shown in the classified heading and the lot is in a desirable area, your heading could indicate this with:

If your lot will appear attractively priced for the area, put the price in the heading.

WESTWOOD—$10,000

WESTWOOD—$150/SQ. FT.

You can combine several attractive features in the heading.

WESTWOOD—ON THE GREENBELT

WESTWOOD—CUL-DE-SAC

WESTWOOD—CORNER LOT

Square feet doesn't mean much to many buyers— Estate-size lot *might be better.*

WESTWOOD—10,000 SQ. FT.

WESTWOOD—½ ACRE

Mobile home zoning is often a strong selling point.

WESTWOOD—ZONED FOR MOBILE HOME

WESTWOOD—WALK TO TOWN

WESTWOOD—ACROSS FROM PARK

ON HWY. 12—$10,000

GOLF-COURSE LOT

ON THE FAIRWAY

WATER ACCESS

100′ SAND BEACH

POTATO RIVER FRONTAGE

Zoning Most residential lots are zoned for single-family residences. When the zoning will permit more units, or special uses, you want the readers to know about it.

ZONED FOR 43 UNITS

ZONED FOR TRIPLEX

FOR YOUR MOBILE HOME

This even has a strong appeal to people who don't own horses.

ZONED FOR HORSES

Commercial or industrial zoning should be indicated in the ad heading if not indicated by ad category. Even when the ad category indicates a general use, better-than-normal zoning should be pointed out.

M—4, 6 ACRES

ZONED FOR HEAVY INDUSTRIAL USE

C—6 30,000 SQ. FT.

Attention Headings While headings that emphasize highly desirable features are preferred, at times you will have lots that don't really have a feature worthy of a heading. You can advertise such lots with attention-getting headings.

PROMISE HER ANYTHING BUT GIVE HER A LOT

THE BEST OF THE LOT

BUY NOW BUILD LATER

LOVE AT FIRST SITE

A LOT TO LOVE

GET A LOT WHILE YOU ARE YOUNG

Ads with sexual connotations will turn off some prospective buyers.

JUST ADD A HOME

ATTENTION: BUILDERS

A LOT NOT TO PASS UP

STRAWBERRY PATCH LOT

A former use can make an attention-grabbing heading.

For ad headings and descriptive language dealing with location, view, terms, bargain sales and so forth, see Chapters Two and Seven.

Terms and Price Residential lots are ordinarily sold at a price per lot, while commercial and industrial lots are usually sold per square foot or per front foot. Terms and price are ordinarily part of the ad closing, but they can be included in the heading when they are or appear to be attractive to a prospective buyer. Before advertising terms, be certain you understand the advertising requirements of Truth-in-Lending (see Chapter Seven).

BUILDERS—LOW DOWN

$1,000 DOWN

If it's new financing, Truth-in-Lending requirements should be considered.

LOW DOWN

WILL SUBORDINATE

Builders in particular are interested in lots where they won't have their cash tied up. Usually the subordination is to a construction loan.

WHOLESALE-PRICED

OWNER SACRIFICE $10,000

55¢/SQ. FT.

Commercial or industrial

$100/FRONT FOOT

Commercial or waterfront

Lot Size Lot area is very important for commercial and industrial sites and should be indicated in the ad by acreage, square feet or front feet. For residential sites, lot size is not nearly as important; in fact, many buyers are confused with sizes shown as square feet or dimensions, though most people understand that an acre is quite large. You can indicate residential lot size in your ad body with words such as:

Huge

Xtra-size homesite

You can use homesite *interchangeably with* residential lot.

Estate-size lot

Garden-size lot

Tribe-size lot

Family-size lot

Family-size homesite

Suited for sprawling ranch home

Room for a pool

Room for tennis court

Special Features Any attractive feature should be pointed out in your ad. You can even take what would normally be a negative feature and make it appear positive.

The steep grade lends itself to an imaginative buyer who wants the ultimate view site.

If a lot owner has received city or county planning approval for a special use or specific structure, then your ad should indicate this.

Approved for 47 units

Tentative approval for 47 units

22 units—plans and approvals included

Feasibility studies completed

Engineering completed

All permits and approvals for restaurant use included

For a subdivision with very few lots remaining, attention-getting headings stress rarity.

RARE EARTH

RARE WESTWOOD LOT

LAST OF ITS KIND

THE LAST LOT

A lot that can be further divided can be a powerful attraction for many prospective buyers.

Can be divided

Can be split into 3 parcels

Possible lot split

If a lot has a structure that provides present income, even though the present use is not economical because of the land value, you can show this as a positive feature.

Present income

LOT + INCOME

INCOME NOW—DEVELOP LATER
Provides income until you are ready to build

The presence of utilities need only be pointed out if there are other lots in the area without them.

Utilities available

This does not necessarily mean the utilities are presently at the lot.

Utilities to lot

Natural gas to lot

Power to lot

Underground utilities

A strong plus factor for residential lots

A large number of lots available within a subdivision is a strong sales feature for a builder. Your heading could be:

BUILDERS—23 LOTS

23 LOTS—BUILDER'S SPECIAL

23 LOTS—DEVELOPMENT-READY

LOTS OF LOTS

7 FINISHED LOTS

Finished *means all improvements are in.*

Other features that can be emphasized in your ad include:

Percolation test

Perc-approved

Lot perked

Protected by restrictive covenants

Cleared homesite

Building pad in

Build your dream home beneath 100-year-old oaks.

Suitable for trilevel

A positive way to describe a hillside lot

Generalized language for the body of a lot ad includes:

This is your opportunity to select the site for your personally designed home.

Create your own masterpiece.

Lot Closings While many of the closings for homes also apply to lots, the following are exclusively for lots:

Blueprint-ready for $________.

Bring your blueprints $________.

It will be ready when you are $________.

Buy now—build later $_________.

The perfect site for your dream home at $_________.

A dream setting for a dream home $_________.

Ready for your dreams $_________.

A lot not to pass up $_________.

Building-ready at $_________.

Buildable now $_________.

Some of the above closings could also be used as ad headings.

Completed Ads for Lots

BENEATH A MAJESTIC OAK

The perfect spot to turn your dreams into reality. One of the last remaining estate-size lots in prestigious Hidden Hills. Unexcelled at $35,000

Clyde Realty **476-8200**

This ad appeals to present owners of mobile homes who are paying high rents in crowded parks. (Note: It sells benefits.)

MOBILE HOME SITE $10,000

Pay no rent as the owner of your own 1/2-acre lot. The park-like setting provides plenty of room for children, pets, garden and, best of all, privacy. Call us about the attractive terms.

Clyde Realty **476-8200**

This family ad stresses safety—quiet cul-de-sac—*and the fact it is close to schools.*

A LOT FOR YOUR FAMILY

On a quiet cul-de-sac, walking-close to elementary and Jefferson middle schools, this is a very special site for a happy family. $27,000.

Clyde Realty **476-8200**

A typical ad for a lower-priced lot. If the lot had other positive features besides the price, they should have been included.

$7,000—WEST SIDE

You read it right. This 80′ lot has sewer and water in and paid for and is priced for immediate sale.

Clyde Realty 476-8200

Obtain the owner's permmission prior to advertising any owner financial difficulty.

This is a bargain ad designed to induce quick action.

First-come-first-served *creates a strong sense of urgency.*

HIDDEN HILLS—LIQUIDATION

Builder needs cash and must immediately dispose of 3 choice estate-size wooded homesites. Offered on a first-come-first-served basis at only $19,000 each.

Clyde Realty 476-8200

This attention-getter should be used under Lot *heading.*

This ad sells the virtue of building.

FUSSY

Why not choose where to live and build your home the way you want it? One look at this extra-size-view homesite in desirable Westwood and you will start planning your new home. It's ready when you are at $47,500

Clyde Realty 476-8200

11 Investment Income Property and Business Opportunities

Investment income properties range from single rental units to huge residential and commercial and industrial complexes. People buy these properties for a number of reasons, including:

- Income
- Preservation of capital in an inflationary period
- Appreciation
- Tax shelter (depreciation)
- Leverage benefits
- Pride of ownership

Investment buyers may be conservative investors looking for a safe long-term investment with a modest return or they might be wheeler-dealers willing to risk everything for the chance of large, quick profits. Or they might fall anywhere in between those extremes.

Investment buyers tend to be practical: They are less likely to be swayed by emotional approaches. Your ads must therefore appeal to the needs of the investor or at least the needs the investor perceives.

Residential and Commercial

Attention-Grabber Headings The following ad headings are primarily to attract attention; they provide little or no information to the reader. Headings such as these should be used when there are no really strong features to be stressed.

OPPORTUNITY

OPPORTUNITY KNOCKS

INVESTOR'S DREAM

A LITTLE IMAGINATION
will pay big dividends if you invest in this. . .

UNIQUE OPPORTUNITY

RARE OPPORTUNITY

TAX REFORM INCOME

SANFORIZE YOUR DOLLAR
Keep it from shrinking by investing in this. . .

SLEEPING OPPORTUNITY

The fact that a property has not been on the market previously is appealing to investors although it really says nothing about the property's desirability.

FIRST TIME OFFERED

SUCH A DEAL $79,900

LOOKING FOR LEVERAGE

This unusual heading is extremely effective.

GET RICH SLOWLY
with the steady income from this. . .

INVEST IN YOUR FUTURE

INVEST IN AMERICA

For a large property

SYNDICATORS' DREAM

ATTENTION SYNDICATES

A good ad for a vacant white elephant

ANSWER AND WIN
What would you do with. . .

BUY NOW—GLOAT LATER
The best investment of your life will be this. . .

YOU WILL NEVER HAVE TO SAY YOU'RE SORRY
if you buy this. . .

BE THE LANDLORD

Informational Headings Preferred headings tell about the property. Investors want to know what you are selling. A heading should tell what the property is and can also give some detail about the property.

7 LOW-MAINTENANCE UNITS

32U—INVESTOR'S DREAM

32U—OCEAN VIEW

This means one bedroom.

8–1s $258,000

32 GARDEN UNITS

PRIME MULTITENANT COMPLEX

7 UNITS—IMMACULATE

20—2BR—GLENDALE

10 UNITS—NETS 10%

24 PRIME RENTALS

MINI-SHOPPING CENTER $300,000

3 STORES—6 APARTMENTS

STUDENT HOUSING

DYNAMIC DUPLEX

DYNAMIC DUO

Duplex ad

2 ON 1

This means there are two units on one lot.

TRIPLE TREASURE

Three units

A ROOF OVER YOUR HEAD
MONEY IN YOUR POCKET

This two-line heading is for rental units with an owner's apartment. The ad is fairly subtle and some readers might not realize what the heading refers to.

TWO-FAMILY TREAT

Duplex or two houses

HALF-PRICE LIVING

These might be a little too subtle for some readers.

BRING A FRIEND

DO YOU HAVE A FRIEND?

A DOUBLE HEADER
DOUBLE SCOOP

If a unit in a two- or four-unit building is vacant, it should be covered in the ad body with language such as Lower now vacant. *It is a strong plus feature for a buyer who intends to occupy it.*

HI-RISE PRIDE

MINIRESORT

Price and Terms in Headings While price and terms are normally covered in the ad closing, appealing ones should be in the heading.

BELOW APPRAISAL—$300,000

$30,000/UNIT

7 UNITS—$200,000

UNDER $30/SQ. FT.

8% DOWN—8% INT.

See Chapter Seven for Truth-in-Lending requirements.

Rents Unsophisticated owners—as well as absentee ones—often are not cognizant of current rental rates. They frequently leave long-term tenants on bargain rentals. Investment buyers get excited over property where they realize rental increases are possible. Below-market rents should be pointed out in the ad body or in the heading itself.

Low-low rents

Below-market rents

Short-term below-market leases

Bargain rents

Raisable rents

Low rents—high rental demand

No rent increases since 1978

If there is rent control in nearby areas but not on the property you have for sale, let readers know.

CONTROL-FREE RENTS

NO RENT CONTROL HERE

When a rental schedule provides for rental increases or is tied to an index such as the consumer price index, say so.

Provisions for rent escalation

Escalating leases

Lease tied to CPI — *Consumer Price Index*

Long-term CPI leases

Inflation-proof leases

Investors love triple-net leases, where the commercial tenants pay the taxes, insurance and all maintenance expenses; and percentage leases, where the rents are a percentage of gross sales and increase as the tenants' volumes increase. Leases of these types can be shown by:

10% NNN

Triple-net lease

NNN—AAA tenant — *Means a highly rated tenant on a triple-net lease (Dunn & Bradstreet rating)*

NNN

Percentage lease

Percentage lease with guarantees — *Usually a minimum rent is required.*

Guaranteed income

Insured leases — *Lease insurance*

Profit The bottom line to many investors is profit. They want to know about the net. Language that can be used in the ad body or heading includes:

$ maker $

Positive cash flow

Bottom line = profit

You can bank on it

Not beautiful—just profitable

No pride of ownership—just profit

Good headings or closings for rundown but profitable property

Bread and butter units

Bread & butter units—meat and potatoes too

Net 12%

12% cash-on-cash

12% cash flow

Makes U money

Rake in the rents

Profit is implied but not stated.

$30,000 spendable

Impressive cash-on-cash return

This low-key statement can be stronger than quoted figures. It invites inquiry.

Nearly break even

Break even—almost

Break even with 15% down

That a property almost or just breaks even is a very positive factor to many investors who are looking for depreciation possibilities.

Gross $45,000

While not profit, the gross gives the investor an idea of the size and/or rental structure of a property.

Cash-on-cash + depreciation

Should rent for 20¢/ft.

For a vacant commercial property

7 × gross

Many unsophisticated buyers use the gross multiplier to evaluate property even though it gives no indication of actual net.

Let the rents supplement your income

$950 comin' in

Tenants The prospect of a continued high occupancy rate adds considerably to a property's appeal. A low risk factor means a lower capitalization rate and greater desirability. Language indicating strong tenants and/or high rental demand includes:

AAA tenant

Refers to high Dunn & Bradstreet rating

Leased to NYSE tenant

A corporation listed on the New York Stock Exchange

Blue-chip tenant

Sale-leaseback

Usually a long-term lease

Seller will leaseback or vacate

Long-term lease

Leased investment

Professional tenants

Strong tenants

National tenant

Always leased

Tenant waiting list

Major tenants occupy 80% of space

National tenants occupy 80% of space

Low vacancy

Close to zero vacancy

Bonded lease

Stable rental area

Income Taxes A good tax shelter is the first consideration to many high income investors. The following would attract these investors:

$30,000 tax shelter

Depreciation shelters income

Tax loss + cash flow

The ultimate tax shelter

Tax-errific

Prepare for the tax auditor

Attn: sophisticated investor

Attention-getter

Uncle Sam will hate you

This 10-unit apt. building will shelter $25,000 of income.

IRS revenge

Tax problem? This. . . may be your answer.

Need shelter?

Protect yourself and your income with this. . .

Location If the location is truly exceptional, such as an apartment building on the beach or a commercial building on the best street in town, it should be considered for the heading. If not the most important feature, location should be covered in the ad body. The following language will help you to express that a location is desirable:

Prime 1st St. location

In the path of progress

Expanding area

Dynamic growth area

High-traffic location

High-traffic corner

High-traffic street

Heavy foot traffic

Downtown

Best rental location

High-rental-demand area

In demand rental area

Prime rental area

Excellent rental area

Highway visibility

High accessibility

This makes a good heading.

Traffic—signage—visibility

Mention proximity to a well-known business or building.

Next to McDonald's

Across from Wendy's

At the intersection of two major highways

Traffic count *23,000* cars per day

Strategically located between. . .

Pride of Ownership Many people delight in letting their friends know they own a quality property. They feel the quality of the property somehow reflects back on themselves. Many owners are actually happier owning a building they can claim with pride than a less prestigious building of similar value that offers a greater net income.

Besides construction quality and location, the history of a building also affects its prestige. It could have historic significance, be designed by a great architect or even have been occupied by a prestigious firm or individual.

Pride of ownership can be appealed to in the ad headings or ad body.

Pride-of-ownership units

If the building is well known

The Caldwell Building

Name of prestigious tenant or former tenant

Former IBM Building

Might be particularly appealing to the nouveaux riche

NAME THE BUILDING
Your firm or family name can be on this prestigious. . .

A landmark

Historic landmark

Older commercial buildings, and even older homes that can be converted for commercial purposes, may carry prestige because of their age. See Chapter Six for language that extols the virtues of older buildings.

Condition A well-maintained building appeals strongly to pride-of-ownership buyers, but any investor knows a well-cared-for property means far fewer headaches in the future. That a property is in better-than-average condition can be expressed in the ad body or heading.

Well-maintained

Immaculately maintained

Like-new

Better than new

Completely up to code

No deferred maintenance

For property in bad repair, you can use the fixer-upper language found in Chapter Nine.

Special Features The following positive features should be covered either in the ad body or in the heading:

Ideal *fast-food* location

For retail buildings

Free-standing

If property has liquor licenses which go with the property

Includes licenses

These are extremely strong, as investors understand this could mean large profits.

Condominium conversion possibility

Could be converted to condominiums

Condominium-conversion approval

Student housing usually means high profit.

Ideal for student housing

Indicates tenants pay their own utilities

Separate meters

Individual meters

Individual utilities

Tenants pay utilities

Separate utilities

Show the number of parking spaces if it is unusually high.

Ample parking

Paved parking area

Parking for 80 cars

Off-street parking for 80 cars

Room for 9 additional units

Mention a possible attractive use.

Ideal for conversion to artists' lofts

This is a good heading for income property where primary value is the land for some other use.

Rent now—develop later

Show the lot size only if it is exceptionally large.

3/4 of an acre

Show the size only when it is larger than normal.

Each unit approx. 1,200 sq. ft.

Redevelopment area

Redevelopment possibilities

Redevelopment loans available

Ideal for *distribution center*

These are attractive for professional people who don't want to be bothered with management.

Professionally managed

Management-free investment

EZ management

Waiting for your business

Have your business downstairs while you live upstairs in this spacious...

The fact that a property is vacant is normally a negative one. However, it is positive for someone who wants the property for his or her own use.

Rezoning possibilities

This will excite buyers who are interested in quick profits.

Low expenses

Maintenance-free

Almost maintenance-free

No risk

Minimum risk—maximum potential

Many of the same headings and body copy shown in the other categories can be used for investment property; therefore, check the index for appropriate language.

Closings The following closings are suggested for investment ads:

A money-maker at $________.

Investment-priced at $________.

Action-priced at $________.

Investor-priced at $________.

Just take a look and you will buy at $________.

For pride-of-ownership property

Proudly presented at $________.

You won't believe the financing $________.

Don't wish when you can own $________.

Don't let this one get away $________.

Outstanding at $________.

Impressive at $________.

A rare offering at $________.

Unexcelled at $________.

The perfect choice for the young investor $________.

Offered at M.A.I. appraisal of $________.

An opportunity waiting to happen at $________.

Unparalleled opportunity at $________.

A rare property presenting unlimited possibilities at $________.

An investment for your future $________.

Inquire now $________.

You won't take a second look at $________.

Seeing is buying $________.

Deserves your immediate attention $________.

Hurry to own at $________.

Demands immediate attention $________.

Merits your prompt attention $________.

Warrants your immediate attention $________.

Definitely worth your inspection $________.

For the investor with vision $________.

An investment for the future $________.

For the future-minded investor $________.

Duplex or small owner-occupied units

Live and earn $________.

Be the first to inspect this rare find $________.

Don't wait till it's gone $________.

Exciting potential at $________.

The place to watch your equity grow $________.

For the future-minded buyer $________.

Tap the potential $________.

What a buy for the future at $________.

Insure your future for $________.

Insure your future today $________.

For the buyer with vision $________.

The bottom line will be profit at $________.

Become the landlord for $________.

Completed Ads for Investment Property

Brick *indicates a sound structure.*

Two-story means there is no elevator maintenance.

Possibility of rental increase

PROFITS NOT PRIDE

Not much pride of ownership with this older, brick, 24-efficiency-unit 2-story in a hi-rental-demand area. Immediate cash flow with current low rents. Assumable $250,000 8% loan. A money-maker at $400,000.

Clyde Realty **476-8200**

This ad does not include price or terms, yet is unlikely to attract bargain-hunters based upon its tone. It is aimed at "heavy hitters." Assuming the buyers have accountants reflects on the quality of the property and prospective buyer. The low-key action statement is an invitation for serious discussion.

AAA TENANT

National tenant on solid lease makes this 24,000-sq.-ft. prime rental a blue-chip investment. An exceptional opportunity for an investor in the maximum tax bracket. We would be happy to provide details for you and your accountant.

Clyde Realty 476-8200

The list of positive features can be very effective, hitting the reader with feature after feature. Price is not essential as the down payment eliminates unqualified buyers.

SHOPPING CENTER— 42 STORES

- Fully leased—percentage + CPI
- Prime growth area
- Positive cash flow
- Room for additional stores
- Professionally managed
- Realistic financing with approximately $1,000,000 down

Clyde Realty 476-8200

If the location was desirable, it should have been included.

HOUSE + INCOME

Live in one and rent the other. Two 2-bedroom units on one huge lot. Immaculate and only $69,500.

Clyde Realty 476-8200

Investors are aware that many tax shelters have been attacked by the IRS and some investors have even been the victims of fraud.

The down payment indicates the price is a great deal higher. Be sure you have the owner's permission before you suggest a down payment that was not specifically agreed to.

WHY GAMBLE?

with risky and dubious tax shelters. This fully leased blue-chip commercial complex takes the gamble out of investing. 12 retail stores on NNN leases that provide for inflationary increases. Professionally managed, this is the ultimate in leveraged tax shelters. Try $400,000 down.

Clyde Realty 476-8200

The ad with its attention-getting heading is aimed at a small segment but would be likely to attract other investors as well.

HAVE A COLLEGE STUDENT?

Put him/her in business while living in style in this like-new, brick, 4-unit (2-2BR/2 baths, 2-1BR/1bath) that's walking-close to the university. Let us show you this investment that makes cash and tax cents at $220,000.

Clyde Realty **476-8200**

This ad should be under the Investment *or* Commercial *category rather than* Industrial *since it is not aimed at the industrial buyer.*

CREATIVE BUYER

needed to discover a new use for this 40,000-square-foot, 1870, 4-story former shoe factory. A rock-solid structure of classic design located close to the center of everything, it is ready for revitalization. Possible loft conversion, boutiques, restaurants, galleries or ? An opportunity not to be missed at $295,000

Clyde Realty **476-8200**

Industrial

Buyers and lessees of industrial property are interested in a number of factors including:

Location:
- Labor market
- Community culture
- Community taxes
- Community services (schools, fire and police)
- Local housing market
- Highway access
- Rail access and sidings
- Public transportation for employees
- Availability of service industries

Structure:
- Size and configuration
- Construction
- Height
- Open or span distance
- Overhead cranes and capacity
- Elevators—freight elevators
- Floor loads

Loading docks
Service door sizes
Sprinkler systems
Heating and cooling systems
Utilities—electricity, gas and water
Office space
Parking
Security
Zoning

NOTE: We don't have uniform zoning. Most cities and counties use a number of zoning symbols and the same symbol is likely to have different meanings in different areas. Industrial zoning allows a range of uses from small clean industries where factories look like offices, to dirty, smelly or unsightly installations. Inclusion of zoning in the ad is not necessary when a leased building is being sold as an investment. If the likely buyer will be the user, zoning is important and should be included, unless you have similar industrial properties of different zoning, so that a prospective buyer can be switched if necessary.

Terms:
- Price
- Down payment
- Interest rate
- Monthly payments
- Special conditions

Headings Headings for industrial ads usually provide factual information and should include the size of the property, as this is of prime importance to any buyer. Additional features can also be included:

10,000 SQ. FT.—LIKE-NEW

Zoning

10,000 SQ. FT.—M-4

50,000 SQ. FT.—SINGLE LEVEL

50,000 SQ. FT.—MINIMUM DOWN

Include an attractive price.

50,000 SQ. FT.—$15/SQ. FT.

50,000 SQ. FT.—$750,000

10,000 SQ. FT.—ROOM TO EXPAND

40,000 SQ. FT.—CRANE SERVED

30,000 SQ. FT.—RAIL SIDING

Advertised as an investment

30,000 SQ. FT.—LEASED

30,000 SQ. FT.—SALE-LEASEBACK

Include location

30,000 SQ. FT.—BLOOMINGTON

30,000 SQ. FT.—HEAVY INDUSTRIAL

30,000 SQ. FT.—WAREHOUSE

30,000 SQ. FT.—LIGHT MANUFACTURING

Special-use structure

FOUNDRY—30,000 SQ. FT.

30,000 SQ. FT.—4 YEARS OLD

30,000 SQ. FT.—ALMOST NEW

30,000 SQ. FT.—CLEAR SPAN

Bargain headings are also appropriate for industrial property.

20,000 SQ. FT.—COURT-ORDERED SALE

RECEIVER ORDERS SALE—40,000 SQ. FT.

BANKRUPTCY SALE—40,000 SQ. FT.

FOUNDRY—CORPORATION ORDERS DISPOSAL

For additional bargain headings ideas, see Chapter Seven.

Body Copy Examples of information to be included within the body of the ad include:

Good column spacing

700-sq.-ft. office

700-sq.-ft. air-conditioned office

10,000-sq.-ft. showroom

Showroom and warehouse space

Large showroom

16′ sidewalls

Clear span

A previous use can tell a prospective buyer a lot about the property.

Previously used as an assembly and distribution center

Ideal for a machine shop

1 level

For employees

Excellent public transportation

4,000-sq.-ft. warehouse or assembly area

Heavy power

Very heavy power

Ample power

31,200-volt/144-amp primary service

400 amps

3-phase power

EPA wastewater system

Situated on a 2-acre site

Parking for 180 cars

Fenced parking for 180 cars

Paved parking for 180 cars

3 acres of fenced parking

3 acres of outside storage

Strategically located

Free-standing building

10-ton crane

3 crane bays

Gas heat

Air-conditioned

Gas pumps

800-sq.-ft. dock

400′-long dock

Bed-level dock

Truck-level dock

Recessed dock

Enclosed dock

Adjustable dock boards

Depressed loading dock with levelators

Drive-in door

Drive-in *16′ × 14′* door

16′ OH door

Freight elevator

Fully sprinklered

Security fence

Electronic security system

Butler building — *A make of steel building*

Tilt-up concrete construction

Reinforced concrete construction

4 years old

Like-new

Closings Some suggested closings for industrial property include:

You won't believe the financing $_________.

Impressive at $_________.

A rare opportunity at $_________.

Offered at M.A.I. appraisal of $_________.

Warrants your immediate attention $_________.

Deserves your immediate attention at $_________.

Merits your prompt inspection at $_________.

Insure your future growth at $_________.

A unique opportunity at $_________.

Bargain closings such as the following can also be used:

Auction-priced at $_________.

Priced well below replacement cost at $_________.

Let's talk $_________.

WARNING: Anytime your ad indicates the price is not firm, you must have the owner's permission.

Must-sell-priced at $_________.

Priced to move quickly at $_________.

Completed Ads for Industrial Property

Indicates it has proper zoning for uses cited

18,000 SQ. FT.—
CLEAR SPAN

Six-years-old, one-story structure features 24′-ceiling, rail siding, sprinklers, electronic security, 4-bay truck dock and 1,500 S.F. air-cond. offices. The 2-acre site provides ample parking and excellent freeway access. Located in the progressive growing community of Middleton. An ideal site for light manufacturing or distribution center. Priced far below reproduction cost at $950,000—submit terms.

Clyde Realty **476-8200**

This property apparently was not used as a junkyard. It is advertised in this manner because the property has zoning allowing a use that will be attractive to many buyers. Advertise for a high-demand use if your property fits that use.

**JUNKYARD—
LOW DOWN**

This 10-acre rail-served site is zoned for auto dismantling. An almost-new 8,000 S.F. metal building would be ideal for parts storage. A double-wide mobile home would make an excellent office. A rare find at $600,000 with flexible terms.

Clyde Realty 476-8200

CLASS A BUILDING

13,000 sq. ft. on 1-acre fenced site. 30′ ceiling with overhead crane and full sprinkler system. Close to airport and Interstate 5. An unusual opportunity at $38/sq. ft.

Clyde Realty 476-8200

This attention-getting heading tells what it is and where it is.

**THE BEST LITTLE
WAREHOUSE
IN AKRON**

18,000-sq.-ft., fully sprinklered, clear-span Butler building with 18′ sidewalls. Two 16′ OH doors and truck-level loading dock. 500-sq.-ft. air-cond. office. Plenty of parking and/or outside storage on the 1½-acre, security-fenced site. Priced at a hard-to-believe $18/sq. ft.

Clyde Realty 476-8200

Business Opportunities

Sale of a business usually involves goodwill, fixtures and stock-in-trade. Real estate usually is not part of the sale since most businesses operate in leased space.

Newspapers generally have a classified category entitled *Business Opportunities.* Some larger papers have special categories for hotels and motels, mobile home parks, resort property and so on. Some newspapers also have a separate category for investment opportunities in which business opportunities are frequently included. The *Business Opportunity* category generally would be the preferred placement for a business opportunity. However, if most of the businesses of the type you are advertising are included in another category, you also should consider that category for ad placement.

Trade magazines and journals often carry a page or more of ads concerning businesses or equipment for sale. Classified ads in these specialized magazines and papers should be considered, as they reach a select group of people likely to be interested in a particular type of business.

Businesses generally are listed alphabetically. Readers of a large paper with hundreds of business opportunities are more likely to just check the headings of businesses of particular interest to them. Therefore, generally it is preferable to start with a simple heading indicating the type of business, rather than an imaginative or cute heading. The best headings for most business opportunities are very simple.

These headings not only give the type of business but also indicate an important feature that is likely to interest a prospective buyer.

MOTEL 38 UNITS

GARAGE—6 HOISTS

SUPPER CLUB—SEATS 250

RESTAURANT—$10,000 DOWN

MOBILE HOME PARK—280 SPACES

MOBILE HOME PARK—5 ★

DOG GROOMING—$80,000 GROSS

Unusual Businesses The general descriptive heading is not likely to get attention for an unusual business. Suppose you wished to advertise a wake-up-call service. It is unlikely prospective buyers would look under *W* for wake-up calls. An attention-grabbing heading is the only route in such a case.

THE BUCK STARTS HERE

UNBELIEVABLE MONEY-MAKER

$ MAKER $

YOUR MONEY TREE

A MONEY MACHINE

COUNT YOUR PROFITS

PROVEN GOLD MINE

A GOLD MINE

IMPRESSIVE TRACK RECORD

BE THE PRESIDENT

BE THE BOSS

FANTASTIC PROFITS

HIGH PROFITS—LOW OVERHEAD

MAKE MONEY

This heading is a natural for a telephone wake-up service.

TELEPHONE DOLLARS

OPPORTUNITY KNOCKS

This is a strong lead where the franchise is not well known. If it is well known, use the franchise name for the heading.

NATIONAL FRANCHISE

This appeals to a hesitant potential buyer. The idea of a partner can provide support.

PARTNER WANTED

NEVER AGAIN
will an opportunity such as this come along.

GUARANTEED JACKPOT
You will be the winner with this. . .

MONEY LOVERS

THE SELLER MEANS BUSINESS

While absence of competition will appeal to many buyers, it does not mean the business is profitable.

CAPTURED CLIENTELE
The only laundromat in town

WALK-IN (TYPE OF BUSINESS)
Take over this hi-volume operation without interruption.

Many brokers like to combine the type of business with an attention-getting heading.

THERE IS A TAVERN IN THE TOWN
and it could be yours.

SEW WHAT
A thriving sewing machine sales and service business

Aiming at the Unemployed Business opportunity ads are also checked by people who are unemployed. Loss of a job often leads to a decision to go into business. Many successful businesses were founded out of necessity resulting from unemployment. Unemployed buyers often have no specific business in mind. You can appeal to them with businesses that don't require specific skills or extensive training.

HIRE YOURSELF

BE YOUR OWN BOSS

IMMEDIATE INCOME

INDEPENDENCE DAY

WORK FOR YOURSELF

BE MASTER OF YOUR FUTURE

FAMILY BUSINESS

PARENT & CHILD BUSINESS

FATHER & SON BUSINESS

MOTHER & DAUGHTER BUSINESS

RECESSION-PROOF BUSINESS

RECESSION SOLUTION

These ads also are attractive to employed individuals who are unhappy with their jobs.

Honesty When an owner wants out of a business, he or she will often make statements that stretch the truth. In order to be honest in your advertising, it is essential that you check any gross figures from the seller's income tax or sales tax returns.

Some owners don't consider depreciation of equipment in the net they give you. Others look at all wages taken by them and their family as net. When obtaining net income, you should question the sellers as well as check federal income tax returns.

Because gross is easier to verify than net, it is preferred for ads. For your own protection, it would be best to state *Owner Reports $________ (gross or net)* or *Owner claims $________ (gross or net).* You should also obtain a signed statement of income from the sellers.

You are supposed to be a professional; merely repeating sellers' figures without checking them might be considered negligence and subject you to damages.

Reasons for Sale Prospective buyers will often look a gift horse in the mouth, asking themselves, "If the business is so good, why are they selling?" The reason for sale can reassure the prospective buyer. Always obtain the owner's permission before you advertise the owner's reason for wanting to sell.

So many business owners use ill health as a reason for sale that it has taken on a new meaning: "Owner is sick of losing money." Because of the overuse of ill health, I suggest it be used only with strong specifics such as:

Hospitalized owner must sell

Invalid owner must sell

Owner's doctor says sell now

Owner's heart condition necessitates immediate sale

When an owner's reason for sale is advanced age, it can be covered with:

A business that is growing too fast is a strong plus—most people consider themselves take-charge executives.

Business has grown too fast for elderly owner. Needs a young take-charge executive

Owner retiring (age 73)

Showing that the owner has been in business for a long time reassures prospective buyers.

Owner retiring after 27 years

79-year-old owner wants out

79-year-old owner retiring

79-year-old owner has no children to take over

Other reasons for sale are:

Divorce settlement forces sale

Partnership dissolution forces sale

To settle estate

Heirs say sell

Owner moving to California to repeat his/her success there

Here is a statement that does not tell a reason but has an element of intrigue, so the reader wants to know more:

Unusual circumstances force the sale of this profitable...

You should avoid *other interest* as a reason for sale; it is overworked and not convincing. Far better is a simple:

While this gives no reason at all, it is effective.

Owner wants out

A statement to help reassure a prospective buyer is:

Retiring owner will sign noncompetition agreement

Part-Time and Absentee Owners That the present owner devotes only part-time or even no time to a business can become a positive feature, suggesting to prospective buyers that their full efforts will lead to prosperity: A profitable business will make even more profit, while marginal and even loss operations will move into the black with their full-time attention.

Such statements as the following promote that perception:

Part-time owner reports $________ gross.

Reports $________ net with absentee owner.

Absentee owner reports $________ net with all hired help.

Absentee owner wants out

A heading for a business that does not require full-time management could be:

PART-TIME BUSINESS

Full-time income

Older Businesses An older business has a definite plus: It has been operating for a long time, so it has been a success. Buyers are likely to feel their chances of failure will be materially lessened in such a purchase. As a matter of fact, they are generally right.

Take advantage of 27 years of goodwill.

Established 1937

4th generation of family ownership

Long-established

This business has been a landmark since 1946.

In operation more than 30 years

Open Books For profitable businesses, statements about the accessibility of the books will give a buyer reassurance and create interest.

Books open to serious buyer

The books are open to you and your accountant on this unique business opportunity.

Asking prospective buyers to bring an accountant is a plus. You are assuming the buyers are professional. Buyers may not bring in an accountant, but will be reassured in that they were offered the opportunity.

Losers Unfortunately, the real reason most businesses are for sale is they are either money losers or unable to provide a sufficient income to the owners.

Positive ways to treat businesses of this type are:

Needs a take-charge owner

Needs a take-charge manager

Needs an energetic operator

Untapped potential

Needs a couple willing to work

Can be expanded

Must see to realize potential

Proven growth record

But not necessarily profitable yet

Buyer Training When you are appealing to prospective buyers who are unlikely to have specific experience in the business, statements such as the following can be very appealing:

Owner will train

Experienced staff

Employees Other information about employees that can be a positive factor in your ad:

Loyal staff will remain

This is reassuring to a hesitant buyer.

Manager of 17 years willing to stay

That the manager has been there a number of years will reassure the buyer.

Our employees know of this ad.

This statement adds a measure of respectability to the ad. It conveys the image of a well-established firm, though it actually means very little.

Special Skills Many first-time business buyers are afraid of businesses that involve selling. A business that does not require sales talent can be appealing.

No selling

No selling experience needed

If a business involves sales, you should consider:

Selling experience helpful

If a business involves a mechanical area but ownership does not require special skills, let the buyer know with:

No mechanical experience necessary

Franchises Because of the success of some franchises such as McDonald's and Kentucky Fried Chicken, to many buyers a franchise means success. Franchises do offer national advertising for identity as well as training and supervision. As a matter of fact, the failure rate among franchise buyers is lower than other businesses. You could cover the plus factors of a franchise with an ad similar to the following:

For well-known franchises, use the name in the heading. If not well known, you can state National franchise.

PRINTING—YE OLDE PRINT SHOP

Gain instant name recognition from national advertising. A turnkey operation with full training and support. No experience necessary. Confident seller will finance part of the $55,000 purchase price. Call now for security tomorrow.

Clyde Realty 476-8200

Home Businesses A number of excellent businesses can be run effectively out of an owner's home. If the business you have for sale is currently run out of the owner's house, make this a positive feature.

Work in your home.

Pay no rent in this home-operated business.

This profitable . . . can be operated right from your home.

So simple, you can operate out of your home

No commuting—your business will be in your home with this . . .

Lease If a business has a favorable lease, this is a definite plus.

Below-market rental

Advantageous lease

Long-term lease

Long-term lease at moderate rental

Favorable lease

Low rent

Inventory Most business sales involve a dollar price plus inventory because inventory is subject to constant change. If a sale price includes inventory, it should, of course, be stated.

$39,000 including inventory

Price includes all inventory

When the price is plus inventory, you can state:

Plus inventory

Plus inventory at cost

Owner Financing Willingness to finance a buyer is an extremely strong indication that the owner is confident about the money-making ability of the business. Such a situation should be prominently featured in your ad:

Call to find out about the unusual owner financing.

Long-time owner willing to finance buyer

Down Payment A low down payment is a positive feature of a business sale and should be included in the ad. To many buyers, the down payment will be more important than the total price. See Chapter Seven for Truth-in-Lending requirements.

The following recently appeared in a business opportunity ad:

No cash required. Your home equity is the key to your independence.

This apparently says the buyer can borrow on his or her home to buy the business.

Other Positive Features That a business has operated for a period of time and has never been offered for sale before would indicate to prospective buyers that the business is probably profitable.

13 years under present ownership

First time offered

The equipment included can be made to seem very positive with statements such as:

Comes with all equipment, furnishings and fixtures for efficient operation

All equipment included for uninterrupted operation

These statements would be applicable for just about any business sale.

If the equipment is fairly new, it is of course a positive feature.

Latest equipment

New equipment

Like-new furnishings and equipment

If a business includes electronic games, consider statements such as:

Game income pays rent

Game income pays utilities

Round-the-clock machine income

14 video games

Location can be covered with:

100% location

This is an idiom for the best retail location in town. It only should be used in ads aimed at sophisticated buyers.

No competition in town

The only *liquor store* within *30* miles

Strategically located between major food store and J. C. Penney

Prominent location

Prestigious location

Corner location

High-traffic location

College town

This is a positive feature for a motel, bar, sporting goods dealer and so forth.

Located in the affluent community of Kaysville

Located in booming Kaysville

Located in progressive Kaysville

Adequate parking is very important in metropolitan areas.

Loads of parking

Ample parking

A positive way to describe a profitable seasonal business would be:

This seasonal business boasts a year-round income.

The type of merchandise carried can be covered with:

All major lines

Top-line inventory

Exclusive dealer for Evinrude

Customers can be covered with:

Steady neighborhood trade

Established clientele

Enjoys a substantial tourist trade

National accounts

National clients

Major clients

Closings Many of the closings in previous categories are applicable to the sale of business opportunities as well as real estate. Some additional closings are:

Provides reassurance — One of the finest business opportunities we have seen $________.

Calls for action — Your security is only a phone call away.

Restaurant closing — Wear the chef's hat for $________.

A good candy store closing — A sweet deal at $________.

Investigate, then buy with confidence $________.

Restaurant closing — Your recipe for success $________.

Your customers are waiting $________.

Ideal for a nursery — Grow with a growing business.

Calls for action — Investigate, then buy at $________.

Hire yourself *has strong appeal to a person who is unemployed. Have the owner's permission to suggest a down payment.* — Hire yourself today. Try $________. down.

A family operation for $________.

A wise family investment $________.

A good operating business that could be even better

Available with a flexible down payment for a take-charge owner

For the take-charge manager $________.

Your own money machine for $________.

For a business including living quarters — A unique opportunity to combine business with good living $________.

Ideal for a recreation or sports-type business — Combine profit with pleasure $________.

Your ticket to financial security $________.

Get ready to count your profits $________.

After a modest down payment, you can start to count your profits.

A business with a future $________.

Potential-packed at $________.

You're in business for only $________.

$________ down and you're in business.

Completed Ads for Business Opportunities

The price is not given, but the approximate down payment is. You must have the owner's permission to suggest a down payment.

The area is a strong plus, as is the beer and wine license.

The ad is designed to make the readers hope they are selected as buyers.

PIZZERIA—
TRY $10,000 DOWN

Owners retiring to Italy are selling their hi-volume pizza parlor in college area. Beer and wine license included. Owners willing to train and finance a hard-working, sober couple. A rare opportunity for a lifetime of security.

Clyde Realty 476-8200

The ad with its attention-getting heading does not even tell the exact type of business, but creates interest in the reader to investigate.

Be certain to obtain owner's permission to reveal personal data.

BETTER THAN BURGERS

An 8-yr.-old, fast-food operation with a phenomenal profit margin must be sold immediately for divorce settlement. Bring along your accountant and you will buy with confidence at $69,500.

Clyde Realty 476-8200

Attention-getting heading. The ad gives an idea of the size of the business and the reason for sale. Significant to prospective buyers without cleaning experience would be that a long-time manager or employees were willing to remain to train a new owner.

CLEAN UP

Long-established quality carpet cleaners (8 trucks—14 employees) must be sold to settle estate. Many large commercial accounts. An excellent business that could be even better. Priced for immediate sale at $190,000.

Clyde Realty 476-8200

You can see it isn't really necessary to tell the type of business. This can be beneficial for businesses difficult to describe in a few words.

Good action closing

WRITE YOUR OWN PAYCHECKS

as the owner of this proven money-making service-related business. The retiring owner will not only train the buyer but is also willing to finance a sincere buyer with approximately $30,000 down payment. Stop reading the want ads and call now for a secure future.

Clyde Realty 476-8200

The simple heading tells what it is.

Good reason for sale

Mixed drinks are more profitable than beer.

BAR & GRILL

The owner of this friendly tavern is retiring after 27 years. With a heavy mixed-drink volume and a limited menu of burgers and steak sandwiches, this proven money-maker enjoys a steady neighborhood trade. An excellent family business at $97,500 with owner financing available.

Clyde Realty 476-8200

Practice Exercises

Here is your opportunity to practice, step by step, what you've learned about writing real estate ads that work. Fourteen listing sheets give you a description and picture of a property and include personal notes the listing agent made during his or her inspection.

Using that information, the worksheets opposite the listings ask you to plan your own targets and approach, then put all the elements together to create a complete ad. Use the index to review applicable text material and examples. You will also want to check the quick reference guide to synonyms and descriptive terms in preparing effective copy.

You may find it useful to use the worksheets, or your own version of them, as a guide when you're faced with the challenge of writing real ads—or practice ads based on your office's own listings.

For each practice listing, we have provided our solution, together with comments on our reasons for making the choices we did. Of course, there is no right or wrong answer to these exercises; our ads are presented as examples of one effective approach. We suggest you compare your ads to the ones in this book, then put yourself in the anticipated buyer's shoes to see whether your ad equals or exceeds ours in effectiveness. If not, some revising may be in order; if so, you've absorbed the lessons of this book and know how to turn your knowledge into practical accomplishment. Congratulations!

1

Clyde Realty 476-8200

LISTING NO. C-46-84

RESIDENTIAL INCOME (COMMERCIAL) INDUSTRIAL

Owner Hendrix Klopper Type of Listing Ex RT - 10% Price $ 78,000 Exp. Date 3-1-88

Annual Scheduled Gross $ 7560

Address 944 W. Andrews

Directions Corner of Andrews and Moyer

To show contact: Lisa Klopper 476-1448

Units	Type	Size	Lease	Monthly Rent
1	Comm	2100 sq. ft.	Exp. 9-85	$370
2	Apt	1 BR	M/M	$125
3	Apt	1 BR	M/M	$125

Parking Rental (1 space) Other Income $ 10

Monthly Scheduled Gross $ 630

Annual Expenses (prior calendar year as submitted by owner):

Taxes $ 590 Trash $ -- Insurance $ 270 Pool/Gardener $ --

Management $ -- Gen. Maintenance $ 200 Utilities $ -- Misc. $ 50

Total estimated annual expenses $ 1110 Expenses verified Yes ☐ No ☒

Property Description:

Lot Size 40' x 130' Zoning C-2 Structure Size 30' x 70' Date Built 1938

Roof New in 1980 Heat Gas Cooling Water Coolers Construction Conc. Block

Basement No Parking

Water X Sewer X Gas X Elec. X

Financing: Owner will finance 80% with 5 yr. balloon - 11½%

Listing Agent: Alice Hopkins

Agent's Remarks Structure appears sound but needs a facelift. Good traffic corner. Parking for 14 cars. Rents appear too low

Who is likely to be the buyer of this property? Young investor - Local shopkeeper who can use location

Features likely to appeal to the eventual buyer: Owner Financing Low price for a commercial - fixer upper

WORKSHEET FOR WRITING CLASSIFIED AD #1

1. After studying the property description and inspection notes on the opposite page, write a brief description of two or three types of buyers who would be attracted to this property.
2. Choose one buyer and try to form a detailed picture of him or her in your mind. Put yourself in the buyer's place. Then make a list of benefits the property offers that buyer and the needs it fulfills.
3. A. Choose one or two items from your list and, using the index, select or modify a heading.

   B. Selecting those features you want to emphasize in the ad body, use the index for appropriate language.

   C. An effective closing either sums up the features, helps set the mood, gives an assurance of value or asks for action. Use your index to help you select or modify a closing based on the type of property or special feature you wish to emphasize.
4. Using the information you've developed, write at least one complete ad for this property. The authors' two versions and commentary are on page 338.

Clyde Realty 476-8200

LISTING NO. R3-18-84

~~RESIDENTIAL INCOME~~ (circled) COMMERCIAL INDUSTRIAL

Owner: Cooley Investments Type of Listing: Exc 6% Price $875,000 Exp. Date 6-1-88

Annual Scheduled Gross $151,476*

Address: 2840 Crestwood

Directions: 1 Block West of Farrel

To show contact: Clyde Realty - Tom Higgins

Units	Type	Size	Lease	Monthly Rent
24	Apts.	2 BR - 2 Ba	All on 1 yr	$480 to
			leases	550
				$12,408

Laundry Machines Other Income $ 215

Monthly Scheduled Gross $ 12,623

Annual Expenses (prior calendar year as submitted by owner):

Taxes $ 7140 Trash $ 744 Insurance $ 1720 Pool/Gardener $ 3120

Management $ 10,760 Gen. Maintenance $ 2300 Utilities $ 1822 Misc. $ 1100

Total estimated annual expenses $ 28,706 Expenses verified Yes ☒ No ☐ (from owners' accounta Reed & Malcolm)

Property Description:

Lot Size 200' x 440' Zoning R-3 Structure Size ____ Date Built 1978

Roof Asphalt Heat Gas Cooling X Construction Brick & Frame

Basement ____ Parking off street 38 spaces

Water X Sewer X Gas X Elec. X

Financing: Assumable 8% loan for $191,000. Owners will carry $500,000 12% 2nd mortgage for 3 years.

Listing Agent: ____

Agent's Remarks *Actual rents last 12 months $138,600 (after vacancies and collection losses)

Who is likely to be the buyer of this property? A buyer in a high tax bracket.

Features likely to appeal to the eventual buyer: Close to hospital. Eye appeal. Prestige property. Pool, spa and lush landscaping.

WORKSHEET FOR WRITING CLASSIFIED AD #2

1. After studying the property description and inspection notes on the opposite page, write a brief description of two or three types of buyers who would be attracted to this property.
2. Choose one buyer and try to form a detailed picture of him or her in your mind. Put yourself in the buyer's place. Then make a list of benefits the property offers that buyer and the needs it fulfills.
3. A. Choose one or two items from your list and, using the index, select or modify a heading.

   B. Selecting those features you want to emphasize in the ad body, use the index for appropriate language.

   C. An effective closing either sums up the features, helps the mood, gives an assurance of value or asks for action. Use your index to help you select or modify a closing based on the type of property or special features you wish to emphasize.
4. Using the information you've developed, write at least one complete ad for this property. The authors' version and commentary are on page 338.

3

Clyde Realty 476-8200 LISTING NO. R-58-84

RESIDENTIAL 2 BEDROOMS + Den

Price $ 119,500 Exp. Date 7-15-88

Owner Mr. & Mrs. Lawrence Bolt

Type of Listing Exc 6%

Address 783 Williamsburg Lane

Directions 1st right after entering Colonial Village is Williamsburg Lane

Key ☒ Sign ☒

To show Clyde Realty (Tom Clyde)

Sq. Footage 1560

Interior	Living	Dining	Kitchen	Bedroom	Bedroom	Bedroom	Bedroom	Closets	Baths
1st Flr.	x	x	x					Den	½
2nd Flr.						2			2

Lot Size N/A Year Built 1982 Garage 2-car RV Parking

Street x Curb x Sidewalk x Driveway x Basement x

Construction Frame Roof Tile

Floor Coverings Carpets Fireplace In Den (used brick) Drapes x

D/W x Range/Oven x W/D Disp. x Micr. Other

Sewer x Water x Gas x Cable TV x Laundry In Kitchen

Landscaping Very lush - Private patio very nice

Pool Assoc. Fencing Transportation

Schools School Bus at gate

Shopping ½ mile Hospital 3 mi. to University Hospital

Taxes $1,080 Financing Owner owns free and clear - Wants all cash. New loan (ARM) will take about $15,000 down

Listing Agent Tom Clyde

Listing Agent's Remarks Very impressive end unit. Presently vacant. Shows very well.

The likely buyer for this property: Young professionals, retirees, empty nesters, or 2 unrelated adults.

Features likely to appeal to the eventual buyer: Luxury appointments- 2 large suites, each with large ceramic tile bath. Wood panelling in den.

WORKSHEET FOR WRITING CLASSIFIED AD #3

1. After studying the property description and inspection notes on the opposite page, write a brief description of two or three types of buyers who would be attracted to this property.
2. Choose one buyer and try to form a detailed picture of him or her in your mind. Put yourself in the buyer's place. Then make a list of benefits the property offers that buyer and the needs it fulfills.
3. A. Choose one or two items from your list and, using the index, select or modify a heading.

   B. Selecting those features you want to emphasize in the ad body, use the index for appropriate language.

   C. An effective closing either sums up the features, helps the mood, gives an assurance of value or asks for action. Use your index to help you select or modify a closing based on the type of property or special features you wish to emphasize.
4. Using the information you've developed, write at least one complete ad for this property. The authors' version and commentary are on page 339.

Clyde Realty 476-8200 LISTING NO. R-138-84

RESIDENTIAL 3 BEDROOMS

Price $ 189,500 Exp. Date 4-1-88

Owner Kilgore Bros. - Builders

Type of Listing Exclusive

Address 1848 Vermont Lane

Directions Take Brown Street to Atlanta, west on Atlanta to Vermont. Right on Vermont.

Key ☒ Sign ☒

To show Contact Clyde Realty

Sq. Footage 1320

Interior	Living	Dining	Kitchen	Bedroom	Bedroom	Bedroom	Bedroom	Closets	Baths
1st Flr.	14 x 20	Area	12 x 14	10x12	12x14	14x14		x	2
2nd Flr.									

Lot Size 90' x 110' Year Built New Garage 2-car RV Parking

Street Paved Curb x Sidewalk Driveway Cement Basement No

Construction Frame Roof Tile

Floor Coverings Carpet/Tile Fireplace Red Brick Drapes No

D/W x Range/Oven x W/D Disp. x Micr. Other

Sewer x Water x Gas x Cable TV x Laundry In Kitchen

Landscaping Front only

Pool Fencing Rear Transportation 4 blocks to bus

Schools

Shopping ½ mi to Sunrise Ctr. Hospital 2 miles - St. Vincent's

Taxes Financing Conventional

Cash to Builder

Listing Agent Harvey Silkwood

Listing Agent's Remarks Brand New - Buyer can choose colors, tile, carpets, etc.

The likely buyer for this property: Younger family - retirees

Features likely to appeal to the eventual buyer: Design - It looks almost colonial but very modern. Cathedral ceiling in living area; rich oak woodwork.

WORKSHEET FOR WRITING CLASSIFIED AD #4

1. After studying the property description and inspection notes on the opposite page, write a brief description of two or three types of buyers who would be attracted to this property.
2. Choose one buyer and try to form a detailed picture of him or her in your mind. Put yourself in the buyer's place. Then make a list of benefits the property offers that buyer and the needs it fulfills.
3. A. Choose one or two items from your list and, using the index, select or modify a heading.

   B. Selecting those features you want to emphasize in the ad body, use the index for appropriate language.

   C. An effective closing either sums up the features, helps the mood, gives an assurance of value or asks for action. Use your index to help you select or modify a closing based on the type of property or special features you wish to emphasize.
4. Using the information you've developed, write at least one complete ad for this property. The authors' version and commentary are on page 339.

L-31-8

5

Clyde Realty 476-8200

LISTING NO. ______

LOTS(S) – LAND

Price $ 62,500 Exp. Date 8-1-88

Owner Thomas Harding

Type of Listing Exc 7%

Location The 1st vacant lot west of Rancho Palmeras on the south side of the street

45-821 Palm Shadow Dr.

Legal Description Lot 17 Block 4 to Petersens 3rd addition to the City of Indian Wells

Size 110' x 120'

Zoning R-1

Street Paved Curb No Gutter No Sidewalk No

Gas x Elec. x Sewer x Water x Cable TV x

Topography Flat lot on south side of 57

View Excellent view of Mt. Eisenhower

Assessed Valuation $14,300 Taxes $143 Financing Owner wants cash

Listing Agent Tom Clyde Agent Remarks Walled Lot between homes in $200,000 price category

Who is likely to be the buyer of this property? Speculative Builder or Buyer who wants a new custom home

Features likely to appeal to the eventual buyer: Prestige location- View of Mt. Eisenhower. 3 date trees, formerly part of date grove.

WORKSHEET FOR WRITING CLASSIFIED AD #5

1. After studying the property description and inspection notes on the opposite page, write a brief description of two or three types of buyers who would be attracted to this property.
2. Choose one buyer and try to form a detailed picture of him or her in your mind. Put yourself in the buyer's place. Then make a list of benefits the property offers that buyer and the needs it fulfills.
3. A. Choose one or two items from your list and, using the index, select or modify a heading.

   B. Selecting those features you want to emphasize in the ad body, use the index for appropriate language.

   C. An effective closing either sums up the features, helps the mood, gives an assurance of value or asks for action. Use your index to help you select or modify a closing based on the type of property or special features you wish to emphasize.
4. Using the information you've developed, write at least one complete ad for this property. The authors' version and commentary are on page 339.

Clyde Realty 476-8200 LISTING NO. R-64-84

RESIDENTIAL 2 BEDROOMS

Price $ 36,500 Exp. Date 5-1-88

Owner Lyle Thorsen

Type of Listing Exc 6%

Address 6841 W. Pioneer

Directions Pioneer runs 2 blocks west of Morrison Dr.

Key ☐ Sign ☒ Lockbox x

To show Clyde Realty (Lester Roemer)

Sq. Footage 920 (main house)

Interior	Living	Dining	Kitchen	Bedroom	Bedroom	Bedroom	Bedroom	Closets	Baths
1st Flr.	x	x	x	x	x				x
2nd Flr.	room for bedroom in walk-up attic								

Lot Size 80' x 140' Year Built 1890 ? Garage 2 RV Parking

Street Paved Curb Sidewalk x Driveway Gravel Basement Partial

Construction Frame Roof Asphalt

Floor Coverings Bare Wood Fireplace Drapes

D/W Range/Oven W/D Disp. Micr. Other

Sewer x Water x Gas Cable TV Laundry In basement

Landscaping Minimum, but several nice trees

Pool Fencing Transportation

Schools 2 blocks to Kincaid School (1-6)

Shopping 2 blocks Hospital 4 blocks

Taxes 218 Financing Unassumable loan. Buyer will need new financing.

Listing Agent Lester Roemer

Listing Agent's Remarks Renter occupied - looks as if it hasn't been decorated since it was built. There is a nice room over garage, now used as a bedroom.

The likely buyer for this property: Fixer upper buyer. It is probably lowest priced home in town.

Features likely to appeal to the eventual buyer: Low Price - Fixer upper. Deep lot with garden.

WORKSHEET FOR WRITING CLASSIFIED AD #6

1. After studying the property description and inspection notes on the opposite page, write a brief description of two or three types of buyers who would be attracted to this property.
2. Choose one buyer and try to form a detailed picture of him or her in your mind. Put yourself in the buyer's place. Then make a list of benefits the property offers that buyer and the needs it fulfills.
3. A. Choose one or two items from your list and, using the index, select or modify a heading.

   B. Selecting those features you want to emphasize in the ad body, use the index for appropriate language.

   C. An effective closing either sums up the features, helps the mood, gives an assurance of value or asks for action. Use your index to help you select or modify a closing based on the type of property or special features you wish to emphasize.
4. Using the information you've developed, write at least one complete ad for this property. The authors' version and commentary are on page 340.

7

Clyde Realty 476-8200 LISTING NO. R-37-84

RESIDENTIAL 4 BEDROOMS

Price $ 114,500 Exp. Date 5-15-88

Owner Mr. & Mrs. William Schmidt

Type of Listing Exc 6%

Address 7230 W. Willow Springs Rd.

Directions 2 miles north of Edgemont on Willow Springs

Key ☐ Sign ☒

To show Call Lester Roemer at Clyde Realty

Sq. Footage 2850

Interior	Living	Dining	Kitchen	Bedroom	Bedroom	Bedroom	Bedroom	Closets	Baths	Den
1st Flr.	X	X	X	X	X	X	X	Family Room	2½	X
2nd Flr.										

Lot Size ½ acre Year Built 1971 Garage 2½ RV Parking X

Street X Curb Sidewalk Driveway Paved Basement X

Construction Frame Roof Wood Shake

Floor Coverings Carpet Fireplace Stone Drapes X

D/W X Range/Oven X W/D X Disp. Micr. Other Trash Compacte

Sewer Septic Water Well Gas Cable TV Laundry In Basement

Landscaping Lawn & several huge Oak trees & 8 fruit trees

Pool Fencing Transportation School Bus at door

Schools Desert Valley School Dist.

Shopping 3 miles Hospital 3 miles

Taxes $1,485 Financing Assumable private 1st mortgage for $84,000 at 9%. Owner might carry a short term 2nd.

Listing Agent Lester Roemer

Listing Agent's Remarks Shows very well - 30' deep garage has huge workroom. Many open fields and woods in area.

The likely buyer for this property: Large family that enjoys semi-rural life semi-rural life.

Features likely to appeal to the eventual buyer: Eye appeal - Size - Condition. Orchard, ridge location, pastoral view from window of family room.

WORKSHEET FOR WRITING CLASSIFIED AD #7

1. After studying the property description and inspection notes on the opposite page, write a brief description of two or three types of buyers who would be attracted to this property.
2. Choose one buyer and try to form a detailed picture of him or her in your mind. Put yourself in the buyer's place. Then make a list of benefits the property offers that buyer and the needs it fulfills.
3. A. Choose one or two items from your list and, using the index, select or modify a heading.

   B. Selecting those features you want to emphasize in the ad body, use the index for appropriate language.

   C. An effective closing either sums up the features, helps the mood, gives an assurance of value or asks for action. Use your index to help you select or modify a closing based on the type of property or special features you wish to emphasize.
4. Using the information you've developed, write at least one complete ad for this property. The authors' version and commentary are on page 340.

Clyde Realty 476-8200 LISTING NO. C-41-84

RESIDENTIAL INCOME (COMMERCIAL) INDUSTRIAL

Owner Dr. Harvey Golden Type of Listing Exc 7% Price $ 890,000 Exp. Date 4-15-88

Annual Scheduled Gross $ 91,440

Address

Directions 7 Blocks west of Hwy 74 on University Ave.

To show contact: Clyde Realty (Tom Clyde)

Units	Type	Size	Lease	Monthly Rent
10	Office	1250 Sq. Ft.-	1-5 yr.	$680 to
	Suites	1550 Sq. Ft.	leases with	$820
			CPI increases	

Other Income $

Monthly Scheduled Gross $ 7620

Annual Expenses (prior calendar year as submitted by owner):

Taxes $ 8650 Trash $ 1200 Insurance $ 3950 Pool/Gardener $ 1860

Management $ X Gen. Maintenance $ 1200 Utilities $ 13,760 Misc. $ 1400

Total estimated annual expenses $ 31,960 Expenses verified Yes ☒ No ☐ (shown books)

Property Description:

Lot Size 140' x 260' Zoning C-1 Structure Size 90' x 90' - 2-story Date Built 1976

Roof Asphalt Heat Gas Cooling Ref Construction Frame

Basement Parking Paved 30 spaces

Water X Sewer X Gas X Elec. 220

Financing: Assumable $350,000 1st Mortgage at 12%. Owner will carry 2nd for strong buyer.

Listing Agent: Tom Clyde

Agent's Remarks Prestige Building; Unique exterior (wood). Tenants are MD's - Attys - CPAs, etc. No vacancies last 2 yrs.

Who is likely to be the buyer of this property? Pride of ownership buyer - Tenant or likely tenant - Possible syndicate

Features likely to appeal to the eventual buyer: Design - Prestige - location

WORKSHEET FOR WRITING CLASSIFIED AD #8

1. After studying the property description and inspection notes on the opposite page, write a brief description of two or three types of buyers who would be attracted to this property.
2. Choose one buyer and try to form a detailed picture of him or her in your mind. Put yourself in the buyer's place. Then make a list of benefits the property offers that buyer and the needs it fulfills.
3. A. Choose one or two items from your list and, using the index, select or modify a heading.

   B. Selecting those features you want to emphasize in the ad body, use the index for appropriate language.

   C. An effective closing either sums up the features, helps the mood, gives an assurance of value or asks for action. Use your index to help you select or modify a closing based on the type of property or special features you wish to emphasize.
4. Using the information you've developed, write at least one complete ad for this property. The authors' version and commentary are on page 341.

9

Clyde Realty 476-8200

LISTING NO. R-54-84

RESIDENTIAL 6 BEDROOMS

Price $ 64,800 Exp. Date 3-15-88

Owner Jean Ledbetter

Type of Listing Exc 6%

Address 42820 Kildare Blvd.

Directions 1 Block west of Madison just north of Williams Road

Key X Sign X

To show Clyde Realty (Harvey Silkwood)

Sq. Footage Approx. 4000

Interior	Living	Dining	Kitchen	Bedroom	Bedroom	Bedroom	Bedroom	Closets	Baths
1st Flr.	x	x	x	Parlor		x	x	walk-in pantry	1
2nd Flr.			sewing room	x	x	x	x		1

Lot Size 100' x 140' Year Built 1900 ? Garage 2 RV Parking

Street x Curb x Sidewalk x Driveway Gravel Basement x

Construction Frame Roof

Floor Coverings Fireplace 2 Drapes

D/W Range/Oven W/D Disp. Micr. Other

Sewer x Water x Gas x Cable TV x Laundry In Basement

Landscaping Neglected - Weeds

Pool Fencing Transportation Backs to Hwy.

Schools 2 blocks to Madison Middle School

Shopping 2 blocks Hospital ½ mile

Taxes 427 Financing Cash

Listing Agent Harvey Silkwood

Listing Agent's Remarks Newer roof - vacant for over a year. Structurally appears sound - needs paint, plaster and a lot of fixing.

The likely buyer for this property: Investor for fix-up - huge family - possible office use, but need zoning change

Features likely to appeal to the eventual buyer: Price for so much space - Distinctive design

WORKSHEET FOR WRITING CLASSIFIED AD #9

1. After studying the property description and inspection notes on the opposite page, write a brief description of two or three types of buyers who would be attracted to this property.
2. Choose one buyer and try to form a detailed picture of him or her in your mind. Put yourself in the buyer's place. Then make a list of benefits the property offers that buyer and the needs it fulfills.
3. A. Choose one or two items from your list and, using the index, select or modify a heading.

   B. Selecting those features you want to emphasize in the ad body, use the index for appropriate language.

   C. An effective closing either sums up the features, helps the mood, gives an assurance of value or asks for action. Use your index to help you select or modify a closing based on the type of property or special features you wish to emphasize.
4. Using the information you've developed, write at least one complete ad for this property. The authors' version and commentary are on page 341.

Clyde Realty 476-8200 LISTING NO. C-12-84

RESIDENTIAL INCOME (COMMERCIAL) INDUSTRIAL

Owner Hillary Babcock Type of Listing EXC 7% Price $ 390,000 Exp. Date 4-15-88

Annual Scheduled Gross $ 36,720

Address 76420 Highland Way

Directions

To show contact: Tom Clyde - Clyde Realty

Units	Type	Size	Lease	Monthly Rent
9	Office Suites - (8 - 3 room)			$240 -
	(1 Front	1200 Sq. Ft. Suite	M/M	$470
			or 1 yr leases	

Other Income $

Monthly Scheduled Gross $ 3060

Annual Expenses (prior calendar year as submitted by owner):

Taxes $ 2980 Trash $ 600 Insurance $ 450 Pool/Gardener $ 600

Management $ X Gen. Maintenance $ 1200 Utilities $ 250 Misc. $ 300

Total estimated annual expenses $ 6380 Expenses verified Yes ☐ No ☒

Property Description:

Lot Size 120' x 210' Zoning C-1 Structure Size approx. 9000 sq. ft. Date Built 1964

Roof Asphalt Heat x Cooling x Construction Stucco

Basement Parking Paved for 16 cars

Water X Sewer X Gas X Elec. X

Financing: Owner will finance $250,000 at 10% for 5 years.

Listing Agent: Tom Clyde

Agent's Remarks Fully rented - Tenants pay own utilities Rentals can probably be increased 10%-20%

Who is likely to be the buyer of this property? Small investor with high income and good cash position

Features likely to appeal to the eventual buyer: Fully rented - will pencil out

WORKSHEET FOR WRITING CLASSIFIED AD #10

1. After studying the property description and inspection notes on the opposite page, write a brief description of two or three types of buyers who would be attracted to this property.
2. Choose one buyer and try to form a detailed picture of him or her in your mind. Put yourself in the buyer's place. Then make a list of benefits the property offers that buyer and the needs it fulfills.
3. A. Choose one or two items from your list and, using the index, select or modify a heading.

   B. Selecting those features you want to emphasize in the ad body, use the index for appropriate language.

   C. An effective closing either sums up the features, helps the mood, gives an assurance of value or asks for action. Use your index to help you select or modify a closing based on the type of property or special features you wish to emphasize.
4. Using the information you've developed, write at least one complete ad for this property. The authors' version and commentary are on page 341.

Clyde Realty 476-8200 LISTING NO. R-50-84

RESIDENTIAL 7 BEDROOMS

Price $ 96,500 Exp. Date 9-15-88

Owner Ezra Higgins

Type of Listing Exc 6%

Address 42511 Padua Lake Rd.

Directions 6 miles north of Hwy 14.
Padua Lake Rd. crosses 14 by K-Mart

Key ☐ Sign ☒

To show Tom Clyde at Clyde Realty

Sq. Footage Approx. 5,000

Interior	Living	Dining	Kitchen	Bedroom	Bedroom	Bedroom	Bedroom	Closets	Baths
1st Flr.	x	x	x	1	Library				1
2nd Flr.				6					1

3rd 3 Large Unused Rooms

Lot Size 140' x 320' Year Built 1880 Approx. Garage 2 RV Parking x

Street x Curb Sidewalk Driveway gravel Basement x

Construction Frame Roof

Floor Coverings Hd/wd Fireplace 3 Drapes x and shades

D/W Range/Oven W/D Disp. Micr. Other

Sewer Septic Water Well Gas Cable TV Laundry In Basement

Landscaping Lush

Pool Fencing Transportation

Schools School Bus at door - 7 miles to schools

Shopping 6 miles Hospital 7 miles

Taxes 487 Financing New financing required

Listing Agent Tom Clyde

Listing Agent's Remarks The best cared for older home I have ever seen. Sparkles inside and out.

The likely buyer for this property: Family that wants a distinctive home with character - Antique Collector

Features likely to appeal to the eventual buyer: Condition - Size - Architecture

WORKSHEET FOR WRITING CLASSIFIED AD #11

1. After studying the property description and inspection notes on the opposite page, write a brief description of two or three types of buyers who would be attracted to this property.
2. Choose one buyer and try to form a detailed picture of him or her in your mind. Put yourself in the buyer's place. Then make a list of benefits the property offers that buyer and the needs it fulfills.
3. A. Choose one or two items from your list and, using the index, select or modify a heading.

   B. Selecting those features you want to emphasize in the ad body, use the index for appropriate language.

   C. An effective closing either sums up the features, helps the mood, gives an assurance of value or asks for action. Use your index to help you select or modify a closing based on the type of property or special features you wish to emphasize.
4. Using the information you've developed, write at least one complete ad for this property. The authors' version and commentary are on page 342.

Clyde Realty 476-8200 LISTING NO. R-75-8

RESIDENTIAL 4 BEDROOMS

Price $ 78,000 Exp. Date 2-15-88

Owner Willard Young

Type of Listing Exc 6%

Address 5738 W. Jefferson

Directions

Key ☐ Sign ☒

To show Tom Clyde - Clyde Realty

Sq. Footage Approx. 1500

Interior	Living	Dining	Kitchen	Bedroom	Bedroom	Bedroom	Bedroom	Closets	Baths
1st Flr.	x	x	x	1					1
2nd Flr.				3					½

Lot Size 80' x 110' Year Built 1934 Garage Det. 1 RV Parking

Street X Curb X Sidewalk Driveway X Basement X

Construction Frame Roof

Floor Coverings Hd/wd Fireplace X Drapes X

D/W Range/Oven W/D Disp. X Micr. Other

Sewer X Water X Gas X Cable TV X Laundry In Basement

Landscaping Extremely pleasant

Pool Fencing Fenced yard Transportation

Schools ½ mile to Jefferson High

Shopping ½ mile Hospital 1 mile

Taxes Financing Owner owns clear. Will require new financing.

Listing Agent Tom Clyde

Listing Agent's Remarks Immaculate bungalow styled home. Fresh inside and out. Well cared for garden.

The likely buyer for this property: Family who wants comfort and space, but can't afford a newer home.

Features likely to appeal to the eventual buyer: Size - Garden

Condition - Design - Location

Woodwork, built-in cabinets, bright, large kitchen.

WORKSHEET FOR WRITING CLASSIFIED AD #12

1. After studying the property description and inspection notes on the opposite page, write a brief description of two or three types of buyers who would be attracted to this property.
2. Choose one buyer and try to form a detailed picture of him or her in your mind. Put yourself in the buyer's place. Then make a list of benefits the property offers that buyer and the needs it fulfills.
3. A. Choose one or two items from your list and, using the index, select or modify a heading.

   B. Selecting those features you want to emphasize in the ad body, use the index for appropriate language.

   C. An effective closing either sums up the features, helps the mood, gives an assurance of value or asks for action. Use your index to help you select or modify a closing based on the type of property or special features you wish to emphasize.
4. Using the information you've developed, write at least one complete ad for this property. The authors' version and commentary are on page 342.

13

Clyde Realty 476-8200

LISTING NO. R-21-85

RESIDENTIAL 4 BEDROOMS

Price $198,500 Exp. Date 10-15-88

Owner Ralph Fasano

Type of Listing Exc 6%

Address 71460 Hwy 47

Directions 8 miles west on Hwy 47

Key ☐ Sign ☒

To show Tom Clyde - Clyde Realty

Sq. Footage 2700

Interior	Living	Dining	Kitchen	Bedroom	Bedroom	Bedroom	Bedroom	Closets	Baths
1st Flr.	X	X	X		Family Room				½
2nd Flr.				4					2

Lot Size 2½ acres Year Built 1980 Garage 2½ RV Parking X

Street X Curb Sidewalk Driveway Basement Rec Room/Gym

Construction Brick and Frame Roof

Floor Coverings Carpets Fireplace 2 Drapes X

D/W X Range/Oven X W/D Disp. X Micr. X Other

Sewer Septic Water Well Gas Cable TV Laundry

Landscaping Huge lawn

Pool Fencing Perimeter Transportation

Schools School Bus to Midvale Dist.

Shopping 4 miles Hospital 9 miles

Taxes 1285 Financing Assumable $128,000

9% 1st mortgage. Owners indicate they won't carry a 2nd

Listing Agent Tom Clyde

Listing Agent's Remarks Separate 250 sq. ft. studio and bath

Not zoned for horses

The likely buyer for this property: Executive who wants a more rural life

Features likely to appeal to the eventual buyer: Size - Beauty - Land - Suburbia

WORKSHEET FOR WRITING CLASSIFIED AD #13

1. After studying the property description and inspection notes on the opposite page, write a brief description of two or three types of buyers who would be attracted to this property.
2. Choose one buyer and try to form a detailed picture of him or her in your mind. Put yourself in the buyer's place. Then make a list of benefits the property offers that buyer and the needs it fulfills.
3. A. Choose one or two items from your list and, using the index, select or modify a heading.

   B. Selecting those features you want to emphasize in the ad body, use the index for appropriate language.

   C. An effective closing either sums up the features, helps the mood, gives an assurance of value or asks for action. Use your index to help you select or modify a closing based on the type of property or special features you wish to emphasize.
4. Using the information you've developed, write at least one complete ad for this property. The authors' version and commentary are on page 343.

Clyde Realty 476-8200 LISTING NO. ______

FARMS – FARMLAND

Owner: Tom Hughes

Price: 140,000 Exp. Date: 8-15-88

Type of Listing: exc

Location: On On Raccoon Road; 4th mailbox south of Pinepoint Drive.

Legal Description:

Size: 90 acres Tillable: 35 Pasture: 15

Zoning: ag Woods: 30 Water Source: artesian well

Frontage: 330 ft

Gas: no Elec.: 220 Sewer: cesspool

Topography: rolling

Equipment included: some old field machinery

Assessed Valuation: 140,000 Taxes: 300 in 1986 Financing: no

Outbuildings: barn(s): small barn in good condition; Dutch style.

shed(s): 2, in need of repair

Other: old chicken coop and milkhouse

House: Lot size ______ Year built: older Garage: 2 car Sq. Footage ______

Basement: yes Construction: wood frame Roof: asphalt Floor Coverings: oak floors

Fireplace: no Drapes: no Range/Oven: elec W/D: no

Disp.: no Micr.: no Other ______ Laundry ______

Interior	Living	Dining	Kitchen	Bedroom	Bedroom	Bedroom	Bedroom	Closets	Baths
1st Flr.	x	x	x						1/2
2nd Flr.				x	x	x	x	ample	1

Listing Agent: Thomas Clyde Agent Remarks:

House in good condition and updated. Land not suited to large-scale farming. House under 100-year-old pine trees. Clear fishing stream runs through property.

Who is likely to be the buyer of this property?

retiree, self-sufficiency, commuters, self-employed

Features likely to appeal to the eventual buyer: picturesque, creek, trees, rolling landscape, modernized house and standing barn.

WORKSHEET FOR WRITING CLASSIFIED AD #14

1. After studying the property description and inspection notes on the opposite page, write a brief description of two or three types of buyers who would be attracted to this property.
2. Choose one buyer and try to form a detailed picture of him or her in your mind. Put yourself in the buyer's place. Then make a list of benefits the property offers that buyer and the needs it fulfills.
3. A. Choose one or two items from your list and, using the index, select or modify a heading.

   B. Selecting those features you want to emphasize in the ad body, use the index for appropriate language.

   C. An effective closing either sums up the features, helps the mood, gives an assurance of value or asks for action. Use your index to help you select or modify a closing based on the type of property or special features you wish to emphasize.
4. Using the information you've developed, write at least one complete ad for this property. The authors' version and commentary are on page 343.

This property lends itself to a number of approaches. These ads represent two of the possibilities.

This ad is specifically designed to attract small and first-time investors. A fixer-upper approach could also be added to property one.

1a

STORE + 2 APTS.
NOT BEAUTIFUL
JUST PROFITABLE

Ample parking and the tenants pay their own utilities on this high-traffic commercial corner. Profitable with below-market rentals. Owners financing is possible at the investor price of only $78,000.

Clyde Realty 476-8200

This ad sells the benefits of ownership to the small business, commercial, occupant-buyer.

1b

MERCHANTS
WHY PAY RENT?

This 2,100-square-foot prime corner store can be yours with a low-low down payment. There is plenty of parking and the 2 apartments upstairs help make your payments. Be your own landlord at $78,000.

Clyde Realty 476-8200

Because of the property's location and quality, this ad is aimed especially at doctors who want to invest in income residential property. The heading appeals to pride of ownership. The body stresses location near a major hospital and gives pride-of-ownership details.

2

24 PROUD UNITS

The most beautiful apartment complex in the city is walking-close to University Hospital. The professionally managed, 2-bedroom, 2-bath luxury units are set in a park-like grove with pool and separate hot spa. With its below-market financing, you and your accountant will agree this is truly an exceptional opportunity at $875,000.

Clyde Realty 476-8200

This ad aims at young professionals and empty-nesters. It assumes the convenience of condo living while creating an image of the privacy and luxury available in a single-family home.

3

COLONIAL VILLAGE —TOWN HOUSE

The privacy and elegance of estate living are yours with this rare end unit. Twin master suites with sumptuous Grecian baths, paneled den with antique brick fireplace, very private patio with delightful landscaping, a powder room for guests and a double garage are just a few of the amenities of this truly magnificent residence. Available now and worthy of your immediate attention at $119,500.

Clyde Realty **476-8200**

This ad gives special nostalgic appeal to a brand-new home by stressing its unique features. It appeals to buyers who want new housing but are put off by the uniformity often associated with it.

4

THE SPIRIT OF NEW ENGLAND

This brand-new 3BR, 2-bath Nantucket traditional captures the craftsmanship of yesterday combined with all the conveniences of tomorrow. You will love the colonial window walls, the warmth of solid oak, the rose brick fireplace and the feeling of spaciousness with its soaring ceilings. Besides having everything on your want list, there is still time to choose carpets, colors and wall coverings for that very special personal touch. Don't delay at $129,500.

Clyde Realty **476-8200**

Though only a lot, this property is given extra appeal by the use of extra words that say quality. *This land is walled for privacy, has a special view and boasts date palms that add to the picture of a truly luxurious site.*

5

INDIAN WELLS

Beneath towering date palms, this walled estate-size lot in the desert's premier community will provide you with a spectacular poolside view of Mt. Eisenhower. This is the irresistible site for that very special home. Proudly offered at $62,500.

Clyde Realty **476-8200**

The heading appeals to those already interested in a fixer-upper—if the price is low for the market, it would also be appropriate for the heading. The house's negative features appeal to young artistic types who find them an exciting challenge. A second group the ad will attract is lower-income buyers with children, who consider location the *major factor in choice of housing.*

6

**FIXER-UPPER—
YOU BET**

This 1890 5-room American bungalow is in desperate need of paint, plaster and nails. Its redeeming features include a rocking-chair front porch, a walk-up attic suitable for an extra bedroom, an old-fashioned root cellar, a separate 2-car carriage house with a second floor artist's studio and a family-size vegetable garden. The only eyesore in a neighborhood of fine homes, it's disaster-priced at $36,500.

Clyde Realty 476-8200

This ad will attract the typical suburban family. It sells family benefits, providing an image of a place where idyllic family living can take place. The targeted family may not need four bedrooms and a den, but the extra space is very appealing and therefore is prominently featured as a heading.

7

**4 BEDROOMS
+ DEN**

On a quiet lane in prestigious Orchard Ridge, this immaculate 2½-bath western-style ranch is sheltered by ancient oaks on its full ½-acre site. Your family will delight in the tribe-size country kitchen and the window-walled family room overlooking the picturesque countryside. Other amenities include an orchardstone fireplace, an oversized double garage with a huge workroom and a mouth-watering family orchard. Exceptional financing makes this your wisest investment in family living $114,500.

Clyde Realty 476-8200

This aims straightforwardly at the large investor or small syndicate. It emphasizes pride of ownership as well as good return on investment with carefree management.

8

PROFESSIONAL BUILDING—100% OCCUPANCY

Doctors, attorneys and accountants love this distinctive architectural masterpiece in its lushly landscaped prestigious setting. The 10 huge suites are all on escalating leases. One look at this building and the books will convince you this is truly a carefree blue-chip investment. Priced at $890,000 with flexible financing.

Clyde Realty 476-8200

This ad has an exceptionally strong appeal to the artistic do-it-yourselfer, someone who appreciates architectural quality and believes older is better. The heading will also attract large families hoping to find lots of room at a bargain price. (Could also have been written aimed at an investor, emphasizing lot size, rental possibilities and highway location.)

9

FIXER-UPPER —VICTORIAN

An abandoned 12-room, 2-bath classic with full wraparound porch, distinctive balconies, 2 fireplaces and all the gingerbread you have dreamed of. While basically sound, the cosmetic treatment to make this grand old lady seem young again will take barrels of paint, a ton of nails and a great deal of imagination. This one is definitely not for the timid at $64,800.

Clyde Realty 476-8200

This bare-bones ad is designed to get the prospective investor on the phone. If the price for the location and number of units appears attractive, it could have been featured in the headline. (Revisable rents could have been included in the ad.)

10

PROFESSIONAL PLAZA

9 private office suites, each with its own entrance in a high-rental-demand area. A unique investment opportunity that will make dollars and sense at $390,000

Clyde Realty 476-8200

This ad is aimed at the upper-middle-class buyer who wants a distinctive home to be proud of, but is not interested in fixing it up or enduring ancient utilities and construction problems. The ad takes advantage of the revival of interest in Victorian buildings.

11

VICTORIAN SHOWPLACE

This 14-room architectural masterpiece has been lovingly preserved from the 1880s. It has been carefully updated with the conveniences and systems of today so as not to detract from the basic charm of days gone by. There are all the nooks and crannies, gingerbread trim, quiet porches, polished hardwoods and high ceilings with elaborate moldings that can make this your oasis for tranquil and gracious living. Set on a lushly landscaped acre, you and your friends will agree this is many steps above anything you have seen at any price. Here is your opportunity to own a real treasure for the price of an ordinary home—$96,500.

Clyde Realty 476-8200

This ad sells the virtues of yesterday to the family of today. Traditional *applies to any older architectural style that cannot be readily classified. Attractive financing is implied by a "friendly" seller.*

12

4 BR—TRADITIONAL

Set on a quiet tree-lined street of fine homes, this sparkling American classic is waiting for your family. You will love its solid hardwood floors, built-in China cabinets, formal dining room, sunny eat-in kitchen, lovely garden plus all the extras you have dreamed about. If you qualify, the owner will help you provide your family with the home they deserve. Full price $78,000.

Clyde Realty 476-8200

This ad is targeted at the rising executive anxious to affirm that he or she has made it to the top of the social order. The heading sticks to a straightforward description, but will draw the attention of the reader looking for an exclusive property. The body of the ad stresses pride of ownership and luxury features such as the fitness center.

13

**4 BR—
WILLIAMSBURG
COLONIAL**

Set on 2½ acres, this almost-new executive estate captures all the charm of colonial America and combines it with the conveniences of today. The 2½ baths, huge family room, massive fireplaces, country kitchen, basement fitness center and 2½-car garage are just a few of its many special features. There is even a separate studio/guest house with an additional bath. If you don't mind being envied by your friends, this home can be yours at $198,500.

Clyde Realty 476-8200

This ad, which provides an attractive image of a pleasant simple farm, is aimed at retirees and people seeking a simpler way of life. The farm is too small to appeal to real farmers.

If financing were available, it should have been mentioned.

14

**GRANDMA'S
FARM—90 ACRES**

The perfect 4-bedroom farmhouse sheltered by century-old pines has been updated for comfortable country living. The charming Dutch barn, family orchard, crystal-clear fishing stream and ample woodlot are reminiscent of an almost forgotten way of life. This is your chance for real country happiness at $140,000.

Clyde Realty 476-8200

Quick Reference Guide To Synonyms and Descriptive Terms

This guide is no substitute for the detailed treatments in the text, but will serve to jog your memory and stimulate your creativity when you are looking for just the right word or phrase to express what you have in mind.

Air-Conditioning—Central air, fully air-conditioned, zone control air-conditioning and heat, climate-controlled environment, electronically controlled environment.

Alcove—Music, sleeping, reading, library, office, sewing room (*See:* Den).

Animals and Birds—Roaming deer and curious raccoons will visit you at this. . . , the backyard features a magnificent oak tree that is home to at least one family of squirrels, deer have been seen on the property, the woodlot is loaded with game, your nearest neighbors are squirrels and a friendly family of raccoons, wild critters abound on this. . . , presently home to deer, quail and pheasant, you will feed the deer in your own backyard, you will look out your windows and see quail and doves at the well-frequented bird feeders, the breakfast area overlooks the well-frequented hummingbird feeders.

Appliances—Like-new, built-in, all built-ins, built-in everything, Maytag, the Maytag appliances reflect the quality appointments of this. . . .

Architectural Types

Brownstone—Brownstone classic, front-stoop brownstone.

Cape Cod—Friendly Cape Cod, captivating Cape Cod, New England Cape Cod.

Colonial—Rhett Butler colonial, Tara, southern manor, pillared colonial, columned colonial, 4-column colonial, southern colonial, southern traditional, New Orleans colonial, double-stairs colonial, colonial with a contemporary flair, substantial colonial, classic colonial, nostalgic colonial, New England charmer, clapboard colonial, federal colonial, colonial splendor, head-turning colonial, distinctive colonial, impeccable colonial, picture-book colonial, proper colonial, a touch of Williamsburg, Williamsburg-inspired, Williamsburg traditional, Georgian colonial, Virginia colonial, Quaker charmer, Pennsylvania Dutch, Dutch colonial, New England saltbox, for the colonial purist, multigabled colonial, colonial grace with modern comfort, a touch of New England, executive colonial, stately colonial, timeless colonial, monumental colonial, Nantucket colonial, saltbox colonial, Quaker Village colonial, pampered Dutch colonial.

Contemporary—Refreshing, dramatic, outstanding, stunning, sophisticated, distinctive custom, California contemporary, Arizona contemporary, New Mexico contemporary, tri-level, split-level, earth shelter, solar home, art deco, excitingly different, imaginative floor plan, contemporary elegance casually designed in the flavor of the Southwest, exuberant design, open-living design, free-flowing floor plan, open concept, versatile floor plan, exciting and spacious, skylit, treetop, California-inspired, beaux-art, stunningly conceived, innovative without being trendy, clean, sleek, uncluttered design, sleek and sophisticated yet warm and cheerful.

English—English manor, English manor house, Cotswold manor, stone manor house, proper English, smashing, a touch of Old England, English brick, Yorkshire Tudor, handsome Tudor, flawless Tudor, country English, English colonial, Queen Anne, Elizabethan, Edwardian, English chateau, English country, English cottage, proper English, proper English brick, Tiffany Tudor, architecturally smashing, smashingly impressive, reminiscent of an English country estate, patterned after the noble houses of England where entertaining and hospitality were inseparable from a gracious tradition.

French—Sassy French Provincial, French colonial, French country home, sumptuous French country home, French Regency, two-story French Regency, French Normandy, turreted French Norman, French manor, French contemporary, chateau, French chateau, Flemish cottage.

Greek—Greek revival, Greek gothic.

Italian—Stately Mediterranean, old-world Mediterranean, Hollywood-style Mediterranean, lavish villa, Italianate, brick Italianate, Mediterranean colonial, Romanesque beauty, Venetian, Venetian gothic.

Ranch—California, raised, exciting rambler, brick rambler, long, low and luscious, sprawling ranch.

Spanish—A touch of Spain, Spanish hacienda, adobe hacienda, Presidio Spanish, old-world Spanish, tons of tile, flowing tile floors, mission tile, adobe fireplace, arches, massive arches, covered walkways, capturing the glory of old Spain.

Traditional—Traditional estate, elegant brick traditional, dignified traditional, American traditional, American bungalow.

Victorian—Country, charming, grand, a dignified lady, turreted, Victorian showcase, stately, bow front, grandiose, vintage, gingerbread, Queen Anne, storybook, commanding.

Architecture (Details)—Exquisite architectural details, handsome detailing, classic detailing, the most authentic. . . we have seen, the aesthetic allure of classic design, blending the traditional with the timeless, built with delightful European flair and style, classical embellishments.

Architecture (General)—Architecturally perfect, architecturally fresh, one of a kind, architectural masterpiece, architecturally designed, distinctively designed, masterful design, exuberant design, Frank Lloyd Wright–inspired, featured in *Architectural Digest,* architectural award winner, design award winner, award-winning design, designed by. . . , awe-inspiring, artistic masterpiece designed by. . . , merging aesthetic form with efficiency of function, capturing nature's essence, architecturally unique, a home that breaks the monotony of the ordinary, excitingly different.

Assumable Loans—Assumable 7%, VA-assumable, FHA-assumable, assume 8½% FHA, $8,500 takeover, paydown to 7½% loan, super assumption, no qualifying—no credit check, large, long-term fixed-rate.

Atrium—Cathedral, glassed-in, fountain, glass-domed, soaring, lush, garden, tropical.

Attic—Walk-up, room for 2 additional bedrooms in walk-up attic, storage, storage attic could be converted to studio or guest room, skylighted, skylit, windowed, dormered, would make ideal artist's studio, perfect loft studio, attic studio.

Backyard—Tribe-size yard, fully fenced backyard, playground backyard, room to romp, room for swing set and sandbox and a gaggle of children, the backyard is just waiting for your children, orchard-size, perfect spot for your garden, garden-size, fenced play area, child-safe fenced yard, family-size, the backyard is just waiting for a sandbox and swing, the old oak tree in the backyard is the perfect place to hang your swing, picturesque and private.

Bargain Property—*See:* Homes—Bargain-Priced.

Barn—Weathered, horse, wobbly, red, old Dutch, gambrel-roofed, ancient, massive, would make ideal studio.

Bars—Wet bar, refrigerated wet bar, pub room, friendly pub room.

Basement—Full, poured, block, 8′, dry, sump pump in. . . , partial, fruit cellar, exposed, walk-out, daylight, finished, expansion room in. . . , partially finished, laundry room in. . . , ready for finishing, roughed-in for bath, perfect for rainy-day playroom, plenty of storage room, room for 2 additional bedrooms in..., expansion room in..., future game room, ready to be finished, plenty of room in dry basement for a hobby shop, wine cellar, 600-bottle wine cellar, temperature-controlled wine cellar.

Basement Unit—English apartment, room for English apartment, terrace-level apartment, could be finished for rental unit, would make possible in-law suite, could be converted to English apartment, possible rental unit.

Bathhouse—Cabana, dressing room with shower, pool house.

Baths—Master, sumptuous master bath, sensuous master bath, sinfully sensuous master bath, deliciously sumptuous baths, tiled, Roman, Phoenician, Grecian, garden tub, luxurious sunken tub, step-down tub, antique tub, antique claw-footed tub, opulent Phoenician bath, skylit bath, enchanting garden bath, bath/fitness center, oval tub, tub with Jacuzzi, double tub, double vanities, double shower, his-and-hers vanities, dual vanities, separate shower, powder room, 1/2-bath, 3/4-bath, floor-to-ceiling tile in... .

Bedroom—26′ master bedroom, master suite, breathtaking master suite, sensual master suite, lavish master suite, 2 bedrooms in children's wing, separate dressing areas, his-and-hers dressing rooms, nursery, teen suite, maid's room, maid or guest room, guest suite, separate guest suite, king-size, queen-size, delightful dormered..., room for additional bedrooms in..., master suite with morning room, master suite with sitting room, sumptuous master suite, dual master suites, master suite plus guest room, master suite features a snuggle-up fireplace, separate suite for guests or live-ins, elegant en suite, lower-level bedroom.

Brick—Used, Tennessee, antique, Norman, warm rose, all brick, maintenance-free brick exterior (*See:* Stone).

Builder's Sale—Builder's closeout, builder's liquidation, builder's final sellout, desperate builder, builder SOS, builder must sell, built by the builder as (his/her) own residence, built by the builder for (his/her) own family (*See:* Homes—New).

Business Opportunities—The buck starts here, unbelievable money-maker, a money machine, count your profits, proven gold mine, impressive track record, fantastic profits, opportunity knocks, national franchise, captured clientele, immediate income, hire yourself, work for yourself, be master of your future, family business, mother and daughter business, father and son business, recession-proof business, take advantage of...years of goodwill, established..., long-established, in operation more than...years, books open to serious buyer, the books are open to you and your accountant, needs a take-charge owner, untapped potential, can be expanded, proven growth record, owner will train, experienced staff, loyal staff will remain, employees know of this ad, below-market rental, advantageous lease, long-term lease, long-term lease at moderate rental, favorable lease, price includes all inventory, inventory at cost, comes with all equipment, furnishings and fixtures for efficient operation, all equipment included for uninterrupted operation, latest equipment, new equipment, like-new furnishings and equipment, 100% location, strategically located between...and ..., prominent location, prestigious location, corner location, high-traffic location, college town, located in affluent community of..., located in booming..., loads of parking, ample parking, carrying all major lines, top-line inventory, exclusive dealer for..., steady neighborhood trade, established clientele, enjoys a substantial tourist trade, national accounts, national clients, major clients, retiring owner will sign noncompetition agreement, unusual circumstances force the sale of this profitable..., owner retiring, 79-year-old owner retiring, business has grown too fast for elderly owner, needs a young take-charge executive, owner's doctor says sell now, part-time owner reports $________ gross, reports $________ net with absentee owner, absentee owner wants out,... generations of family ownership, this business has been a landmark since..., needs a couple willing to work, no selling, no mechanical experience necessary, this profitable...can be operated right from your home, exclusive dealer for... , your security is only a phone call away, a good operating business that could be even better.

Carpeting—Top line, plush Karastan, all wool, sculptured wool, deep shag, Stain Master, plush sculptured, plush neutral, luxurious, wall-to-wall Berber.

Ceiling—Lighted, softly lighted, illuminated, skylighted, cathedral, soaring cathedral, impressive cathedral, beamed, open-beamed, exposed beam, 10′, two-story living room, the 10′ ceiling adds a feeling of spaciousness and light, a soft ceiling of light gently illuminates the charming kitchen, coved, vaulted, dramatically vaulted, colossal, double-height, tin, the 14′ vaulted ceiling enhances the ambiance of the great room.

Ceiling Fan—Ceiling, plantation, paddle, Bermuda.

Church—Just a short walk to..., just down the road from..., walk to..., walk to worship,...parish.

Clean—Better than a model, shows like a model, immaculate, impeccable, flawless, spotless, move-in ready, squeaky clean, reflects caring owners, owner's pride, whistle-clean, handsomely kept, antiseptic clean, white-glove clean, it sparkles, pristine condition, blue-ribbon condition, superbly maintained, reflects owner's pride, better than new.

Closets—Huge, his-and-hers, walk-in, lighted, outrageous, mirrored wardrobes, double sliding wardrobes, mirrored doors on the sliding wardrobes, more closets than you have ever seen, loads of closet and storage space, built-in shoe racks in..., closets you can get lost in.

Colors—Soft terra-cotta tones, rich terra-cotta tones, warm and rich color scheme, warm medley of colors, muted tones, soft tones, softly decorated, basic earth-tone decor, golden earth tones, warm earth tones, muted earth tones, desert colors, desert decor, cool and fresh, cool tones, bright and light, peaches-and-cream decor, a happy decor of..., tasteful neutral tones, subdued tones of ivory and beige, decorator-perfect, decorator colors, decorator-fresh, decorator-sharp.

Columns—Doric, Corinthian, Greek, Roman, soaring, fluted, pilaster.

Condominium—Condomaximum, choice corner unit, impressive end unit, at last—a corner unit, free-standing unit, garden unit, villa-style, fantasy villa, upgraded...model, sought-after ...model, a hard-to-find... model, upgraded unit, upgraded appliances, upgraded beyond belief, walk to everything from this..., walk to..., strategic location, rental service available, monthly assessments only $________, low monthly assessment, low condo fee includes everything, maintenance fee includes heat, never a rent increase, very private balcony, 18 windows welcome the sunshine in this immaculate corner unit, manicured greenbelt, soundproofed walls, you won't have to whisper in this soundproof..., whisper no more—fully soundproof building, elevator building, doorman, concierge, full-service building, a condominium that gives you the privacy of a single-family home, an exciting alternative to apartment living, a resort-style life-style with big-city sophistication, sophisticated yet so comfortable, for a uniquely comfortable urban life-style, free from the burden of maintenance, all the amenities of a fine resort, more than just a place to live—it's a whole new way of living, resort environment, a world of fun and leisure, for comfort and uncomplicated living, the closest thing to carefree living, offering the excitement of city living in an almost country-like setting (*See:* Security, Privacy, Vacation Homes).

Cooperative—(*See:* Condominium).

Courtyard—Stone, brick, paved, fountain, flower-bedecked, charming.

Darkroom—With sinks, with stainless-steel sinks, ideal for photographer's darkroom, would make the perfect darkroom.

Deck—Wraparound, inviting sun deck, secluded, extensive deck area, extensive decking, redwood, cedar, redwood balcony, wrapped on three sides by redwood deck, sunset, sunrise, barbecue, cantilevered, garden, warm, sunny, secluded, privacy, a very private sun deck.

Decorating—Lavishly decorated, tastefully decorated, professionally decorated, decorated by..., dramatically decorated, decorated in peaches and cream.

Den—Lion-size, walnut-paneled, courtroom-paneled, study, paneled study, library, English library, music room, English drawing room, drawing room, office, home office, office/den, estate office, convertible, the warm paneled den features a friendly orchard stone fireplace, floor-to-ceiling bookcases line one wall of the richly appointed study, the separate entrance makes the den the perfect home office, your perfect quiet spot, your "sneak-away" place.

Dining Room—Separate dining area, formal, elegant, chandeliered, crystal chandelier adorns the formal dining room, banquet-size, gallery, window-wrapped, room for a family reunion in the. . . , solarium-style, breakfast room, cheerful breakfast room, greenhouse-windowed breakfast room.

Doors—Double doors, pocket doors, double pocket doors, solid oak entry, massive hand-carved, handcrafted, sculptured double-door entry, 9′ doors, massive 9′ doors, double glass doors, sliding glass patio doors, sliding French doors, classic French doors, stained-glass entry door, leaded-glass entry door, leaded-glass accents, crystal doorknobs.

Driveway—Paved drive, concrete drive, cobblestone driveway, circle drive.

Entry Hall—Foyer, tiled foyer, slate foyer, impressive slate foyer, soaring foyer, two-story soaring foyer, split foyer, vestibule, the lovely slate foyer beckons you into this magnificent residence.

Entryway—Courtyard, arched, shaded, dramatic, slate, turreted, dramatic turreted, massive, grand, gallery, gracious, picturesque columned entry enhances this. . . , cathedral, portico, gated, enter through a stone portal, drive-through portico, the estate entrance frames this. . . .

Estate Sale—Estate clearance, heirs say sell, heir's selling, estate settlement, priced to settle estate, probate sale, probate-ordered sale, heirs want cash now.

Exterior Siding—Low-maintenance Masonite siding, no-maintenance aluminum siding and trim, maintenance-free vinyl siding, western cedar siding, maintenance-free redwood siding, natural cedar siding, natural textured wood siding, handsome brick exterior, brick and cedar exterior, brick beauty, brick-and-stone exterior, native stone exterior, solid stone construction (*See:* Brick).

Family Room—30′ game room, club room, recreation room, daylight recreation room, billiard room, marine room, playroom, family playroom, drawing room, salon, fitness center, home gym, private gym, family room opens onto. . . , the family room centers on a massive stone fireplace, warm, window-wrapped, leisure room, pub room, English pub room, cozy pub room with stone fireplace, adult playroom, magnificent salon, grand salon, lounge.

Farms (Farmers')—A farmer's farm, family farm, real farmer's farm, double cropper, grade A dairy farm, irrigated alfalfa farm, poultry ranch, apple orchard, diversified farm, farmin' bargain, high producing soybean farm, a working farm, a working ranch, 220 acres under plow, 400 acres of pasture, 600 acres tillable, 100 acres in government program, 90% tillable, 800 deeded acres, 10-acre tobacco allotment, balance woodlot, 120 acres currently in alfalfa, leased grazing rights on 3,000 acres, BLM lease for 3,000 additional acres, pasture for cows, will carry 700 cow units, capacity for 800 feeder pigs, 120 bushels of corn per acre reported last year, said to be one of the best-producing farms in the area, a self-sustaining cattle operation capable of carrying 600 cattle units, improved pasture, unimproved pasture, native pasture, 4″ drilled well, 3 wells, natural flowing spring, year-round flowing river, seasonal stream, 1/2 mile of river frontage, irrigation lines, 120 acres irrigated and tiled, irrigation allotment, creek could be used for irrigation, creek presently used for irrigation, drip irrigation, overhead irrigation, includes ample water rights, 4 ponds, land is well watered, blessed with ample water, milking parlor, automatic feeders, fenced and cross-fenced, 80-stanchion barn, 42-stall barn, 6 silos, 4 Harvester silos, three 60,000-bu. grain bins, 30′ × 120′ machine shed, 40′ × 100′ pole barn, 40′ × 100′ open-loft barn, 11-room house, modern 11-room house, newer 11-room house.

Farms (Gentlemen)—Family showplace, country squire, weekend farm, picture-postcard farm, Currier and Ives farm, Old West ranch, executive farm, 300-acre empire, for the blue-jeans executive, agricultural estate, the best in town and country living, farm in style, flying cowboy/cowgirl ranch, flying farmer, possible landing strip, miles of white board fencing, abundance of wildlife, just the place for purebred cattle and thoroughbred horses, mouth-watering orchard, historic farm, storybook farm, be lord or lady of the manor, start a dynasty on this. . ., shades of the Old West, Old West ranch, Zane Grey would have felt at home in this. . ., be monarch of the range, the Old West is alive and well on this. . ., established by a federal land grant issued in 18__, manor house built in 18__, this is the first time this farm has been on the market in. . . years, formerly owned by. . ., Dutch barn, complete cattle-working facilities were specifically designed for easy management, farm pond stocked with bass, trout-filled stream, abundance of wildlife, professional management available.

Farms (Hobby)—Mother earth farm, self-sufficiency farm, self-sufficiency retreat, cornucopia hobby farm, organic farm, organic orchard, grandpa or grandma's farm, beginner's farm, starter farm, farmette, minifarm, ranchette, pioneer farm, retirement farm, old-time farm, farmlet, your escape from the city, back to basics, 40 acres and independence, find your roots, harvest the good life, traditional farm home, old-time farm home, solid 5-room home, windmill-powered well, hydropower possibilities, possible water generation site, possible dam site for lake and hydropower, contains marketable timber, full complement of modern well-maintained equipment, easy drive to..., not just a home—it's a way of life, a better place to raise a family, escape from city crime and grime, harvest the good life, for the life you deserve, hayloft barn, gambrel barn, massive barn, on a country lane, on a quiet country lane, country living at its tranquil best, offering pastoral tranquility.

Farms (Investment)—In the path of progress, farm now—develop later, $90,000 1st-year depreciation, owner will leaseback, lessee available, $200,000 of depreciable assets, 1/2 mineral rights, development possibilities, exciting potential, the ultimate tax shelter, impressive investment, tax farm, owner will leaseback, tenant available.

Fencing—Cyclone, white board, cedar rail, split-rail, white picket, charming white picket, stockade, privacy walls, block walls, completely fenced, fully fenced, perimeter and cross-fencing, fenced and cross-fenced, old stone, high-walled garden, hedged with stone walls, embraced by stone walls, estate-rail fencing, ranch-rail fencing, wrought iron fencing.

Financing—Less than $________ down, try $________ down, can you afford $500 per month?, old-fashioned financing, down-to-earth financing, no money down, hardly anything down, possible 10% financing, no-down VA, low-down FHA, seller pays points, seller pays points and closing costs, locked-in interest rate, payments like rent, financing has been arranged, financing available, offering extraordinary financial arrangements (*See:* Assumable Loans).

Fireplace—16′ floor-to-ceiling, wood-burning, fieldstone, split-stone, orchard stone, native stone, massive stone, massive walk-in, majestic stone, California driftwood, Tennessee stone, antique brick, warm rose brick, marble, cheerful, corner, 2-way, see-thru, Heatilator, with heat exchanger, free-standing, dramatic Danish, stove insert, Franklin stove, marble hearth and mantle, solid walnut mantle, massive mantle, brick hearth, raised hearth, heartwarming brick, toe-warming, cheerful hearth, travertine, river rock, soaring.

Fixer-Uppers—Fix 'n' save, sweep and reap, weed it and reap, prewar wreck, magnificent wreck, a shambles, demolition derby special, bit of a mess, executive-fixer, worst house—best street, the worst-looking house, an eyesore, peeling-paint special, leaking-roof special, bring your toolbox, bring your paintbrush, fix or tear down, bring your hammer, wrecking-bar special, paintbrush needed, needs love, needs a labor of love, needs a face-lift, ugly duckling, Pygmalion—needs Dr. Higgins, in terrible condition, neglected, neglected giant, neglected ranch, neglected—oh yes!, needs everything, high-class disaster, quality construction in need of cosmetic surgery, but the structure is sound, solid construction, presently livable, barely livable, livable but..., make no mistake—there is work to be done, needs a few bushels of nails and barrels of paint, loaded with potential but needs a barrel of paint, bring your imagination and some elbow grease, a neglected beauty awaiting a Prince Charming, this home boasts 3 bedrooms and 2 baths—what it doesn't boast about is its horrible condition, wear your old clothes and bring along aspirin, a jungle of overgrown shrubs and trees, it looks like it fought in World War III and was the loser, we scraped the bottom of the barrel to come up with this. . ., deserted, abandoned, semi-fixer-upper, fire-damaged, rambling wreck, abandoned artist's chalet, it's a lemon, handyperson's special, diamond in the rough, toolbox special, needs TLC, dumpy duplex, forgotten cottage, fixer-upper possibilities, dilapidated disaster, ruin, paint, patch and profit.

Flooring (Tile)—Terrazzo, quarry, Mexican, Mexican quarry, sun-baked Mexican, travertine, Portuguese, easy-care, no-wax Congoleum, vinyl, pure vinyl.

Flooring (Wood)—Hardwood, random-plank, random-width, hand-pegged, pegged hardwood, gleaming, parquet, solid oak, maple, soft-tone maple, mellow pine, pine plank, heart oak, varnished oak, dazzling oak, graced with gleaming hardwood and richly carpeted floors.

Foreclosure—Foreclosure sale, near foreclosure, stop foreclosure, beat foreclosure sale, foreclosure pending, last chance before foreclosure, lender forces sale, beat-the-sheriff sale, lender wants sale now, lender orders sale, bank repo, out of foreclosure, government foreclosure, for sale by lender, lender sale.

Fountain—Fountain courtyard, fountain atrium, shimmering, bubbling, Spanish, Mexican, tiled, garden, fountain pool.

Furnished—Completely, completely and exquisitely, magnificiently, magnificent furnishings, extravagant furnishings, extravagant appointments, exciting accessories, custom-furnished without regard to cost, most of the custom furniture stays, decorator-furnished, designer-furnished, fully . . . and accessorized, . . . with everything, . . . available, charmingly furnished, a wealth of luxurious appointments, toothbrush-ready, lavishly appointed, decorator appointments, California decorator, decorated and furnished by. . ., turnkey-furnished, richly detailed interior appointments, impeccably decorated and furnished.

Garage—Heated, 2-car, double, attached, 2½-car, oversized double, 2+ car, coach house, carriage house.

Garden—Gardener's showcase, harvest in your own backyard, family-size garden, super-size vegetable garden, productive, private, English, private walled, terraced, organic, lush tropical, excellent garden spot, great spot for vegetable garden, sunny garden spot, perfect spot for your. . ., space for an herb garden, old-fashioned grape arbor, courtyard. . ., solar greenhouse, your own greenhouse, the perfect plant and putter place, rose, formal rose, Hawaiian, oriental, bonsai, perennial, a quiet garden spot, resplendent in a myriad of colors.

Gate—Wooden, security, wrought iron, gate-guarded, the gateposts stand like stone sentinels (*See:* Security).

Gazebo—Garden, delightful, charming, screened, gazebo with wet bar and BBQ for your summer entertaining.

Glass—Double-glazed, triple-glazed, intricately etched, frosted, stained, leaded, vintage leaded, oval, insulated (*See:* Windows).

Golf—Just off the 7th tee, on the fairway, walk to the clubhouse, golf-cart distance from the course, just a chip-shot from the course, just off the emerald green fairways, the golf course is right in your backyard, executive course, 27-hole course, designed by. . ., championship golf course, PGI course, world-class golf course, in the exclusive golf community of. . ., in the golf-course community of. . ., in a country-club setting.

Guest Quarters—Guest room, guest suite, private guest suite, self-contained guest house, separate guest unit could be rented, in-law suite, in-law unit, servant or guest room, delightful dormered guest room.

Heating—Forced-air, hot-water, hydronic, baseboard, hydronic baseboard, zoned heat control, climate zone control, 4-zone hydronic, 5-ton heat pump for economy and comfort, the economy of natural gas, wood-burning stove, combination wood/gas furnace, wood-burning furnace with auxiliary gas heat, wood stove heats entire house, economical wood heat, wood stove with catalytic converter, energy-saving wood heat, wood heater fireplace insert. Franklin stove, solar heat, partial solar heat, passive solar heat.

Hedge—English, sculptured, privacy, rose.

Hills—Nestled in the. . ., on top of the. . ., hilltop showplace, above the smog, the gently rolling hills create a haven for this. . ., perched atop a high knoll, knolltop. . ., sited high in a one-acre knoll, above all, top of the mountain, hilltop showplace, be king or queen of the hill.

Homes (Bargain-Priced)—Unbelievable price, super buy, wow! what a value, auction-priced, foreclosure-priced, panic-priced, priced for immediate sale, must-sell-priced, "pinch-me" priced, priced below appraisal, speculator priced, desperate owner, the bargain of Westwood, exciting value, owner transferred, absentee owner wants out, partnership dissolution forces sale, bankruptcy sale, near-bankruptcy sale, attorney orders sale, court-ordered sale, corporate owner must sell, corporate liquidation, buyer backed out, one house too many, below cost, below builder's cost, below reproduction cost, below appraisal, price drastically reduced (*See:* Estate Sale, Builder's Sale, Foreclosure, Value).

Homes (Country)—On a country lane, country-fresh, town-close—country-fresh, pastoral perfection, country magic, bird-watcher's paradise, a new way of life—country-style, God's half-acre, heaven's acre, country squire's estate, estate in the country, country-quiet, hassle-free country life, a friendly life-style, city conveniences with country charm, commuter's dream, refuge from the city, discover the joy of country life, charming countrified home, old-fashioned country home, everything you need for country living, your nearest neighbors are squirrels and a family of raccoons, brings city conveniences to the country, country living with city flair, combines country charm with city conveniences, the country is right outside your door, matchless country beauty, where hawks soar high and the air is crisp and clean, endowed with country charm, Currier and Ives estate, calendar-scene estate, you will discover the joy of country life in this. . . , old-fashioned country home, a happy alternative to city living, the charm is country and so is the quiet, enjoy the simple pleasure of American rural life combined with big-city conveniences, country ambiance with all the conveniences of the city, your family will breath the clean air of rural America, blends harmoniously with the peaceful country surroundings, leave the city lights behind, for a simpler life, old-fashioned country living can be yours, country living as it should be, enjoy the security of country living.

Homes (Family)—A happy home, family home, roots for your family, children wanted, designed for children, a kid's home, for the growing family, needs boys and girls, you provide the family, room for the family, room for a pony, get settled before school starts in this. . . , move before school starts, your kids will love this. . . , a home for family love, room for the family, across from the park, 1 block to the playground, fenced play area, on a child-safe cul-de-sac, teenager's suite, playroom, rainy-day playroom, nursery, tribe-size backyard, child-safe backyard, room for bikes and trikes, a very special family home, this. . . reflects the time when the family home was the center of one's existence, a much-loved home of the past for your family future, trees for climbing, a place where children can still run free, if you are tired of driving your children to school, you will appreciate this. . . , family-size yard, fully fenced, a place to raise your children in all the old ways, the backyard is just waiting for a sandbox and swing, the old oak tree in the backyard is the perfect place to hang your swing, ready for your family, a happy home, a spouse-pleaser, a spouse-saver, a very special family home, a home that will secure your family's future, buy today and your family will thank you forever.

Homes (General)—Dream house, executive home, a house with personality, a rare opportunity, captivatingly beautiful, instantly appealing, eye-appealing, bewitching, seductive, elegant, overwhelming, sophisticated, handsome residence, refreshing, dramatic, outstanding, stunning, excitingly different, charming, a home to cherish, enchanting, picturesque, trend-setter, enticing, friendly, breathtaking, refreshingly different, versatile floor plan, built in the European tradition of fine craftsmanship, offering heart-stirring warmth that will win you over, sophisticated design, unassuming charm, offering a charm that complements the environment, captures your vision of tomorrow, romance and flair run rampant in this..., captivatingly different, stunningly conceived, amenities to enhance your living pleasure, featuring all the amenities you have dreamed of, wall-to-wall comfort.

Homes (Large)—Space odyssey, room for everything, the biggie, room to roam, room to spare, big is beautiful, elbow room, L-A-R-G-E, H-U-G-E, the big house, space abounds inside and out in this..., a whopping...square feet of living space, plenty of room for collectibles in this..., you won't squeeze the children in this..., embassy-size.

Homes (Low-Priced)—Budget-balancer, budget-pleaser, a first home, starter home, EZ on the budget, dollar-stretcher, easy to own, castle on a budget, wallet-watcher, elegantly affordable, kiss your landlord good-bye, take the landlord off your payroll (*See:* Homes—Bargain-Priced).

Homes (Luxury)—Prestigious, only the finest, sheer elegance, overwhelming, tres elegant, the ultra in executive homes, a great house, private estate, showplace, lavish estate, palatial estate, home extraordinaire, a showcase home, sleek and sophisticated, magnificent estate, one of Akron's great homes, conservatively elegant, understated elegance, subdued elegance, a world-class residence, the ultimate in prestigious living, unexcelled, epitome of elegance, the Dom Perignon of fine estates, just a little better, suited for royalty, impressive, a handsome estate, far from the ordinary, absolutely awesome, muted elegance, top-of-the-line, the standard of excellence, just a little better than anything you have seen, uncompromised quality, uncommon luxury, graciously elegant, quiet elegance, masterpiece, magnificent in its scale and design, thoughtfully planned to provide the ultimate life-style, for those accustomed to the very best, built for a life-style to be envied, refined elegance, a home that mirrors your achievements, reflecting the goals and ambitions of today's achievers, providing an unexcelled quality of life, reflecting the classic taste and subtle sophistication of the most discriminating buyer, truly an unparalleled home, a charismatic blending of regal splendor with delicate charm, truly a feast for the senses, for the life-style you deserve, a home that echoes achievement, the home for those who appreciate the fine art of living, elegance personified, the unmistakable air of elegance is expressed eloquently in its..., a home that knows no compromise, you need compromise no more, what civilized living is all about, an ambassadorial residence, providing a new definition of elegance, a remarkable blend of authentic character and luxury amenities, dramatically combining the best traditional detailing with high-tech amenities to provide the ultimate life-style, all the appointments one would expect in a home of this caliber, resplendent with magnificent detail, while life is filled with compromises—you need compromise no more, just a step above anything you have seen, the look of prestige is captured eloquently in this stately. . . , once in a rare while a home such as this will appear on the market, a gracious style of luxury that soon may no longer be available, provides a new definition of elegance, offering the utmost in gracious living, enjoy the life-style others can only hope to match, a new dimension in gracious living, truly the culmination of all your dreams, the ultimate statement of your success, if you promised yourself the best in life—there is no better time than now to keep that promise.

Homes (New)—Builder-fresh, brand-new classic, young and beautiful, new is better, never lived in, be the first to live in. . . , still time to pick the colors, muddy-shoes opening, be the first owner of this. . . , a future classic, a new home with a dramatic flair, one of the most exciting new homes we have seen, you will smell the newness in this. . . , a rare opportunity to buy one of the original models at. . . , a sparkling-new rendition of a. . . , price guaranteed for. . . (*See:* Builder's Sale).

Homes (Old)—A bit of history, the grandeur of yesterday, grandpa or grandma's house revisited, step back into yesterday, timeless elegance, heirloom estate, nostalgic showplace, preserved from yesteryear, ageless beauty, circa. . . , better than new, 19th-century perfection, turn-of-the-century ranch, a centurion, a century young, antique treasure, antebellum, antebellum beauty, timeless beauty, bed-and-breakfast potential, inn potential, has been admired since it was built . . . , embodies the charm and romance of a bygone era, reflects the pride of 6 generations of family ownership, time-mellowed, built to endure,. . . sq. ft. of traditional charm, enjoy the charm and warmth found only in older homes, gracious turn-of-the-century charm, gracious old-world charm, its beauty has increased for 100 years, old-fashioned space and grace, you will be struck by the excitement and romance . . . , many families have been raised in this . . . , it truly represents the grandeur of the past with all of the modern conveniences of tomorrow, style and tradition are captured in this. . . , registered with the National Register of Historic Places, landmark-eligible, possibly eligible for National Registry, steeped in history, a home with a history, a lady with a past, better than new, the old manse, historic treasure, the best of the past, time will stand still in this. . . , yesterday's dream, old-world charm abounds in this. . . , artistically restored to functional and aesthetic perfection, painstakingly restored, tastefully restored and updated to meet the living standards of the most discriminating, in museum condition, museum-piece, restored with imagination and elegance, museum-quality restoration, refurbished with state-of-the-art conveniences, new everything, with old-world detailing and modern amenities, 19th-century elegance combined with 20th-century convenience, unobtrusive improvements . . . , the meticulous and imaginative renovation offers . . . , masterfully renovated, a once-in-a-lifetime opportunity to secure a piece of America's heritage, a diorama of yesteryear, offering an elegance unobtainable in today's homes,... generations have meticulously maintained this..., every room is filled with classic appointments, a patina of love and care shines from this gentle reminder of the good full life of a long-ago time, offering the charm of yesteryear with the conveniences of tomorrow, your chance to live in a legend, reflects...years of loving care, offering a quality of life that only the past can provide, a unique vestige of the past, an opportunity to live in the opulence that recalls the grandeur of ages past, horse-drawn carriages and parasols recall the days when this...was young, one of the finest specimens of... -century architecture carefully preserved so you can enjoy its future, reflects a spectacular era in America's past, reminiscent of the Gatsby era, you will step back in history as the owner of this..., for the special few who desire the ultimate in unabashed charm of the early 1900s, the elegance of yesterday can be yours for tomorrow, built in ...when quality counted, built in the tradition of a bygone era, the opulence of yesterday refreshingly provides the perfect atmosphere for gracious living, this...reflects the time when the family home was the center of one's existence, a much-loved home of the past for your family's future (*See:* Architecture).

Homes (Small)—Cottage, honeymoon cottage, enchanted cottage, grandpa or grandma's cottage, secluded cottage, writer's cottage, Hansel & Grethel cottage, cute and cozy, artist's studio, single's hideaway, single's pad, retiree's delight, retirement-size, sophisticated adult home, fairy-tale cottage, gingerbread house, mini-chateau, la petite maison, maisonette, mini-estate, a home for the mature adult who deserves a more luxurious environment, the perfect home for a very sophisticated life-style.

Horse Property—Great place for horses, a place to hang your spurs, horse-lover's delight, equestrian estate, equestrian enchanter, zoned for horses, training ring, riding area, lighted riding area, a pipe corral, 2 corrals, perimeter and cross-fencing, fenced and cross-fenced, horse barn with ...stalls, double stalls, tack room, tack room with shower,...acres,...acres of pasture, ...acres of watered pasture, make your horse happy, get a horse—or several to fill this...barn, hey cowboy/cowgirl! There is room on this range to keep several horses, hold your horses in the three corrals that go with this..., bring your horse, paddocks with accommodations for brood mares, put your brand on this spread.

Hot Spa—Hydrotherapy spa, titillating hot spa, tantalizing hot spa, sumptuous hot spa, hot bubbly spa, sensuous hot spa, Jacuzzi, very private spa, therapeutic whirlpool spa for total relaxation, hot tub holds 6–8, redwood hot tub, California hot tub.

Humidifier/Dehumidifier—Power humidifier, furnace with power humidifier, automatic humidifier, automatic power dehumidifier.

Industrial—1,000 sq. ft., single level, 4 years old, rail siding, heavy industrial, light manufacturing, warehouse, the best little warehouse in . . . , zoned M4, 700-sq.-ft. air-conditioned office, 10,000-sq.-ft. showroom, 10′ sidewalls, clear span, previously used for . . . , excellent public transportation, very heavy power, ample power, 400 amps, 3-phase power, EPA wastewater system, . . . acre site, parking for . . . cars, fenced parking for . . . cars, free-standing building, crane-served, 10-ton crane, 3 crane bays, gas heat, 800-sq.-ft. dock, bed-level dock, truck-level dock, recessed dock, enclosed dock, depressed loading dock with levelators, drive-in door, 16′ OH door, freight elevator, fully sprinklered, security fence, electronic security system, room to expand, good column spacing, showroom and warehouse space, ideal for . . . , paved parking for . . . cars, air-conditioned, gas pumps, adjustable dock boards, Butler building, reinforced concrete construction.

Insulation—Fully insulated, R-19 insulation, super-insulated, double-insulated, extra insulation, 6″ sidewalls, 12″ of ceiling insulation, state-of-the-art energy efficient construction.

Investment Income Property—Opportunity, opportunity knocks, investor's dream, unique opportunity, rare opportunity, sleeping opportunity, leverage, invest in your future, syndicator's dream, attention: syndicators, be the landlord, possible student housing, possible artists' lofts, possible condominium conversion, prime rentals, a roof over your head—money in your pocket, raisable rents, should rent for $2/sq. ft., low rents, high rental demand, no rent increase since 1978, no rent control here, NYSE tenant, AAA tenant, blue-chip tenant, tenant waiting list, sale-leaseback, strong tenants, always leased, low vacancy, close-to-zero vacancy, bonded lease, lease tied to CPI, escalating leases, inflation-proof leases, NNN leases, percentage lease, percentage lease with guarantee, $________ coming in, positive cash flow, bottom line = profit, not beautiful—just profitable, bread-and-butter units, nets 12%, 12% cash-on-cash, 12% cash flow, makes U money, $30,000 spendable, impressive cash-on-cash return, nearly break even, break even—almost, break even with 15% down, let the rents supplement your income, $10,000 tax shelter, $50,000 1st-year depreciation, tax loss + cash flow, the ultimate tax shelter, a money-maker, an investment with a future, exciting potential, the place to watch your equity grow, the bottom line will be profit, Sanforize your dollar—keep it from shrinking by investing in this . . . , get rich slowly with the steady income from this . . . , you will never have to say you're sorry if you buy this . . . , below appraisal, control-free rents, provision for rent escalation, long-term CPI leases, guaranteed income, insured leases, no pride of ownership—just profit, rake in the rents, bread-and-butter units—meat and potatoes too, should rent for $________, 7 × gross, $950 coming in, leased to NYSE company, blue-chip tenant, seller will leaseback or vacate, long-term lease, professional tenants, strong tenants, national tenants, always leased, major tenants occupy 80% of space, national tenants occupy 80% of space, stable rental area, Uncle Sam will hate you, IRS revenge, protect yourself and your income with this . . ., in the path of progress, expanding area, dynamic growth area, high-traffic location, high-traffic corner, heavy foot traffic, best rental location, high-rental-demand area, in-demand rental area, prime rental area, highway visibility, traffic—signage—visibility, next to. . ., across from. . ., traffic count of. . .cars daily, strategically located between. . ., well-maintained, immaculately maintained, like-new, better than new, completely up to code, no deferred maintenance, free-standing, ideal fast-food location, condominium conversion possibility, separate meters, tenants pay utilities, ample parking, paved parking, parking for. . .cars, off-street parking for. . .cars, room for. . .additional units, ideal for loft conversion, rent now—develop later, each unit approximately 1,200 sq. ft., redevelopment loans available, professionally managed, management-free investment, EZ management, rezoning possibilities, maintenance-free, almost maintenance-free, the perfect choice for the young investor, an opportunity waiting to happen, for the buyer with vision, profit, the place to watch your equity grow.

Kitchen (Appliances)—Maytag appliances, like-new appliances, all the built-ins, built-in washer/dryer and dishwasher, double ovens, self-cleaning oven, built-in microwave, Jenn-Air range, double-door refrigerator with ice maker.

Kitchen (Cabinetry)—Custom cabinetry, oak cabinetry, custom birch cabinetry, custom hardwood cabinets, an extraordinary amount of handsome wood cabinetry, soft-pine cabinets, the original pine cabinets, old pine cabinets, European oak, imported European, rich cherry, hand-finished oak, an extraordinary amount of handsome wood cabinetry.

Kitchen (General)—Gourmet, dreamy gourmet, chef's. . ., a real cook's. . ., garden, greenhouse, designer, dream island, island cooking center, updated, space-age, super-new, St. Charles, glamorous, friendly, open, kitchen/family room, country-fresh, bright and airy, sun-filled, sun-drenched, brick and copper, energy efficient, breakfast bar, dining counter, convenient dining counter, built-in dining nook, superb culinary center, the gourmet kitchen is a cook's delight, European, European-inspired, Eurostyle, spouse-saver, work-saver, skylit.

Kitchen (Large)—Table space, eat-in, gigantic eat-in, country, breathtaking country, cheerful country, farm-size, ranch-size, spacious, down-home-size, tribe-size, French country, a real old-fashioned....

Kitchen (Small)—Step-saver, efficient step-saver, cozy, galley, efficient galley, one-step.

Landscaping—Professionally landscaped, estate-like setting, park-like grounds, unrivaled, native, natural landscape, desert landscape, impeccable landscape, flawlessly maintained, easy-care, extensively landscaped, lush, likely the most beautiful yard in town, you will picnic in the park right in your own backyard, grounds feature exotic plants from all over the world (*See:* Gardens, Lawns, Trees).

Land (Undeveloped)—Future city, all utilities available, natural gas available, utilities to property, power and phone available, utilities close to property, engineering work completed, completed feasibility study for..., zoned..., master-planned for industry, gently rolling, good drainage, favorable percolation tests, beech- and oak-covered, development-ready, all mineral and gas rights included, potential for subdividing, subdivision possibilities, parcel split possible, an impressive investment, exciting potential, agricultural lease available, wilderness trails for riding or hiking, unspoiled splendor, possible dam site for your own lake, you might find arrowheads along the sparkling creek that crosses this..., located in the center of a hunting and fishing paradise, enjoy camping, fishing and swimming now and build later, a great swimmin' hole, carve your homestead out of the wilderness, marketable timber, timber has not been cut in over...years, absolute seclusion, enough lumber to build and heat your home forever, timber, fish and game—everything you need is here, possible hydropower site, several excellent homesites, shaded building site, subdivision potential, subdivision-ready, land with a future, in path of progress, in path of development, in path of annexation, annexation-ready, center of..., squeezed between rapidly growing...and, possible future RV park, future shopping center?, your own wilderness, wilderness domain, forest preserve, private preserve, hunting refuge, game refuge, outdoors-person's paradise, bird-watcher's paradise, duck-hunter's paradise, duck-hunter's happiness, undisturbed, forest primeval, your private campground, unspoiled splendor.

Lawns—Expansive, expansive emerald, sweeping emerald, park-like setting, finely manicured, green velvet, croquet-size, a green velvet setting, lush green, breathtaking grounds, luxuriously manicured, sweeping lawns and towering trees.

Lease—Assumable, below-market, short-term, long-term, long-term with escalations, long-term lease at moderate rental, advantageous, AAA tenant, NNN lease, triple-net lease, seller will leaseback, sale-leaseback, strong tenants, blue-chip tenants, national tenants, always leased, 100% occupancy, major tenants occupy 80% of space, national tenants occupy 80% of space, low vacancy, close-to-zero vacancy, bonded, insured, guaranteed, . . . tied to CPI, long-term CPI leases, inflation-proof, escalating, provisions for rent escalations, short-term below-market, raisable rents, percentage.

Living room—26′, great room, dramatic great room, step-down, sunken, elegant, grand-piano-size, entertaining-size, mirrored . . . with conversation pit, conversation area, intimate conversation area, 2-story, vaulted, room for a grand piano in this . . . , dramatically proportioned, open-concept living area, romantic conversation pit in this . . . , intimate conversation area (*See:* Alcove).

Location—Be first to discover . . . , a . . . address, . . . trend-setter, heart of . . . , prestigious, the beauty of . . . , the luxury of . . . , . . . 's finest, move up to . . . , in highly prized . . . , in sought-after . . . , in the small exclusive community of . . . , prestigious address, preferred address, the right address, an elegant address, a success address, elite location, estate-like area, fairy-tale setting, coveted location, very "in" area, elite area, gold-coast address, the Bel Aire of . . . , the Beverly Hills of . . . , exciting, premier, superb, millionaires' row, established neighborhood, established community of fine homes, family-oriented neighborhood, on the edge of . . . , bordering . . . , across from . . . , around the corner from . . . , walk to . . . , bike to . . . , minutes to . . . , . . . school district, adjacent to . . . , just steps to . . . , short drive to . . . , down the road from . . . , nestled in the hills, knolltop setting, majestically perched, in a Williamsburg-like setting, in a pleasantly secluded neighborhood of winding boulevards and intimate culs-de-sac, postcard setting, storybook setting, sited for excellence, in the coveted community of . . . , the most prestigious street in . . . , for the price of an ordinary home you can live in . . . , the only available home in much-sought-after . . . , on a private lane in . . . , set in the estate area of . . . , in the friendly community of . . . where neighbors still know each other by name, in the master-planned community of . . . , in the masterfully planned community of . . . , on the best block of the most sought-after street in . . . , location—location, walking-close to . . . , cut your commute, borders . . . , short drive to . . . , across the street from . . . , adjoins . . . , set in the pastoral seclusion of . . . , set in a serene residential enclave, in a select community of fine homes, sited for excellence.

Loft—Sleeping, swiss, balcony sleeping area, balcony studio, artist's studio, library, loft apartment.

Lots—Tribe-size, country-size, estate-size, double-size, garden-size, orchard-size, children-size, huge lot, room for (pool/tennis courts), wooded, corner, cul-de-sac, zoned for . . . , approved for . . . , possible lot split, blueprint-ready, building-ready, protected by restrictive covenants, water access, across from . . . , walk to . . . , M3 zoning, owner will subordinate, . . . % down, ideal for sprawling ranch house, the steep grade lends itself to an imaginative buyer who wants the ultimate view site, feasibility study completed, all permits and approvals for . . . included, engineering completed for. . . ,tentative approval for. . . , suitable for tri-level, buildable now.

Maintenance—Well-maintained, meticulously maintained, superbly maintained, exquisitely maintained, handsomely kept, reflects owner's pride, reflects caring owner, no deferred maintenance, up to code.

Management—Professionally managed, professional management available, management-free investment, EZ management, maintenance-free, tenant makes all repairs, almost management-free.

Marble—Italian, carrera, carrera—the sculptors' choice, travertine, cultured, sheathed in travertine. . . , Grecian, carrera marble enhances the. . . , carrera marble accents. . . , extensive use of, real marble vanities.

Mobile Home—Double-wide, super-double-wide, triple-wide, $24' \times 50'$, wide-wide—double-wide, 5-star park, located in the family section of one of the area's most desirable parks, walk to community center, steps to pool, choice corner lot for spacious privacy, established park, reasonable rent, space rent only $________, space lease available, $10' \times 40'$ covered deck, 2-car carport, storage building, full skirting, ground-level entrance, paved parking.

Negative Ads—Not for you, you don't need this. . . , don't read this ad, don't look at this ad, procrastinators—this is your chance to miss buying this. . . , want to be sorry—then fail to check on this. . . , masochists—if you enjoy hurting yourself don't see this. . . (*See:* Fixer-Uppers).

Neighborhood—Friendly, on the prettiest street and the friendliest neighborhood in. . . , sought-after, highly prized, exclusive, desirable, family, family-oriented, established, established neighborhood of fine homes, quiet, in the small exclusive community of. . . , in a pleasantly secluded neighborhood, in the friendly community of. . . , where neighbors still know each other by name.

Open house—Open for admiration, hey! look us over!, come and see, visit, 1st showing, 1st offering, premier showing, first presentation, open to public, open—come buy, dusty-shoes preview, come and appreciate this. . . , don't be a drive-byer, it's bigger than it looks, come inside—you'll be surprised, don't drive by.

Owner or Former Owner—Doctor's home, lumberyard owner's home, millionaire's hideaway, architect's own home, architect-owner, artist-owner, the Jones estate, owned by a renowned. . . ,built with care for (his/her) own family by a master builder, owner/builder designed and built this. . . for (his/her) own family, owner's pride shows throughout this. . . .

Paneling—Cherry, solid cherry, tongue-and-groove, mellow wood, warm wood, courtroom, hardwood, imported hardwood, gleaming mahogany, wainscoting, extensive wainscoting, solid walnut wainscoting.

Pantry—Walk-in, butler's, old-fashioned.

Park—Almost in the park, around the corner from the park, borders national park, walk to the park from this..., park view.

Parking—Off-street, covered, protected, carport, double carport, indoor, indoor parking for 2 cars, secure underground, RV, room for your RV.

Patios—Brick, flagstone, tiled, family, inviting, picnic-perfect, flagstone terrace, covered terrace, courtyard, enclosed, canopied, stone terrace, sun terrace, raised patio overlooks..., covered, awning-covered, breakfast, magnificent terrace enhanced with a secluded pool and spa (*See:* Courtyard).

Planning—In the master-planned community of..., in the masterfully planned community of..., in the planned residential community of....

Porch (Enclosed)—Screened and glassed, glassed-in, sun-room, California room, Arizona room, Florida room, garden room, conservatory, enclosed lanai, solarium, enclosed patio, summer room, sun gallery, sleeping, enclosed, glassed-in, jalousied.

Porch (General)—Old-fashioned front, country, old-fashioned gallery, columned portico, fully screened, lanai, sleeping, wraparound, veranda, columned veranda, white-columned veranda, captain's, widow's walk, bring your rocking chair, rocking-chair-ready, just the place for your rocking chair or porch swing, swing on the porch and lull your troubles away, you will love the large front porch of this..., a screened porch just made for summer dreaming, lemonade-sipping front porch, pillared front porch, enjoy summer evenings on the veranda of this..., the pillared front porch welcomes you to comfortable living.

Privacy—Ultimate in seclusion, hideaway, escape, serene hideaway, serenity, end-of-the-road seclusion, a private world, sanctuary, secluded, absolute privacy, close-in seclusion, a private world, private oasis, oasis of privacy, nudist's delight, the sound of silence, private road, secluded road, walled estate, absolute privacy, in the private world of..., in a very private corner of..., very private pool, tucked away amidst the pines, on 3 very private acres, privacy garden, ancient oaks create a screen of privacy, a secluded place where there is time to ponder, privacy so complete one could swim in nature's garment, in a private wooded enclave, in a private wooded preserve, your own world of private elegance, cloistered behind high stone walls, scenic and secluded setting, providing pampered privacy, where the air is cleaner—water bluer and privacy still exists, one-way walls of glass, a most rare private setting, very private patio, a very private end unit, a very private sun porch.

Recreational Vehicles—RV hookups, RV hookups for your traveling friends, room for your RV, RV parking, plenty of room for your RV, plenty of parking for your camper and boat, RV-park possibilities.

Redevelopment—Redevelopment area, redevelopment possibilities, redevelopment loans available, ripe for redevelopment.

Reduction—Down to your price, now at your price, reduced for action, price drastically reduced, price substantially reduced, substantial reduction, reduced $________, second reduction, last reduction, final reduction.

Remodeled—Stunningly, completely rebuilt, better than new, with new everything, elegantly modernized, dramatically updated, thoughtfully updated to combine the best of the old with the new, updated systems, 19th-century elegance combined with 20th-century convenience, combines antique charm with today's conveniences, unobtrusive improvements include. . ., offering the charm of yesteryear with the conveniences of tomorrow, it truly represents the grandeur of the past with all the modern conveniences of tomorrow, this classic offers a tour through yesteryear with the conveniences of tomorrow.

Renovated—Totally, partially, completely rebuilt, tastefully, handsomely, the meticulous and imaginative renovation offers. . ., masterfully.

Restored—Totally, superbly, exquisitely, charmingly, meticulously, faithfully, completely and beautifully, restored to combine old-fashioned elegance with up-to-date amenities, completely restored to capture the aura of yesteryear, tastefully, restored nostalgia, . . .to its former splendor, lovingly, restored with the antique-lover in mind, 90% restored, restored colonial, restoration under way, partially, restored by, restorer's treasure, worthy of restoration, ready for restoration, a masterpiece in need of restoration, restorable, artistically restored to functional and aesthetic perfection, painstakingly, tastefully restored and updated to meet the living standards of the most discriminating, museum-quality restorations, restored with imagination and elegance.

River—Meandering, fish and float, clear mountain stream, lazy fish-filled, sparkling stream, babbling brook, a babbling brook runs merrily at your doorstep, you will go to sleep with the gentle sound of the babbling brook, rocky stream.

Roads—(*See:* Streets and Roads).

Roof—Red tile, Spanish tile, mission tile, slate, hand-split cedar shakes, gambrel, Dutch gambrel, Pennsylvania Dutch gambrel, mansard, French mansard roof, multigabled, a real slate.

Rooms (Large)—Mammoth, Texas-size, baronial-size, tribe-size, family-size, magnificently proportioned, dramatically proportioned, castle-size, rooms of grand proportions, 16′ × 40′ living room.

Sauna—Finnish, Danish, Swedish, automatic gas, redwood, cedar, . . .for healthy relaxation.

Schools—In the. . .school district, walking-close to schools and shopping, super schools are walking-close to this. . .,late for school—not from this. . . .

Second Home—(*See:* Homes—Country, Vacation Homes, Water-Related Property).

Security—Guard gate, 24-hour guard gate, security gate, 24-hour doorman, secure residential area, behind the gates, hi-rise security, behind guarded walls, behind a gate-guarded entry, a safe haven, 24-hour security patrol, key-operated elevators, latest in electronic security, 24-hour parking attendants, underground security parking, smoke detectors, intercom security system, 'round-the-clock electronic surveillance, sonic alarm system, security cameras, ultrasonic security system for your peace of mind, alarm system on all windows and doors, central security system, police-connected alarm system, armed response alarm system, Honeywell alarm system, worry-free security, foyer security system, behind electronically controlled gates, state-of-the-art security, monitored security, video security, security gates open to reveal. . .,full security system, sophisticated security system, security gates with intercom, behind a decorative wrought iron security gate, cloistered behind high walls.

Shed—Hobby building, storage shed for your. . ., ideal as an artist's studio, would make an ideal workshop, could be converted to guest house, plenty of room for the collector, storage for your. . ., potting shed, garden shed, English garden shed.

Shutters—Plantation, colonial, Bermuda, privacy, security, French, full.

Soil Type—. . .acres silt loam, . . .acres productive silt loam, . . . acres deep loam, . . .acres rich loam, . . .acres productive bottomland, . . .acres fertile bottomland.

Sprinklers—Underground, automatic, automatic sprinkler system, fully watered by automatic system.

Stairs—Angular staircase, center staircase, wide center staircase, curved staircase, graceful curved staircase, dramatic curved staircase, spiral staircase, circular staircase, the circular staircase spirals to. . ., sweeping staircase, floating staircase, dramatic floating staircase, mirrored staircase, cantilevered staircase, grand staircase, grand walnut staircase, banistered staircase, solid cherry balustrade, intricately carved banisters, hand-carved banisters, circular staircase of oak and cherry.

Streets and Roads—All-weather road, improved road, paved road, county-maintained road, private road, down a winding road, country lane, on a country lane, on a quiet country lane, a country lane weaves its way through this. . ., tree-lined street, quiet tree-lined street, tree-canopied street, quiet no-thru street, end-of-the-road seclusion, coach-lighted street, dead-end street, on a private lane in. . ., no-traffic street, well-lighted quiet street, on a very special street in. . . , the most prestigious street in. . . , on the best block of the most-sought-after street in. . . , on the prettiest street and the friendliest neighborhood in. . . , in a pleasantly secluded neighborhood of winding boulevards and intimate culs-de-sac, tucked away on a quiet cul-de-sac, peaceful cul-de-sac, wooded cul-de-sac, shaded cul-de-sac, children-safe cul-de-sac, the right address, an elegant address, prestigious address, major highway frontage.

Stone—River rock, orchard stone, crab orchard stone, native stone exterior, solid stone construction, cut, solid granite, lannon, cut limestone, Tennessee, California driftwood, massive, split-rock, brick and stone, stone and cedar.

Studio—Artist's, skylit, sky, loft, balcony, attic, would make ideal artist's studio.

Sunlight—Sun-drenched, sun-filled, filled with sunlight, light and bright, flooded with afternoon sunlight, bright with the morning sun, warm and sunny, 18 windows welcome the sun in this. . . .

Swimming Pools—Olympic-size, family-size, kidney-shaped, oval, world-class, in-ground, Gunite, skinny-dipping, crystal-cool, dazzling, inviting, cool blue, shimmering, sparkling, heated, heated and filtered, private, secluded, solar-heated, glassed-in, caged, lap, fully fenced, free-form.

Taxes—Low taxes, low-low taxes, taxes only $382 in 1986, benefit by Clearwater's low tax rate, the lowest tax rate in the county.

Tennis—Night-lighted court, illuminated court, sunken tennis court, championship tennis court, world-class tennis court, close to courts, room for tennis court.

Terms—(*See:* Assumable Loans, Financing).

Tile—Fully tiled, sleek ceramic, ceramic, Italian, Venetian, Mexican, Portuguese, travertine (*See:* Flooring—Tile).

Timeshare—Interval ownership, special shared ownership plan, you want your cottage for 2 weeks—why pay for 52. (*See:* Vacation Homes, Water-Related Property, Condominiums).

Trees—Your home in the woods, beneath towering pines, nestled beneath the towering trees, nestled in the forest, tall timbers, lofty pines, hardwood haven, wooded wonderland, in the oaks, sheltered by towering pines, shaded by a grove of native hardwoods, mature orchard, organic orchard, young orchard, producing orchard, mouth-watering family orchard, young orchard just coming into the most productive years, the backyard is enhanced with. . . , the backyard is a tropical oasis of palms and citrus, many fruit and nut trees embellish this rolling parcel, maple trees for augering,. . . your own maple syrup from the sugar maple in. . . , there's a great place for a hammock between the elms in the pleasantly shaded backyard, lawn graced with shade and flowering trees, century-old oak, a tranquil wooded setting envelops this. . . , a Paul Bunyan–size forest, rustic wooded, sprinkling of hickory and oak trees in the sunlit meadow, sprinkled with oak trees, cut your own Christmas tree in your family woods, virgin timber, mature hardwood, marketable timber, timber cruised at an estimated $________ per acre, no timber has been cut in over 40 years, your woodlot will keep you warm for many winters, ample wood lot for home heating, meandering drive through your scenic woodlot, captivating setting adorned by huge shade trees, tucked away in the trees, nestled on a large lot beneath mature shade trees, flanked by towering magnolias and graceful cedars, towering trees form a canopy over this..., towering trees and flowering shrubs, 100-year-old oaks shade this..., tucked away on 3 enchanted wooded acres, set among huge and capitivating hardwood trees, framed by flowering dogwoods, cherry blossoms and maples surround this..., age-old trees and manicured lawns, flanked by ancient maples, nestled in a peaceful wooded setting, cloistered behind towering hemlocks, nestled in the pines, a tapestry of flowering shrubs and magnificent trees, a lush oasis of towering trees and flowering shrubs, hammock-ready trees, the perfect backyard spot to hang your hammock, specimen trees, specimen trees and shrubs, where the trees grow tall and the sun meets the sea, set in a sun-streaked wooded glen, woodlot is loaded with game, mature hardwoods.

Trim—Solid oak trim, solid oak woodwork.

Unfinished Areas—Bonus room, storage attic could be converted to studio or 4th bedroom, ideal spot for darkroom, ready for finishing to meet your needs, could be converted to guest facilities, expansion room in..., a perfect playroom.

Urgency—Won't be around long at..., can be yours today but it will be gone tomorrow, if you wait it will be too late, call now for you are not the only one reading this ad, be first or be sorry.

Utilities—City water and..., county..., natural gas, economical natural gas, available,...to property, underground.

Vacation Homes—Retreat, northwoods retreat, mountain retreat, family retreat, corporate retreat, hideaway, artist's hideaway, country escape, escape the rat race, refuge, your quiet place, getaway house, chalet, northwoods chalet, for weekends or weeks on end, country quiet, lodge, mountain lodge, northwoods lodge, buy the sun, your place in the fun, start a family tradition with this extended family-size summer home, enjoy those lazy days of summer in this..., every day will be a holiday at this..., the place for your weekend getaway, where winter is just a memory, slow down the tempo of your life, the place for a relaxing country weekend, an experience with nature for weekends or a lifetime, loaded with peace and quiet, less than...from..., you will feel at peace with nature in this ..., located in a 4-season vacationland, your escape hatch from the city (*See:* Water-Related Property, Homes—Country).

Value—A great value at $________, an obvious value at $________, realistically priced at $________, competitively priced at $________, well-priced at $________, priced right at $________, rock-bottom-priced at $________, priced to sell at $________, action-priced at $________, down-to-earth price of $________, excitingly priced at $________, solid value at $________, all this for only $________, yours for only $________, unmatchable at $________,hard to believe at $________, a tempting value at $________, value-packed at $________, packed with value, a must-see for the buyer who expects more, unprecedented value, an uncommon find at $________, an uncommonly fine home at $________, the price is right at $________, offered at an amazingly reasonable $________, truly worth seeing and worth owning at $________, hard to believe at only $________.

View—Above the lights, sea of lights, city lights, above all, ocean view, a view of the world, exhilarating, incomparable, million-dollar, smashing, cinemascope, panoramic, 360°, sweeping, mile-wide, permanent, guaranteed, seductive, incredible, unparalleled vistas, bird's-eye, eagle's-eye, white-water, river, unreal, awesome, magical, dazzling, unsurpassed, forever serene vistas, pastoral vistas, serene pastoral vistas, fairy-tale, seventh heaven, picture-book, glorious, commanding, overlooks a variegated fairyland of lights, tranquil, unspoiled, unobstructed, breathtaking, watch the sailboats from the deck of this. . . , overlooking. . . , sunrise, sunset, an almost fairy-tale diorama, surrounded by stunning vistas, celestial.

Wainscoting—Walnut, solid walnut.

Walkways—Quiet, flagstone walk, lighted, shaded walks, covered, quaint cobblestone paths, ancient stone.

Wall Coverings—Imported, textured, decorator, designer, lavish use of. . . , coordinated.

Water-Related Property—Creekfront dazzler, riverfront sanctuary, beach retreat, on the waterfront, lakefront Shangri-la, beach house, a place on the beach, white sand beach, spectacular white sand beach, wide sand beach, gradual sand beach, gentle wading beach, child-safe wading beach, stroll on the sand, miles of sand beach for barefoot walking, 200′ of choice sand frontage, a tranquil setting, the gentle sound of rushing water will lull you to sleep in this. . . , the view of the sunset over the water is unsurpassed, pounding surf is at your front door, fish-filled river, fish off your own dock, spring-fed lake, crystal-clear spring-fed lake, sparkling stream, swimmin' fishin' lake, shimmering water, lake access, meandering stream, cool mountain stream, lazy fish-filled river, 30′ dock, 30′ dock with electric hoist, boat house with hoist, wet boat house, covered dock, permanent pier, deep-water dock, bulkheaded frontage, protected anchorage, on the perfect lake, at the water's edge, fish and float river, fish-filled creek, for the Tom Sawyer in you, sailboat water, walk to beach, stroll on the sand, stroll on the beach, on the sand, blue water and white sails, beach retreat, beach house, buy the sea, commanding waterfront site, practically in the water, for those who appreciate the beauty and serenity of waterside living, overlooking the tranquil waters of..., babbling brook, a babbling brook runs merrily at your doorstep, you will go to sleep with the gentle sound of the babbling brook, only a short stroll to catch the waves, listen to the surf and watch the waves from this..., sandy beaches await you at this..., watch the reflections of the changing seasons in the tranquil waters of lake..., enjoy the tranquility of wide waters and quiet beaches, promenade on a spectacular stretch of white sand beach, bike to beach, swim and fish in your own backyard, ice-cold flowing spring, clean mountain stream, beach privileges, private mooring, mooring rights, beach rights, waterfront esplanade, steps from the sand, dock and davits, heavy-duty davits, beach access, dedicated beach access, seawalls, protective docking, private lake access.

Water (Well)—Pure well water, sparkling well water, you will relish the cold pure water from your own well.

Wheelchair Access—Handicapped conveniences.

Windows—Wall of glass, windowed wall, majestic wall of glass, 30′ window wall, one-way walls of glass, knee-to-ceiling, one-way, Palladian, window-wrapped solarium, soaring window walls, Anderson window wall, greenhouse, picture, picture window overlooks..., picture window frames a picturesque and private backyard, clerestory, mullioned, glassed-in, skylight, diamond-lite, glass-domed atrium, glass-enclosed atrium, the sliding glass doors open to..., French doors, double glass doors, leaded glass, leaded-glass accents, vintage leaded glass, beveled glass, beveled and jeweled glass, etched glass, intricately etched glass, frosted glass, stained glass, oval glass, colorful window boxes, old-fashioned bay window, Thermopane, double-glazed, triple-glazed, solar bronze, self-storing storms and screens.

Workshop—Separate workshop in..., built-in workbench, ... would make ideal workshop, hobby shop, huge 24′ workshop, workshop area in..., plenty of room in the dry basement for a hobby shop.

Zoning—Zoned C3, zoned for horses, rezoning possibilities, adjoining property zoned M3.

Index